The New Corporate Activism

Harnessing the Power of Grassroots Tactics for Your Organization

Edward A. Grefe

Marty Linsky

McGraw-Hill, Inc.

New York   San Francisco   Washington, D.C.   Auckland   Bogotá
Caracas   Lisbon   London   Madrid   Mexico City   Milan
Montreal   New Delhi   San Juan   Singapore
Sydney   Tokyo   Toronto

Library of Congress Cataloging-in-Publication Data

Grefe, Edward A. (date)
    The new corporate activism : harnessing the power of grassroots
tactics for your organization / Edward A. Grefe, Martin Linsky.
      p.   cm.
    Includes index.
    ISBN 0-07-024431-6
    1. Business and politics—United States. 2. Corporations—
United States—Political activity. I. Linsky, Martin. II. Title.
JK467.G76   1995
659.2—dc20   95-7805
                                                  CIP

1 2 3 4 5 6 7 8 9 0 DOC/DOC 9 0 9 8 7 6 5

ISBN 0-07-024431-6

*The sponsoring editor for this book was Betsy N. Brown, the editing supervisor
was Caroline R. Levine, and the production supervisor was Pamela A. Pelton.
This book was set in Baskerville by Victoria Khavkina of McGraw-Hill's
Professional Book Group composition unit.*

Printed and bound by R. R. Donnelley & Sons Company.

McGraw-Hill books are available at special quantity discounts to use as
premiums and sales promotions, or for use in corporate training programs. For more information, please write to the Director of Special
Sales, McGraw-Hill, Inc., 11 West 19th Street, New York, NY 10011. Or
contact your local bookstore.

 This book is printed on recycled, acid-free paper containing a
minimum of 50% recycled de-inked fiber.

To Lynn, Nicole, and Keith Grefe
Lynn, Alison, Sam, and Max Linsky
For their constant patience and encouragement

Contents

Contents

Preface

The strategies for influencing public policymaking are undergoing fundamental change. Until recently, when corporations, professional associations, or nonprofit organizations wanted to affect legislation, they would hire a high-priced, capital-based lobbyist to make it happen. When they wanted to affect the outcome of a referendum question on the ballot, pollsters and media buyers would get the call.

Now people who want to make a difference in legislation or ballot questions increasingly are using a whole new approach, which we call *The New Corporate Activism*. The essence of this new way is to marry 1990s communication and information technology with the 1960s grassroots organizing techniques. The philosophy behind it is simple enough: given the explosion of hired gun lobbyists and media consultants trying to make themselves heard, success in public affairs can no longer be assured from top down.

Even when it works, the old-style public affairs advocacy achieves only short-run success, leaving no ongoing presence. Often what does remain is a bad aftertaste. Usually, the objective is a negative one, kill a bill or defeat a referendum. So there are no positive messages left behind, and all of those people who were not a part of the closed-door old-boy conversations which produced the desired result feel appropriately left out.

Recent events bear out our thesis starkly. The Clinton Administration, mistaking its plurality for a mandate, attempted a top-down approach to legislative decision making which failed, the Administration's health care program being but one example. The Republicans capitalized on a grass-roots, bottom-up frustration with the way things were not working in Washington to reverse a 40-year hiatus from power in the House of Representatives. Talk radio reflected the views of those who felt they were being left out of the conversations taking place about how the government would solve their problems.

What works in today's world is a three-step process: the creation of a message based on reliable information, the organization of a coalition of real people at the street level who are committed to the enterprise, and a realistic plan for mobilizing people so that their voices will be heard by the right people at the right time.

Since the late 1980s, many companies and organizations have tried their hand at some form of grassroots coalition building. Some have worked and some have failed. Some have used technology well, and some have wasted their investment or not used it at all.

The purpose of this book is to document this experience, examine it, find the cutting edge examples, and assess where the next steps in public affairs are likely to go. Our audience includes CEOs of organizations large and small who are affected by decisions made in state legislatures, in Congress, in City Halls, and at the ballot box. It includes the public affairs specialists, both independents and those inside of organizations, whose business it is to be effective in influencing those decisions. And it includes reporters and news organizations, academics and students of politics and public affairs, and anyone else who needs to understand who is influencing whom, and how, in the world of policymaking in the 1990s and beyond.

This is an optimistic book. We believe in the system. And we believe that the more people are involved and the greater number of people who are mobilized on behalf of issues affecting themselves, the more democratic values are served and self-government is strengthened.

What we are talking about in this volume are tools of democracy, reinvented to meet the constraints of a modern complex technological society. The techniques we discuss here are available to individuals and groups whatever their resources. Using them is not only important to success in public affairs, it is an essential ingredient in reconnecting people to their government, a critical element of citizen responsibility in a democratic society.

There is an old saying: Those who know, do, those who don't, teach. It may be an unfair statement, but what it suggests is that many who seek to inform or to educate have never themselves been actively involved in the activity, having only observed others from afar.

In our judgment, this book could not have been written had both of us not only observed, but, more critically in our judgment, actually been involved in the process of building grassroots organizations—for causes, candidates, and corporations, for profit as well as for not-for-profit organizations. We believe these experiences have given us a unique vantage point from which to draw examples of how we see and have seen organizations build a constituency, either, in our judgment, poorly or properly.

Ed Grefe has been a consultant for over 25 years, some 10 before joining the Philip Morris Company in 1975, and some 15 years since leaving that company to cofound, with Lynn Grefe, International Civics, Inc. Many of the anecdotes he has added to this book come from situations in which his firm was directly involved, either on a project basis or on a continuing retainer.

These include consulting assignments for Hershey Foods Corporation, ARCO, the General Mills Restaurant Group, IBM, Coors Brewing Company, Continental Insurance Company, the National Association for the Specialty Food Trade, the Australian Soft Drink Bottlers Association, Planned Parenthood, CIBA-GEIGY, and others.

During the past 30 years, Marty Linsky has been a legislator, teacher, journalist, and government official, always based in Massachusetts. He has also worked as a consultant for public and private-sector organizations throughout the United States and abroad. Some of the stories in this book came from his own experience and others from his observations of other organizations' experience during his career.

We debated writing this from the perspective of "… and then we said this to the client." That is certainly a valid way to proceed, but what we have discovered in each instance of our consulting is that the net result—good or bad—is a collaborative process. We provided insight based on experience, our clients fused our ideas into an existing modus vivendi. Hence, only where it is necessary have we injected our names to clarify a perspective.

Otherwise we trust that the reader will accept the notion that, in a sense, this book represents what we would say to a potential client if he or she asked us how to proceed. Where we have seen good programs, whether we have been involved in them directly or we have learned about them while doing our research, we have posited them as good examples; similarly, where we believe mistakes have been made, whether we were involved or not, we have added them as examples.

We trust our involvement has not inhibited our candor. In any event, the thrust of how we view the way organizations should proceed remains constant.

Ed Grefe
Marty Linsky

Acknowledgments

No work of this kind could be undertaken without the assistance of some very good people. We are particularly indebted to John Brown for his guidance on lifestyle clustering and affinity groups; to Peter Broadmore and Paul Klie for their insights on Canada; to F. Peter Model and J. Bernard Robinson for their counsel on our conceptual approach; to our researchers, Nicole Sardanis Zelma, Michelle Schettino, and Melissa Wade; to Susan Behm Walrich for her assistance in preparing the Index; to Don Bates, Lew Lobosco, and Lynn Underwood for their technical assistance; to our editor, Betsy Brown; and, to the staff of the Public Affairs Council, especially, Ray Hoewing, its President, and Leslie Swift-Rosenzweig, Executive Director of the Foundation for Public Affairs.

But beyond all these is one person who did more than anyone to make this project a reality—from developing, managing, and analyzing the survey for Chap. 10 to pointing out details that had been missed or overlooked in the manuscript. For that unique dedication we especially thank Lynn Grefe. She applied the same professionalism to this project as she does to her clients.

Introduction

Up in the state capitol of Sacramento, some five years after it went down, they're still talking about "Big Green," the dream, everything-you-ever-wanted-but-were-afraid-to-ask-for environmental proposal. Its proponents called it that because, like the heroic mountain man of *Big John,* Jimmy Dean's classic ballad, Proposition 128 seemed so strong, so virtuous, so *good* for Californians. Indeed, its framers proclaimed it "ballot-proof"—impervious to outside attack by lesser mortals.

"This is a done deal!" exulted Robert Mulholland back in April 1990. "There's no way we can lose . . . unless there's an earthquake that stops California."[1] Mr. Mulholland was one of Prop. 128's principal architects and campaign manager, as well as the state's Democratic Party political director.

Instead of talking about Richter scales, he should have been studying the straw polls. Because when the earthquake did strike at the ballot box, it wasn't a geological but a political disaster. Big Green lost. Big.

This temblor had been set in motion months earlier by a bunch of well-financed activists and organizers whose strategy for toppling Big Green was, simply, to try to undermine it, to tunnel beneath the mountain of presumed support, remove its underpinnings, and let it implode.

The guerrillas smartly set out to depict Prop. 128 as the handiwork of a clique of well-intentioned but self-righteous political élitists, incapable of compromise. Theirs was the Right Way, the *only* way of saving Californians from themselves. Noblesse oblige.

But having staked out ecological purity as their high ground, Mulholland's troops were, in fact, encamped atop a political fault line. And by looking down their noses at the enemy below, they made themselves terribly vulnerable. So when the voters spoke, it was like the mountain crushing Jimmy Dean's selfless "Big John"—swiftly and quite unexpectedly.

The victors were members of a new breed of public policy wonks drawn from a wide spectrum of interests in both public and private sectors who recognized that in the 1990s, success in the political arena—the ultimate marketplace of ideas—would no longer be a top-down proposition. Further, that success—be it at the ballot box or over-the-counter—would depend not just on crafting a credible message but on *building a working coalition* in support of that message. Without such grassroots support, there can be no trust, no credible course of action.

This new breed of guerrilla warriors works on public policy issues. Some for *Fortune* 500 companies, some for smaller firms, some for public agencies, some for nonprofit organizations, and some for associations, but all with experiential and intellectual roots in the community-organizing movements of the 1960s, which were as authentic then as their loyalties are now to their current employers.

Those so oriented are creating public affairs programs that by any measure are excellent. Their approach to public outreach and coalition building stands in sharp contrast to the approach to public affairs in vogue until the mid-1970s.

Back then, it was standard for organizations to conduct their government relations in accordance with a "fix-it" mentality. They had a problem. They hired a lobbyist. They said, "Fix it!" What they meant was "Kill it or make it go away."

The idea that problems faced by organizations in the arenas of lawmaking or regulating could be "fixed" led to a meaning for the word *fix* other than "repair." It was "influence peddling," quite simply—that is, finding the person who knew the legislator or regulator and getting him (it was always a "him" in those days of the old-boy network) to bury the problem.

It was an approach to influencing government decision making that remained dominant until about a decade ago, even though for some time before that, grassroots movements designed to curb corporate and societal abuse and limit the influence of the old-boy network were gaining more and more success. Not only was the top-down philosophy increasingly ineffectual, but even when it worked there were problems.

It was only a short-run solution at best. With success being measured more by legislation stopped than by laws enacted, the persona of lobbyists as nothing more than naysayers or "aginers" left a bad aftertaste for the organization they represented, portrayed, as it often was, as being tinged with a touch of sleaze if not actual corruption.

Further, in a democracy, always playing defense ensures a net loss. It's only a question of how much and when.

Slowly, in the light of the mounting evidence that the fix-it approach was no longer adequate, a shift began in the way organizations began to think about how to play on the field of public policy-making. A new breed of public affairs professionals began emerging who recognized that to build grassroots constituent support, it was necessary to present potential coalition allies with a positive program they could support. Following the example of successful grassroots organizers, these professionals fostered strategies that would be not simply against something but equally *for* something.

They would document a plan that showed them to be for the community, for the consumer, for the taxpayer, for the little guy. In short, they would do the opposite of what proponents of such measures as Big Green were doing and demonstrate that their position was not simply against a good notion but equally for those whose lives and livelihoods could be seriously fractured if the proposal became law.

"Lobbying" became "public affairs," and employee power became a key strategic idea. Leading practitioners of the new wave began to talk to one another and with a wider audience through articles in business journals and the popular press. Institutionalized forums, particularly the Public Affairs Council, provided an opportunity for advocating that people in the corporate world make use of the same techniques that had become so effective against them.

Chronicling the shift in its early stages was a book for professionals by Grefe, *Fighting to Win: Business Political Power* (New York, Harcourt Brace). Published in 1981, *Fighting to Win* was both a rationale for establishing a public affairs program as well as a primer on how to succeed. The book synthesized much of the material that had been published to that time and recounted many of the ideas that had been launched.

Today, most organizations, private and nonprofit alike, have a public affairs program and some way of involving people other than senior executives and the principal lobbyists in their battles over public policy issues. Some programs are informal. Some are highly structured. Some are good, some bad, some so-so.

All public affairs programs intrigue us. It makes no difference where they are located, or how large their geographical scope is, or how well financed they are, whether they are in a criminal justice advocacy organization, a university, or a *Fortune* 500 giant. Important lessons are as easily learned from a shoestring operation as from a multi-million-dollar program.

We are students of the process with, between us, 60 years of experience in journalism, education, politics, public relations, and public affairs. What intrigues us is not where various public affairs programs are coming from or how much or little they spend but whether or not they succeed, and why.

When we started this project, our goal was to report on who had been doing what since 1980. Our initial thought was that it might be possible to simply update *Fighting to Win*. It soon became evident that a revision would not be possible. The public policy world has changed dramatically, and the ideas about employee power that drove the reorganization of the public affairs function in the early 1980s were already beginning to be out-of-date when *Fighting to Win* was published. So, instead, we have decided to approach the subject of public policy from a different perspective and to attempt to inform a broader public as to the dramatic changes in the field.

Many public affairs programs have not been critically reexamined since they were launched over a decade ago. Some pay lip service to the ideas that created them, but they have never really operationalized anything other than a top-down approach.

Some still hire lobbyists and public relations counsel in Washington, for example, who maintain that they've created a grassroots coalition simply by obtaining the endorsement of like-minded organizations within the beltway surrounding the nation's capitol. Those that merely pay lip service to true grassroots rarely consider the fact that real people living outside the beltway may have an opposing view with the consequence that their possible involvement is never addressed.

In contrast, we discovered programs we could point to as truly excellent, especially when judged in the context of their public policy goals. We found that the very good programs share a common approach to their involvement in the public policy arena. They do the same things; and, they do them very well.

Thus, our purpose in writing this book is threefold:

First, we want to report on those programs that we have found to be worth emulating, regardless of one's budget.

Second, we want to exhort those organizations, both private and nonprofit, not now emulating the practices of the excellent public affairs program to do so.

Third, this book is about applying the idea of grassroots activities in a simpler time to the challenges of organizing and communicating in a complex world. For the best follow a simple blueprint for getting their message out, having it heard, and carrying the day. It is a blueprint worth reconsidering given that the revolution that changed the practice of public affairs a decade or more ago is both unfinished and out-of-date; given, too, the changes that have occurred in the public policy arena during the intervening years that have made the need for grassroots coalitions even more compelling.

The six most important of those changes for our purposes are:

1. *The Reagan revolution.* At least two major consequences of the Reagan era have impact on how an organization must structure its public affairs. First, and by far the most critical, is the decentralization of the governing process.

Prior to the Reagan presidency, the primary focus of most public affairs programs was Washington, D.C. The federal government, both in its legislative process and its administrative procedures, was all-pervasive. All problems were to be debated and resolved at the federal level.

The Reagan era changed all that. Today, problems are being debated and resolved at the state, county, and local levels with far greater consequences. Now, national organizations must have, at least, a multistate strategy. And, depending on the product, service, or issue, that strategy may also need to be more localized at a city or county level. In fact, the solution at the federal level often requires a coordinated approach that includes local political involvement.

The advent of the Clinton era arguably increases, in our judgment, the number of battlegrounds that must be addressed. Even the much-heralded budget battle, won by the narrowest of margins, may have been a fluke. Some votes were obtained by promises that may not disprove our thesis when they finally see the light of day, some by an appeal that the Democrats could not embarrass their new President on his first crucial test, and some votes were heavily influenced by successful grassroots activists.

2. *The end of the economic windfall.* A second consequence of the Reagan era was the momentary economic blast followed by what many believe will be a longtime financial chill. The good times are over for the foreseeable future.

Kevin Phillips detailed in *Politics for the Rich and Poor* (New York, Random House, 1990) how the rich got richer, the poor much poorer. But, we believe that the ultimate residue of the Reagan economic legacy will be that those large numbers of people who think of themselves as middle class, most of whom lauded and voted for Reagan in droves, will be the ones whose own lives will be most permanently and negatively affected by the consequences of Reaganomics.

Far from being in the temporary trough of a recession, we are, in fact, in the throes of a permanent retrenchment. One signal is the fact that this recession is asset driven. What assets the middle class were holding onto for their retirement or a rainy day are losing their value at the same time costs are escalating to pay for government-mandated programs, especially in the environmental and health areas. It is this tax *and* asset squeeze that will catch the middle class most directly in its vise.

3. *The new press orientation.* A decade ago when people in business complained about the press, their comments were usually from the perspective of readers and viewers, consumers of the news who didn't like the tilt of some reporting, particularly reporting on the political scene. If it was not the chroniclers of Watergate, Woodward and Bernstein, themselves, it was all the wanna-bes who followed them.

There was a time when there seemed to be little criticism of the business press from the corporate community, and with good reason. It appeared as though many financial reporters were of a mind simply to reproduce the release prepared by the corporate flack. Many criticized journalistic digging, probably unfairly, as being limited to their garden on weekends.

Today, that's changed forever. We've lived through an era of junk bonds, the flim-flam of Milken, the wholesale theft of people's savings from S&Ls, perhaps the imminent collapse of the banking industry, massive layoffs due to, among other things, stupidity in financial planning, excessively insulated decision making by private-sector leaders, and the overreaching greed of the Boesky types on Wall Street.

Currently, the big story *is* the economic story. Reporters, now schooled in business jargon, ask the same jarring questions of corporate types as they once asked of political types. Pulitzers may soon be awarded for the same investigative efforts as in Watergate, but they may be awarded now for various financial "gates."

This is especially true when the story apparently involves conspirators from both business and politics. As an example, take a Knight-Ridder News Service piece entitled "Junk-bond Lobby Wines, Dines, Wins and the Middle Class Picks Up the Tab."[2] A decade ago, such an indictment of the Congressional indifference to the middle class might have been consigned as a "ho-hum, another one of those stories" to a back page. Today, it's Page One.

Thus, the need now is for gifted communications strategists and spokespeople from both the public affairs and executive operations of an organization prepared to deal at the same level of competence with reporters who cover business, finance, and politics, as well as the substantive issues of concern to the organization. The evidence we uncovered in our study of excellent programs suggests that those so equipped will prevail in the nineties and beyond.

4. *Role of the United States in the world order.* There may come a new world order. It may usher in a Pax Americana unrivaled in world history. On the other hand, it may be a world order none of us truly wants. The United States may retreat, as some critics of the Clinton-Christopher policies are contending, from any significant role in the new world order. Whether that happens or not is dependent on many forces, but the impact on individual organizations, in our judgment, will depend in large measure on intelligent guidance by public affairs people of special breadth.

There are public affairs programs, and practitioners, whose mark of excellence is anchored in a dual belief: that there is an international dimension to the public affairs process, one that becomes more apparent as issues sweep across borders becoming truly transnational; and, that the same practical skills that make one a successful professional in public affairs in Albany, New York, Sacramento, California, or Frankfurt, Kentucky, make one equally successful in public affairs in Tokyo among the Japanese Diet or in Brussels among the European Parliament.

The world is a global village. We are not the first to point that out. What we do hope to convince the reader about is that truly excellent public affairs programs, whether existing within for-profit or not-for-profit organizations, must take into account the governmental decisions that are made outside the United States.

A decision made in Tokyo or in Brussels can have as much impact on an organization as one made in Washington. The smartest public affairs organizations recognize this fact and have structured themselves to deal with a multination, as well as a multistate, situation.

5. *Computerization to a new level of sophistication.* One reason smaller organizations and small staffs in large organizations are able to handle increasing amounts of public policy issues in multiple jurisdictions is the use of computers with an ever-increasing ability to manage and manipulate the data necessary for targeting a message to specific groups in specific jurisdictions.

Computerization has been a boon to efficiency. It has also been a bane to employment. But, if there is ever a silver lining in a situation in which companies are downsizing, it is that in the areas of corporate communications—public relations, public affairs, community relations, investor relations, and government relations—computerized applications have enabled organizations to handle the larger load with a smaller staff.

These applications represent a whole new process for managing successful public affairs strategies. What have emerged are systems that enable a company to handle multiple tasks simultaneously to track problems, to identify key people, to monitor attitudes and opinions, to mobilize friends, to assess results. These functions can now be computerized, enabling limited staff to direct multijurisdictional operations.

There is a direct correlation between a well-managed public affairs program and the creative use of computers and data to enhance an organization's opportunities and minimize threats in multiple communities simultaneously. Computers used intelligently provide a program with the margin of excellence that gives an organization the edge in dealing with the same problem in several state or national capitals.

6. *The growth, legitimacy, and consequence of community-based organizations.* Another phenomenon of the eighties was the increasing number and strength of community-based organizations.

Many trace their proud lineage to Saul Alinsky and their success to the concepts for mass organization for power he practiced and wrote about in such works as *Rules for Radicals* (New York, Random House, 1971). But, the degree of their militancy and sophistication has increased dramatically, driven by the Reaganesque hands-off approach to the role of government and the natural advantage of community-based organizations in a decentralized world.

Some industries have been brought to their knees. Two, in particular, spring to mind: the nuclear industry and the fur industry. Others have been kept on the ropes, notably the insurance industry and all industries affected by environmental issues. The techniques used by the better-run community-based groups reflect Alinsky's approach.

These activists can be ignored, to one's detriment; or, they can be addressed in a forthright manner with measurable degrees of success. How this has been done, both poorly and with great success, is explored throughout the book.

There is an irony here. As community-based advocates have taken advantage of the changing relationships among levels of government to compete with large organizations that have cultivated pipelines to governmental authority, so have the best corporate public affairs programs learned from the activists' successes and adopted both their organizational skills and their insights about the nature and use of power in public affairs.

Thus, the heirs of Saul Alinsky can be on both sides of the equation. Organizing at the grassroots level is open to anyone who makes a compelling case. That's the way it ought to be. We should ask for nothing less from the democratic process, especially at a time in history when so many newly emerging democracies are looking to the United States to see how to make their system work.

Nevertheless and intriguingly, many of these excellent corporate public affairs programs are also part of those organizations Tom Peters and Bob Waterman identified on their quest *In Search of Excellence* (New York, Harper Collins, 1982). Success in public affairs in the 1990s and beyond requires a melding of the Peters-Waterman lesson to *trust your people* and Alinsky's notion to *trust the system.* If used well, both the system and one's people can be resources in furthering one's mission and contributing to one's success.

Our trumpet call then is to organizational leaders, both corporate and nonprofit, that wish to claim their legitimate interest in the world of public affairs. There are principles worth considering and programs worthy of emulation. There are ideas worth adopting. There is a process that is genuinely beneficial and demonstrably excellent.

Basically, the process is about building not mere alliances but solid relationships—how that is done, why it is done, and with whom. In the corporate world, what we found were programs that were excellent because management's level of interest was matched with visionary public affairs leaders.

These visionary leaders believe that organizations that trust their people to design good widgets, manufacture good widgets, sell good widgets, and, while so doing, create in the community a sense that their organization is a trusted widget-maker, that the same employees can be trusted to help shape and deliver the public affairs messages in the community.

In the not-for-profit world, we learned a lot about organizing and delivering a powerful message and the differences between moral and economic arguments.

What we will do in this book is demonstrate how truly successful public affairs efforts have married the ideas from Peters-Waterman and Alinsky to modern communications technology to stay on top of and ahead of events in the public affairs arena. Hence the title, *The New Corporate Activism: Making Grassroots Lobbying Work for Your Organization.*

This book shows how well-managed organizations have incorporated, as part of their management philosophy, a strategy for dealing with public issues that makes certain the organization is *actively* plugged in: connected both to those who make decisions at every level of government as well as those who influence the decision makers;

capable of determining swiftly who among its allies is positioned best to make the case, and to what audiences in each particular case; and, attentive to the nuances of the message that is to be communicated.

We have divided the book into four parts. The first part focuses on what to think about before launching a program. Part 2 explains how to determine which ducks go in what rows. Part 3 explains how to get them there. Part 4 looks at situations that seem out of control and suggests ways of reining them in.

Our audience is those people in organizational settings of all kinds who seek to excel in the world of public affairs. They are individuals who buy into the two ideas that underline our approach to public affairs: anticipate and adapt to current realities and broaden the base of those involved in advocating the organization's best interests.

We believe that these ideas are beginning to drive not only public affairs programs but also the culture of our profit and not-for-profit organizations as well. In the final chapter, we explore some notions of how in the years ahead those ideas may reshape the relationship between businesses and their employees and between businesses and the communities in which they are located.

Notes

1. Associated Press, "California Politicians Backing 'Big Green' Environmental Initiative," Thursday, April 26, 1990, p.m. cycle.

2. Donald L. Bartlett and James B. Steele, "Junk-bond Lobby Wines, Dines, Wins and the Middle Class Picks Up the Tab," last of nine articles entitled "America, What Went Wrong?" Knight-Ridder News Service, *The Record*, November 1, 1991, pp. A-1 and 14.

PART 1

Get Ready

What to Think About Before You Begin

1
"All Politics Is Local"

Tip O'Neill made that statement over 30 years ago. He was right then, and he's even more right today. Influencing public attitudes over the long run has always been a grassroots enterprise. But, in these times, the successful advocates of an issue have demonstrated support at the voter level. For they understand not only Tip O'Neill's poignant observation but also the equally compelling, if more recent admonition: "Think globally. Act locally."

Top-down strategies are sometimes useful, particularly for defeating a specific piece of legislation that surfaces unexpectedly. But such crisis-driven operations represent a failure of long-term planning. Worse, if such operations are viewed as legislative solutions favoring only a few, they are usually doomed if counterattacked by a bottom-up grassroots voter coalition. Ronald Reagan took care of that.

From health care to insurance issues to the environment, today the action is at the state and local level. That is where the battles for the hearts and minds of the public are being fought. And that is where such battles are being won.

That makes sense if one clearly understands what the former Speaker of the U.S. House of Representatives meant. For the notion that "all politics is local" means, in one sense, that, ultimately, the winning side must be plugged into—read "in sync with"—the consciousness and action of voters at the grassroots level.

But it also means humbling oneself in order to listen and become attentive to the hopes, fears, aspirations, and anxieties of the people within the community. In that sense, it means becoming part of the bottom-up direction to public policy.

Those who favor a top-down approach eschew being part of a *vox populi* approach to problem solving. They can usually point to selective battles won without public involvement to bolster their claim that they know best how to proceed. But, by ignoring the grassroots participation in their handling of an issue, they run the risk of losing when they might win or even achieving more than they originally thought was politically possible, by appearing arrogant and élitist, often the cause of their undoing.

What intrigues us is noting that such apparent élitism or arrogance is not restricted to any one group in our society. On any given issue and at any given time in the evolution of that issue, those viewed as directing the process from above—rather than being part of the solution from below—can, and often do, vary.

It may be the corporate community at one time on one issue, a specific industry at another time on another issue. But not being in touch with the community is not restricted to the corporate community alone.

Reagan proved that some union leaders were out of date and out of touch. Grenada proved the press can be out of touch. And we are now finding that on even the most contentious issues the ground can shift as those who appeared to be part of the bottom-up solution become viewed as part of the top-down problem. Virtue is a crown worn lightly.

Take just one issue over which opposing sides can become apoplectic, the cleanup of the environment. Initially, the public viewed the corporate community as the arrogant, top-down group who not only cared little about the community but who also seemed to prove their opponent's case both by their reckless handling of the environment *and* by the way they handled their critics.

The good guys were the government activists and the environmentalists who both cared about the cleanup and were working with the community as part of the bottom-up solution. That initial contrast may still be the case in some instances. But it is changing. For what we are finding is that both the government itself and many of the environmentalist organizations are losing touch with people's priority concerns.

Let's examine first how the federal government is losing sight of the basic political fact that "all politics is local." In the next chapter we will examine how the environmentalists have repositioned themselves as the élitist group held suspect by local groups.

Progovernment Early Origins

Historically, the environmental cleanup issue was framed in such a way as to suggest that there were but two sides: those who felt the government was doing too much and those who felt that the government was doing too little.

The battle centered around the direction, or lack thereof, of the cleanup efforts by the U.S. Environmental Protection Agency (EPA), and, in particular, its administration of the Superfund law. The corporate community, that is, those accused of being the polluters, tended to feel that the EPA was doing too much; the environmentalists' groups, that EPA was doing too little.

The creation of the Environmental Protection Agency in 1971 was in response to a growing consensus nationwide. People had become aroused. They were tired of breathing dirty air, swimming in, and possibly drinking, polluted water, and living amidst land whose contamination at times created pockets of degradation resembling the surface of the moon.

Public interest on the subject had been fueled initially by those in the community who were most active in the environmental movement. People wanted someone to be held accountable for the mess and be required to make it whole, to return our environment, if possible, to a preindustrialization, pristine state. Public feelings on the issue grew to outrage as those most obviously involved in polluting the environment adopted an attitude that denied any culpability for the problem.

One notable example—occurring during the incipient days of the EPA, long before the discovery of tragedies such as Love Canal—was a utility company that chose an interesting approach to fight the EPA: advertising. The company spent $3.1 million trying to convince the public that an agency rule requiring scrubbers on their sulfur dioxide belching smokestacks was wrong. They lost.

The campaign gained much notoriety, and public reaction was generally negative. But their failure was not limited to an unconvinced public. What was also bad was the fact that their advertisements poisoned any hope of cooperation or conciliation with the Environmental Protection Agency.

Even worse, such an approach added to the simplistic notion that there were but two sides to the issue: the environmentalist's "white hats" versus the corporate polluter's "black hats." Further, this approach implied that the federal government, especially the EPA, was an advocate of the public interest. If corporate intransigence created the notion that the EPA was the friend of the public, Love Canal cemented it.

Mounting cancer and birth defect rates had aroused local suspicions, which were later confirmed, that the deteriorating health of the residents of that area of Niagara Falls, New York, could be directly tied to the contamination of the land and water. The health problems were sufficient to raise public concerns.

What triggered the demand for corporate reparations was the reaction of the Hooker Chemical Company. Some hinted that the company's attitude bordered on being cavalier, raising questions about the company's apparent wavering between denials of responsibility and accountability. The first was dismissed by the environmentalists. The second was credited for passage of a new law, Superfund, which was enacted in 1980.

Superfund was to be the answer to all the problems that had accumulated over the years. Land and water that been contaminated or polluted would be made whole, and those who had caused the problem would be made to pay. Sounded like a simple process. Find the Love Canals of the country, determine who caused them, clean them up, and send the offenders an invoice.

Sounded also like an ideal solution. The government would do the work, find the polluters, and make them pay. Few doubted that it was the corporate community that would be held liable and made to pay. And from the early evidence presented for public consumption, it seemed that this scenario would match facts with strongly held beliefs.

No one early on supposed that polluters might include other government bodies—cities, counties, states, and, in several instances, the federal government itself. Nor did anyone think through that such governmental pollution would be cleaned up at a price that would fall as heavily, if not more heavily, on the individual taxpayer.

In the heady days following passage of the Superfund, homeowners in some affected areas saw the new legislation as their landscaping lottery come true. It would be a time for new shrubs, trees, lawns, and possibly a new fence to replace the one torn down when the old sod was replaced as part of the contaminated soil removal program.

None thought that they, too, could be, or would be, held accountable. Or, if not held accountable, held hostage to draconian agreements that were sufficiently onerous as to make people wonder whether the EPA was truly on their side.

Government's Involvement Questioned

The feeling that somehow someone else will foot the bill is changing these days as more and more people begin to fully realize that the politics of any issue is ultimately local. In state after state, homeowners are beginning to get the message that the cost of sewage, water, and garbage disposal services alone may triple by the mid-1990s because of regulations aimed at cleaning up the environment.

In New Jersey, for example, a study released in September 1991 by the state's Department of Environmental Protection and Energy accurately predicted that the average annual cost for those services would rise to $1227 in 1994 for each homeowner from $432 in 1989.[1] Staggering enough, it still is not as high as it would have been if it included the higher costs for goods and services passed along to consumers by companies accused of polluting.

Now, instead of a corporate "they" with deep pockets to pay for the cleanup of New Jersey, there is emerging a public "us" being held accountable. It is a trend that many in industry herald. As Hal Bozarth, Executive Director of the Chemical Industry Council of New Jersey, noted following publication of the study:

> We have been saying for some time that sooner or later, the public will get a taste of what environmental protection is all about, and this study is it. The responsibility for a cleaner environment does not just fall on industries like ours, but on communities and individuals.[2]

What happens when the responsibility falls on the shoulders of individuals? Well, for sure, it changes the political dynamics. Sometimes to a point where a staunch environmental legislator does a 180-degree turn. For if anything is certain about elected officials who survive, it is that they heed Tip's advice. And when the politics of the issue begin to affect the pocketbook of individual voters at the local level, even the most ardent elected environmentalist pauses to ponder the dilemma: second thoughts or no second term?

Aspen's Smuggler Mountain

The case in point is Aspen, Colorado. The legislator is Tim Wirth.

If someone were to list cities in the United States in which homeowners would rebel against the EPA and a proposed Superfund cleanup, Aspen would probably not make the list. Its image is that of a highly issue involved town. So much so that a resident columnist for a local newspaper recently wrote that to be branded an "Aspenite" had become "an epithet, a term of opprobrium and scorn":

> Aspenizers are the ones who are taking jobs away from autoworkers in Detroit, loggers in Oregon, forcing the closure of vital military bases by spending tax dollars on frivolous elections to ban fur coats and bigger hotels.[3]

It was not always so, and perhaps it is that distant pioneer past that is returning. For it was silver mining that created Aspen. The precious ore was discovered there in 1879, and between 1887 and 1893 Aspen was the richest silver mining center in America.

But, in 1893, silver was demonetized, and the silver boom was over. One by one the mines closed, and by 1930 the population, which in boom times had numbered 12,000, was down to 705. Then, in the 1930s and 1940s, new investors created a new boom out of another natural resource. This time it was snow instead of silver.

Today, Aspen oozes a century-old Victorian architectural charm. It places at least third annually as the choice of readers of *Ski Magazine.* Its popular image is that of movie stars and millionaires. Stories of properties worth millions are legend. But there is another side of Aspen. It is where the working people live, where property values are more modest. And it is there that our story begins in 1981.

An Early Study

David Boon was a graduate student at the time working toward his master's degree at Colorado State University (CSU). His particular interest as a researcher was in lead and cadmium.

As a part of his studies, he participated in a soil testing program for the CSU extension service. It was all part of a normal program offered to interested Colorado residents who were preparing their spring gardens. Through the county extension service, residents would query CSU as to which fertilizer to use to make their gardens more fertile.

Out of curiosity, Boon decided to boost the level of his testing apparatus for soil samples sent in by residents of the Smuggler Trailer Court in Aspen. He had not been asked or told to do so. There had been no reports from public health officials that would lead him to believe the new test levels were necessary. But he did the tests and found that the soil from the Smuggler Trailer Court area registered high concentrations of both lead and cadmium.

Following on his initial findings, a press release was issued by the Colorado State University dated August 28, 1981. It cautioned individuals and families whose gardens were located near the Smuggler Mountain Mine site that the soil might have toxic quantities. The release particularly warned that children should not have direct contact (play) on the mining waste or be fed vegetables from contaminated gardens due to the risk of lead poisoning.[4]

But, as *The Aspen Times* reported in a story entitled "EPA Superfund: A Ten Million Dollar Mess," "that chance discovery led to a $13.7 million EPA Superfund cleanup project that calls for digging up some 60,000 cubic yards of dirt from residential areas in Aspen over a two year period and entombing it in nearby repositories" located at the base of the Smuggler Mountain. It also called for thousands of residents within the site to be relocated for up to a week while their back yards are excavated, hauled away, and replaced.[5]

It would have happened too, had not Patti Clapper, a homemaker, mother of two small children, practicing nurse at the local hospital, and, at the time a political neophyte, begun asking questions. For by the time she was finished asking questions the EPA could not or would not answer, an entire community's leaders, including the local medical establishment, were part of a grassroots movement whose anti-EPA fervor was best expressed by Aspen's mayor, John Bennett, when he said, "If they start work on this project, I'll lie down in front of the bulldozers to stop them."[6]

Fortunately, before Mayor Bennett had to demonstrate his version of a greater love for his fellow citizens, Senator Wirth saw the light. But we're ahead of ourselves in the story.

Alarmed by the CSU press release, Tom Dunlop, environmental health officer for both the city of Aspen and Pitkin County, performed his own tests. His tests corroborated those performed by Boon. The problem both men now realize is that despite the toxicity of the soil, no one then or since has gotten sick. But, as later events proved, such wellness would not be welcomed by the feds.

The county commissioners responded as any right-thinking county officials would given the evidence in hand and their knowledge of environmental affairs in 1981. They agreed with a proposal by the county engineer, Pat Dobie, that he extend an invitation to the EPA to list Smuggler Mountain as a Superfund site.

After all, they reasoned, Superfund status would provide for the cleanup of a bona fide public health threat *without cost to the community*. (Emphasis added). What they also assumed, logically, but erroneously, was that, once clean, the site would be delisted, and life would return to normal. In June 1984, the EPA announced its initial plans for a cleanup.[7]

One intriguing anomaly is that the EPA initially said that they lacked jurisdiction. According to Mr. Boon,

> The EPA told us that they were responsible only for cleaning up organic chemical dumps such as Love Canal, NY, Valley of the Drums, KY, or Times Beach, MO. Mine sites were the responsibility of a separate Federal law, the Abandoned Mines Lands program.

No one questioned initially whether the site should, in fact, be cleaned up; whether left alone it posed any sort of a health threat; whether the cleanup process would cause more of a health problem than leaving the site alone; or whether it could be cleaned up to a point that the EPA would guarantee that no health hazard existed—a point bankers would insist upon in order to make loans. What bank in its right mind would make a loan on a property that might end up in default, thereby making the bank both the owner of the property and the one liable for a portion of the cleanup costs?

Not until local residents began to raise questions did anyone wonder aloud why only the less prestigious parts of Aspen were cited for Superfund, why the million-dollar-plus properties that also sat on sites of abandoned mines were scrupulously (some would argue, politically) left off the EPA's list. In short, it began to appear to some as though the EPA was picking on the financially less endowed folks to harass.

What no one knew then, and Aspenites only learned in the past year or so, is that once a community is on the list, it takes an act of Congress to get delisted. This is especially true if the proposed solution is to rebury the alleged contaminated soil in the same area to be cleaned; more especially, if finding clean soil to replace the old sod is next to impossible in a region like the Rocky Mountains that has had lead and cadmium deposits in abundance probably since the beginning of time. That the site may never be delisted, even after cleanup, casts a continuing financial cloud over homeowners.

But should the site have been listed in the first place? According to Boon, now a professor and co-chair of the Hazardous Materials Technology Program at Front Range Community College in Westminster, Colorado, "The EPA listing of the Smuggler Mountain area as a Superfund site was a mistake because the health threats from the mine dumps have never been substantiated. In fact, I fought like crazy to get it off the list."[8]

One way he fought was to devise a reclamation plan that would have established a soil cleanup standard of 500 parts per million, which is cleaner than the 1000 parts of lead per million standard that the EPA either requires or promises to accomplish. His proposal would have cleaned the land around Smuggler to a lead level of 500 parts per million. His proposal, which called for a private developer to remove the tainted earth and bury it beneath a foundation of concrete and asphalt, would also have been undertaken at no cost to the federal government. Unfortunately, saving tax dollars, as many who are tracking the EPA today are finding out, is not one of the interests of the agency. Boon's offer was rejected.

For what people are learning is that once the EPA is involved, the agency is there forever, regardless of any reasonable alternative plan, and, most certainly regardless of whether the listing can be proven to be an erroneous one. The federal bureaucratic process leaves no room for denial of a problem an agency has targeted for over a decade. And with that uncertainty of ever being delisted comes the realization that bank loans for any purpose will become increasingly impossible to obtain.

What was erroneous about the listing in Aspen was that the toxicity in the soil had never impacted human health, nor, some think, should it ever. It has to do with the bioavailability of lead. Seems there are differences among sources of lead in terms of how they may or may not affect human health. Lead-based gasoline fumes that are breathed in when airborne may affect the respiratory tract. Lead-based paint chips, eaten by children, will directly impact various organs. But, lead left in the ground seems not to have any appreciable impact.

Stefan Albouy, who currently leases the Smuggler Mine from the original owners, notes:

> There are mineral deposits of lead and cadmium scattered all around the Rockies. Just don't whack off a piece and have it for lunch. . . .
> There are natural outcroppings of the minerals all over the mountainsides. It occurs naturally. Generations of kids grew up playing in the mine dumps. It didn't hurt them and it shouldn't hurt you unless you eat it by the plateful.[9]

Albouy is not a medical person. But the science available backs him up, which it did when the community finally got sufficiently aroused to begin looking into the medical evidence, the financial implications of the Superfund siting, and what some local people alleged was the less-than-truthful approach undertaken by the EPA.

The Bottoms-Up Protest Begins

Patti Clapper had started the ball rolling. She had fought, almost single-handedly since 1988 when she first became concerned, to find out why, in her words,

> We were being threatened by the EPA. We had moved here knowing that it was a Superfund site. But, to us and our neighbors, that simply meant that someone, probably the government, was going to clean up what they said was a problem. We had trouble focusing on any problem since everywhere we looked we saw lush lawns, a beautiful setting.
> We knew of no history of health problems, and we certainly couldn't understand why the EPA was saying to those of us who were homeowners that, by law, we were responsible. How could we be held liable when we had nothing to do with whatever the problem was?

The EPA lawyers threatened us. If we didn't sign a consent decree which would clear EPA of any future liability, then EPA would sue us as a party to the clean-up. But, the consent decree was also a gag order. It said we could not contest any decision they might make or any explanation they might give.

Under the rules of the consent decree, if we challenged any decision or explanation made by the EPA, the EPA could sue us as being liable for the clean-up. So, under the Citizen Consent Decree, we clear the EPA of any future liability, agreeing in effect that we can't sue EPA even if EPA screws up.

They also hedged as to whether there would ever be a delisting or a certifiable clean-up. They would make no guarantees of what life would be like two or three years after they completed their work, whether we would ever be in a position where the banks would feel comfortable loaning us money and using our homes as collateral.

We wanted something in writing that we would not be sued, a document that would protect us financially. EPA refused. The most they would do is give us something that said we could be held harmless if some third party sued us, but that theory has never been tested in court, and if challenged we would have to pay for our defense of a document they had drawn up.

In short, all we knew for certain is that we would be nowhere in the end, and that our neighborhood would be disrupted from morning to night with earth-moving equipment.

Worse, we learned, as we studied other Superfund sites and asked the right questions, we would be subject to a greater health risk from the dust stirred up by the earth movers than from just leaving the land alone. In Utah, for example, blood lead studies there showed that the amount of lead in people's blood *after* the clean-up was far greater than before due to the airborne lead particles ingested from the dust of the clean-up operation.

The hardest part for me to accept was that my own government was going to force me to do something that didn't need to be done, that I didn't want done, and that would create a greater health risk to my children.[10]

A Local Organization Emerges

Patti Clapper would probably still be railing against the federal establishment without any satisfaction had not a few things come together that made what was initially a one-woman crusade an Aspen-wide cause. The first was a luncheon. The second an election. The third, an imminent deadline.

The deadline was August 1. That was the day the EPA's bulldozers were to begin tearing up the land. Virtually all the signoffs that were needed were in place. Those who had been fighting had just about given up. After years of battling the giant EPA, those few homeowners, like Patti, who opposed the cleanup had been written off as quacks. The city and county fathers had said, in effect, "Why fight 'EPA' Hall."

As *The Aspen Times* noted in its April 25 headline story on the history of the project, "In a community known for its confrontational politics and environmental awareness, public comment on this major project is relatively mute."[11]

Then, Terry Hale got involved. Hale is a dentist. He's also a member of one of those no-name luncheon clubs that exist in many communities and that probably have more clout simply because they have no fixed agenda, no dues, and no axe to grind unless they get riled up. This particular luncheon club attracts not only the local power structure but also a national power élite who'll "drop by" when they're in town for more important things, like skiing or other relaxing endeavors.

Hale invited Patti Clapper to address the luncheon group. Her story aroused their interest, but, as he says:

> We didn't believe her. So she challenged us to check out her facts. We did. We checked with the Colorado School of Mines. We checked with leading toxicologists in the United States. We checked with people in other Superfund sites. What we found was that Patti was right and the EPA had been feeding us a pile of_____.

Dr. Hale also has courtesy staff privileges at the Aspen Valley Hospital, a small, 50-bed facility known more for its orthopedic work than anything else, but staffed with as fine a group of physicians as may be found anywhere. Hale took his findings to the hospital medical board. They were somewhat aware of the issue as Patti Clapper is both a nurse at the hospital and a person who had been asking many of the specialists similar questions in her quest to learn as much as she could about lead, how it is absorbed, how it can be detected, and the like.

Hale prevailed upon his medical brethren to take responsibility for determining the answer to the basic question they, as physicians, should be able to answer: Does Aspen have a health problem? They agreed and formed a committee of seven physicians, headed by Robert E. Hunter, M.D., to study the issue. The result of their study lent credence to the opponents of the cleanup.[12]

Hunter's committee issued its report in July. It said:

> In the past 35 years, there has been no documented case of lead poisoning, nor has Aspen seen evidence of abnormal births or growth and development issues that would suggest that lead has been an ongoing problem.
> Based on the blood levels obtained and the clinical experience of the medical community, it is our belief that lead does not represent a significant health threat to the residents of the Smuggler site nor the remainder of the Aspen area. We can see no justification for the

identification of the site as a Superfund clean-up target and in fact, have significant medical concerns regarding an attempt at remediation. It would seem that the bioavailability of lead now present in the mine tailings is extremely low. This equilibrium could be radically altered should a clean-up be undertaken which converts lead in tailings to lead in dust and in small particles which could be more easily ingested or inhaled.[13]

The Hunter committee had done its homework. They made a number of inquiries. They read as much as they could obtain from scientific journals. They may even have read a report printed in the *Rocky Mountain News* put out by the American Lung Association and *Science Magazine* concerning the chances of dying in any one year based on a specific activity. The goal of the report is to reduce one's participation in such activities to 1 in 1 million, especially if one is currently taking a 1 in 10,000 risk. Here's the chart:[14]

1 in 200	Smoking a pack of cigarettes a day
1 in 4000	Breathing radon gas
1 in 5000	Living in Boston—air pollution
1 in 10,000	Drinking a bottle of wine a week—liver disease
1 in 166,000	Living in a brick building—radiation
1 in 166,000	Living in Colorado—background radiation higher than normal
1 in 700,000	Drinking contaminated well water from a Colorado Superfund site per toxic chemical
1 in 150 million	Living close to a nuclear power plant

Clearly, there appeared to be little, if any, health hazard. The general belief was that lead in the soil caused little problem if left buried, but that it could cause problems if dug up and moved. The Hunter committee called for a moratorium on any cleanup, at least until additional and more conclusive studies could be done.

The final piece of the Clapper-cum-community-cause was an election in May. Those opposed to the EPA gained a new champion. The new mayor, John Bennett, ran on a platform in which he said that, if elected, he would listen to people and he would act to bring the community together. He might not have acted had Patti Clapper been alone.

But, the resounding endorsement of the medical community, plus the information Dr. Hale and his associates had found out about the EPA and its activities in other communities, made Mayor Bennett a believer. Together with new and recently converted incumbent city council members, the Aspen city leadership voted against cooperating with the EPA.

Enter Tim Wirth

There's an old cartoon that shows a person donning his coat as he hurries out of the room. To a quizzical onlooker he explains his haste: "I must hurry. I am their leader and they have left." Enter Tim Wirth.

If any member of Congress ever deserved the appellation, Mr. Environment, it was Colorado's former junior senator. He coauthored the Superfund law as a congressman. He remained a true believer that the Environmental Protection Agency could do no wrong.

On more than one occasion the senator directly, or through his staff, told first Patti Clapper and then Dr. Hale, in effect: "Stop being a cry baby. The EPA knows what it is doing. You don't. So get with the program."

Dr. Hale in particular recalls the senator's aides as being especially confrontational:

> They seemed unable to comprehend that the EPA was, in effect, destroying our civil rights.
>
> We had no borrowing power so long as they would make no guarantees. They never saw the EPA for the police state that it is, bludgeoning people into signing away their rights without, in turn, protecting the individuals. Nor did they understand that the EPA has no credible medical standing.

In his defense, Wirth is not a scientist. He relies, as does any politician, on what he believes to be correct scientific judgment. Whether he had ever thought to hold hearings to air what appears to be a major discrepancy between the clinical scientific community, as represented by the Centers for Disease Control, and the EPA's regulatory scientific community, is unknown.

But, Wirth knows Tip's dictum. He might not do a 180. But, he'd do a 179-degree turn. He decided to back his constituents against the EPA after personally inspecting the site and realizing that, perhaps, the residents were right.

In July, he wrote the EPA regional administrator, Jim Scherer, asking that the agency obtain the opinion of a third party as to the health risk and to hold off on doing anything in the meanwhile, adding:

> It is clear to me that many members of the community have significant reservations about some elements of the proposed remediation plan, and that the implementation of those actions this summer would incite even greater controversy, and, very possibly, confrontation.
>
> [For] the proposed remediation plan has sparked a controversy that spans the length and breadth of Pitkin County. I do not believe that such a situation would well serve either the community of Aspen or the Environmental Commission.[15]

Wirth was aware of the growing antipathy against the EPA in the community. Confrontation at public meetings was heated. Outside the meetings, "EPA Go Home" floats in local parades and colorful anti-EPA telephone answering recordings added to the fervor. Many people refused to return documents mailed to them. Others refused EPA inspectors access to their property. In one situation, an EPA inspector was arrested for trespassing.

Wirth's letter concluded: It is

> . . . possible that the independent third party will conclude that a less intrusive cleanup action plan is adequate to protect human health and the environment. In that case I am confident that EPA would want to reconcile its proposed remediation plan to reflect the third party's recommendations.[16]

The headline in the Aspen *Times Daily* on August 7, 1991, said it all: "EPA Blinks in Superfund Duel." And for that moment, the residents *appeared* to have won. The EPA sought no funding for the site for 1992.

But, as Aspen residents were learning, the battle may have been won, but the war would continue. The reason? As noted before, once the EPA is involved, the feds know they'll be there forever, absent an act of Congress.

The Heart of the Issue

That said, the Smuggler Mountain case in Aspen may yet prove to be a pivotal one, according to attorney Brooke Peterson. Peterson specializes in real estate and land-use law as well as litigation. His previous bouts with the EPA on behalf of an Aspen homeowner's association led to his being retained by the Smuggler Caucus, the group organized to represent the homeowners in their negotiations with the EPA.

Peterson maintains that the Aspen battle demonstrated one strategy he would recommend elsewhere. It also started the ball rolling on two issues that, if resolved, will be significant accomplishments.

The two potential accomplishments include a way of holding harmless the residential landowners who clearly never contributed to the contamination as well as a way of eliminating the potential liability of the banks if they lend to such homeowners. Both proposals are being reviewed by the EPA and the Congress. Wirth, while a member of the U.S. Senate, came to support the proposal to hold residential landowners harmless.

As to the strategy, Peterson maintains that when confronting the EPA on behalf of a client, the strategy should be on two tracks simultaneously: one legal, the other political.

> What Patti Clapper, Terry Hale, and John Bennett did could not have been done by me acting as their counsel. They focused on the

political aspects of the situation, notably the question: Does the clean-up of Smuggler Mountain make sense?

We were able to gain some concessions over the bargaining table, but at some point, it takes political clout and I doubt that Senator Wirth would have listened to me as counsel. He would only respond to those I was representing as they presented their case as constituents.

That the process is probably more political than legal is a point with which the midwife of the Superfund law, Lois Gibbs, might agree. Today, Gibbs is the executive director of the Citizens Clearinghouse for Hazardous Waste, a group that counsels communities on how or how not to proceed when seeking Superfund status.

A decade ago, she was the enraged homemaker living in the Love Canal section of Niagara Falls, New York, whose efforts led to the passage of the Superfund law. She and her organization maintain that environmental matters are 10 percent legal and 90 percent political.

> Of the 1200 plus sites on the Superfund list as of 1991, some 30% got there because of citizen action. If they had asked my advice before proceeding, I would have advised them not to get on the Superfund cleanup list, to avoid it like the plague. Not because the intent of the law was not good, but because it's totally ineffective— it just plain doesn't work.

As of 1991, only 54 sites, some 4 percent, had been cleaned up.[17]

Perhaps the community leaders of Aspen should have asked the question in 1981: Do we really need a federally directed Superfund cleanup? But that's perfect hindsight. It is a question, however, that needs to be asked in communities today that have Superfund status.

And if the answer is no because there is no demonstrable health hazard or because the cleanup will cause a worse problem than now exists, then there is a need to organize and to bring pressure upon the elected officials who can change the law.

A decade ago, such grassroots opposition to the EPA and Superfund would have been unthinkable. It may even be next to impossible today, given the staying power of the EPA and the inertia of Congress. But what is fairly safe to predict is that as more and more individuals feel the flight of dollars from their wallet to undertake tasks they previously thought the responsibility of someone else, new coalitions will be formed that align individual citizens like those in Aspen with corporations against the federal bureaucracy.

What drives individuals to coalesce into coalitions is the combination of economic threat to one's wallet plus a sense of alienation from whatever system—big government, big organization, big whatever as we shall subsequently discuss—that appears to be in control and unresponsive to queries or criticisms. The coalition forms because those who feel both personally alienated and financially deprived begin to find that they share a common bond among others who feel they, too, are likewise being abused.

That's the essence of grassroots politics. That's also the genesis of Tip O'Neill's observation. That's why strategists speak of dealing thoughtfully with an issue globally but applying it sensibly locally. People intellectually respond to an issue globally. They emotionally respond locally.

The Aspen case is clearly one in which the people felt that they were being forced to accept a course of action in a top-down manner without any regard to the feelings, views, or concerns of the people. To some home-owners, the EPA, no doubt unwittingly, now appears to be the arrogant enemy, an élitist group that has chosen to ignore the basic O'Neill tenet.

There was a major financial issue at stake for the homeowners in Aspen. But most people were willing to ignore the dollar issue as long as they truly believed (1) that an overriding health issue existed, (2) that the inconvenience would be minute, (3) that the problem would go away once the proposed cleanup was finished, and, (4), that they could, in fact, trust the people who worked for the EPA.

Once the trust factor was destroyed, once people began believing that anything said by anyone from the EPA (or its cronies, the lawyers from the Justice Department and the consultants out for a buck) was suspect, the coals to ignite a raging grassroots coalition were lit. And once the damper of a health argument became highly suspect, the financial issue took over.

The trust factor is critical. It is lost when people begin believing that a group is trying to muscle its will, in a top-down sense, as the EPA is doing in Aspen. The feds may ultimately win, but the price will be high.

Trust is also being lost, and for the same reasons, by many environmental groups. We shall see how that occurred in California and how many corporate executives almost missed an opportunity because of their inability to trust the system or the people.

Notes

1. Leo H. Carney, "Homeowners Said to Face Rise in Costs to Clean Up Environment," *The New York Times,* New Jersey Weekly, September 29, 1991, Sec. 12, pp. 1 and 8.
2. Ibid.
3. Richard Compton's column, "The Aspenization of Name-Calling," Aspen, Colorado, *Times Daily,* July 15, 1991, p. 7.

4. In an article entitled "Researcher: 'Superfund Not for Smuggler'," *The Aspen Times* (vol. 112, no. 17, April 25, 1991, pp. 1-A and 2-A) suggested that it is a release and a study Boon now seems to regret.

5. Paul Andersen, "EPA Superfund: A Ten Million Dollar Mess," *The Aspen Times*, vol. 112, no. 17, April 25, 1991, pp. 1 and 3-A.

6. American Political Network, Inc., *Greenwire*, July 18, 1991.

7. Andersen, "EPA Superfund," p. 3-A.

8. *The Aspen Times,* op. cit., April 25, 1991, p. 1-A.

9. Mary Eshbaugh Hayes, "Generations Co-existed with Mines," *The Aspen Times*, vol. 112, no. 17, April 25, 1991, p. 7-A.

10. From an interview with Patti Clapper.

11. Andersen, "EPA Superfund," p. 3-A.

12. What they found is that Aspenites are generally healthier than people living elsewhere if one is looking at the amount of lead in their blood. The Centers for Disease Control in Atlanta told them that if one's blood lead level is below 9, there is no concern, but that if it is 10 to 15, there is a need to identify and remediate the source. They learned from the University of Cincinnati about other communities.

    The University of Cincinnati has the oldest research unit in the country for the study of lead. Their people told the Aspen committee that the average citizen in the United States has 6 to 8 deciliters per millimeter of lead in their blood; that people in New Jersey have 18, people in Cincinnati 16, and people in Boston 22.

    The Hunter committee conducted blood lead studies in Aspen. The average adult had 3.1 deciliters per millimeter. The average child 2.6. Beyond the blood lead level, the committee learned from air monitors that Aspen had one-tenth the allowable federal standards and that groundwater tested from wells in the area showed no high traces of lead or cadmium.

13. Robert E. Hunter, M.D., Chairman, Ad Hoc Committee, Lead Toxicity in Aspen, *Position Statement,* Aspen Valley Hospital, July 1991.

14. Bill Scanlon, "Superfund Spending Eclipses Results," *Rocky Mountain News,* Greater Denver & The West, Special Report: "A Costly Strategy," September 27, 1991, p. 8.

15. Timothy E. Wirth, U.S. Senator, "Wirth to EPA: Drop the Shovels for Just a Minute," *Times Daily,* Letters, vol. 4, no. 140, July 15, 1991, p. 6.

16. Ibid.

17. Debra K. Rubin and Steven W. Setzer, "The Superfund Decade: Triumphs and Troubles," *Engineering News Record,* November 26, 1991, vol. 225, no. 21, p. 38; and "Fixing Superfund," American Political Network, Inc., *Greenwire,* Focus section, August 20, 1991.

2
A Rationale for Noninvolvement

The concept explored in the previous chapter, namely, that "all politics is local," can be explained in another way: People respond to what affects them in their daily lives.

Their garbage is not being picked up. The air they breathe is foul. They can no longer swim in places they grew up enjoying because of pollution. There is not a light at the corner so that their children can cross the street safely on their way to school. They have lost, or believe themselves to be in imminent danger of losing, their jobs. They are sick and have no medical coverage. They are facing old age with the prospect of inadequate medical coverage. These situations represent reality for them—one or more things that affect them daily and to which they will respond.

If people respond to what affects them in their daily lives, then in order to know what people are going to respond to, it is important to be out among the people, in touch with their feelings, and communicating with them about those things that are affecting their daily lives. It's really not so complicated. In fact, it is the core and distinguishing feature of the kind of public affairs we believe all corporate executives must practice. We call it simply, "engagement."

It is possible, of course, to learn of the concerns of people in an indirect way. One can take public opinion and market surveys. One can even conduct focus groups. But, while helpful as tools to buttress the astute personal observation or to rebut common misconceptions, they are simply indicators of *ways* to become engaged. They are not substitutes for engagement.

Engagement is about attitude and process. Both require a willing-ness to engage: to build alliances with unusual bedfellows, to cross boundaries of race and gender and ideology, to be willing to challenge opponents and risk sharp confrontation, to think about managing yourself as well as managing the situation you are in, and to use all the personal resources available, intellectual and emotional, in pursuit of the mission. Frightening stuff to types we'll describe here whose atti-tude presages avoidance behavior. A welcome challenge to those oth-ers worth emulating, whose success in the public affairs arena stands in sharp contrast and answers the question, "Why do it our way?"

With engagement all things are possible. Without some engagement, long-term public affairs success is problematic. A total lack of engage-ment can spell trouble. To make the point, let us examine momentarily a corporation, a profession, and a group of social programs that lost their funding during the Reagan era. For each have shared a lack of engagement as the cause of their problems in the community. Quite simply, they have each shared the problem of not being in touch with the community they hoped to sell to, to lead, or to serve.

The Coors Brewing Company at one time in their recent history is the corporate example. It was a time in the early and mid-1980s when their share of the market in many of their regional markets was drop-ping from the mid-60s to the mid-20s, and their hold on their home-town market of Denver was plummeting from first place to third.

The cause was obvious. They were losing market share because of active boycotts by groups that felt that the Coors management was, among other charges, antiunion, antiblack, anti-Hispanic, antifemale, anti-Native American, antigay, and anti-just-about-any-minority-group one could name.

The company has since battled back, and we will recount in the chapter on dealing with crisis—Chap. 8—how they have successfully built bridges to any group that could include potential beer drinkers. But the point is clear. At the time of the boycotts, the company was viewed as not being engaged in the community.

Despite having a good product and, as *60 Minutes* verified, excellent working conditions—also recounted more fully later, when we discuss dealing with the media in Chap. 4—the company continued to be por-trayed by some, albeit incorrectly, as insensitive, its family manage-ment as arrogant. They paid a terrible price for a long while as their critics went unchallenged.

It is a price we believe any organization can expect to pay if it is viewed as similarly disengaged by virtue of a nonexistent or inert pub-lic affairs program. An unfavorable public image can have a dramatic impact on an organization's share of the market, sometimes eliminating it entirely. It can force the organization or group to do business in a way it may view as inimical to its purpose or best interest.

The medical fraternity is the profession we believe will ultimately be doing business in a way they disdain. In our lifetime there will be some form of universally accessible health care—despite the failure of the Clinton administration and the Democrats in control of the Congress to arrive at some modest compromise in 1994—and federal controls of the fees charged by the medical profession. These changes will be brought about not because most of us don't agree with the notion that the doctor-patient relationship should remain free and unfettered but because of the arrogance of some medical practitioners who view their own self-worth as being beyond the rest of ours. The failure of the health care reform legislation, we believe, may have been due more to the messenger than to the message. Republican rhetoric about big government simply postponed the inevitable because the public still wants a level playing field in dealing with their physicians and a reduction in the cost of medical care.

In an article that appeared in both the Outlook section and the National Weekly Edition of *The Washington Post*, the author refers to comments from "randomly selected telephone interviews conducted between 1989 and 1991 by the Gallup Organization for the American Medical Association." The views expressed by the respondents we believe remain relevant today. In particular, 63 percent "felt that doctors are too interested in making money" and "almost 70 percent felt that people are beginning to lose faith in their doctors."[1]

In the political process, perception is reality. Given the fact, we wonder if the public's perception of physicians is not helped by those doctors whose actions add to the questionable view many hold. We have a friend who attended a fertility clinic presentation at a hospital in New York City in the fall of 1992. The discussion centered around in vitro fertilization. The cost was $7300. The physician making the presentation told those in attendance that since insurance did not cover in vitro implants, the attending physicians would note on the insurance form that the actual event taking place was the removal of a cyst. That way our friend and all attending the forum who desired to pursue the in vitro fertilization process could be reimbursed by their insurance carrier.

We have also attended meetings with physicians bent on getting a legislative or political solution to the problem of the sky-rocketing costs of liability insurance. One practical solution: a cap, or dollar ceiling, on the amount that could be collected for negligence. Seems fair.

But, when we've asked if they would pass along to their patients, in terms of fees charged for office visits, procedures, and the like, the savings they would enjoy from lower insurance rates, physicians decline.

The physicians want public support for their position, but they are unwilling to offer their patients a modest quid pro quo for that support.

What many in the medical community seem not to understand is the need for an alliance with the people they serve, an engagement in their lives to understand what is bothering them, namely, the escalating cost of medical care, while physicians apparently do little to reduce the costs. The additional question of concern to patients is why the best medical system in the world is unable to care for those most in need. Many people have the sense that as long as the doctors get their share of the economic pie, the rest of us can pay their fees and get little in return.

The charge of a lack of engagement in the community can also be attached to many worthwhile social programs. While they were doing well, they lost touch with the support base they needed to continue.

The leaders of many community organizations seeking support for worthwhile causes worked exclusively at the state house level and only with legislative leaders and key committee chairs. As a consequence, when the economy turned and cutbacks were necessary, there was no grassroots support for those programs, and therefore, no protection. They, too, like their corporate brethren, had forgotten the need to establish a constituent base. They not only forgot that "all politics is local," they also ignored the economic warning signs, assuming their safety net was secure, because, after all, they said, "We're on the right side of the issue."

Judith Meredith, author of *Lobbying on a Shoestring* (Massachusetts Poverty Law Center, Boston, 1982), and one of the leading lobbyists in Massachusetts for nonprofit causes, speaks of the problem:

> During the 1980s, when the lunch bucket liberals were still in control of the legislature in Massachusetts, we were able to get money simply by defining the issue. Whether it was a program for the elderly, the poor, the disadvantaged, unwed mothers, or undocumented residents, some money could be found for a pilot project.
>
> At one point I calculated that out of a $12 billion budget, we had some $50 million, not a bad sum for projects and people who had little voice and lot of need. At the time there was a lot of money around, a feeling that things were going to continue to get better, and a legislature that was run from the top down. If we convinced the leadership, we got the money. We didn't take the time to build a bottom-up coalition.
>
> Then the fiscal crisis hit and we were seen as expendable. We had previously never had to build public consensus. I knew it was bad when I was visiting my mother and she said to me, 'What's wrong with these people? Why don't they just go out and get a job?' My own mother didn't understand the need!

Hence, the problem of nonengagement is not limited to corporations, or to professions, or to associations of any kind. No. In our observation, lots of executives are unwilling to take this step. And it's understandable.

First, they were not trained for this role. They are managers, people who think up and down and not out. They learn to boss people and to be bossed, to respect boundaries, and to bring only those people into their environment who agree with their perspective.

Second, as few are trained or encouraged to be entrepreneurial, they tend to repel any suggestion that they break out of this mold and to take the risks that go along with it. They fear they will be out there competing for attention with people who by training or instinct, understand how to succeed out on the street. They fear public exposure—a mixed blessing for any executive, but hardly unavoidable in an issue-driven situation—seeing the potential of becoming a public spectacle, either because they take unpopular positions or because they unwittingly do or say dumb things.

They fear rejection; after all they might very well lose. Unlike the door-to-door salesperson who learns early to accept rejection, move on to the next house, and exude again the confidence with which the day started, these executives live in the constant fear that being said no to is the worst thing that can happen, a putdown of their psyche from which they can't recover. They find it impossible to understand the bounce-back agility and staying power of either the salesperson or the politician.

They rationalize that engagement in public affairs takes time and effort which seems better directed toward preserving the short-term bottom line. Public affairs doesn't seem like what they are paid for, what the job was supposed to be.

In short, these executives suffer from either what has been described as "the wimp factor," or from the misconstrued notion that issue engagement can be handled by what we shall shortly describe as "the quarterback process" of public affairs.

The Wimp Factor

In many ways, when it comes to active engagement in the public affairs arena, these organizational heads resemble George Bush during his 1992 reelection campaign. Like the former President, they came to their position, not of their own accord as some Perot-type entrepreneur, but by appointment. They attended all the right schools, got all the right degrees, and in the process took as gospel "the numerative, rationalist approach to management [which] dominates the business schools. It teaches us that well-trained professional managers can manage anything."[2]

But if the chief executive officer (CEO) or the certified association executive (CAE) of an organization never walked a precinct asking for a person's vote (or, its corollary in the business world, gone door to door asking for an order), if they've never tried to work out an accommodation with a group whose view of the universe is the opposite of their own, or if they've never truly trusted people who don't talk, think, act, or look like they do, then like the flustered President at the debate in Richmond, they can never answer the reality-check question: "How has this societal problem affected you directly?"

Like former President Bush, they have leadership ability in non-people-related arenas—production, finance, or marketing (as opposed to sales which may have taught the future executive how to deal with rejection)—but treat the outside world much as Peters and Waterman say they treat their own people, giving "an infinite number of reasons why workers can't be trusted [and assuming that] the *average* worker is an incompetent ne'er-do-well, just itching to screw up."[3]

Bush suffered from the same problem. Unable to identify with people who suffered, unable to credibly articulate a clear vision of where he would lead America, uncomfortable in audience participation TV appearances in the role of asking people to vote for him, he suffered, as one newspaper series commented on the former president, from being tagged a leader one day, a wimp the next:

> In his blood, in his patrician roots, and in his behavior, Bush appears not to feel any particular need to speak out to the country, to seek a public mandate that could strengthen his position with opponents in and out of the Congress.
> Rather, people who watch him closely say, he considers the presidency something of a private affair, best conducted among small groups of powerful, right-minded people. It is an élitist, corporate-style, very personal approach.[4]

As was demonstrated in November 1992, that approach fails.

CEOs of corporations and CAEs of organizations that are facing public policy issues are often among those who operate this way. Certainly, the Exxon Corporation in its handling of the Valdez spill stood accused by many as having taken an élitist approach.

But professional groups, like the trial lawyers or physicians, and not-for-profit groups, are also equally culpable, especially when they fail to reach out to build community support for their position. They are used to making unquestioned decisions in the privacy of their executive suite or examining rooms. They assume no one will accept their position on the issue, so by not asking others to join them, they prove to themselves that no one will. They think they'll be viewed as a wimp for asking, mistaking true leadership as capitulation rather than as mutual accommodation.

Organizational heads avoid publicly visible involvement because it takes commitment, an act often alien to them. No doubt they fear rejection, allowing the small percentage of those who will always view them as suspect to hold them hostage to any reasonable course of action. Some CEOs say it is not their job because public affairs goes beyond the bottom line. Evidently, they've not read *In Search of Excellence.* For in that seminal work Peters and Waterman maintain that

> Innovative companies are especially adroit at continually responding to change of any sort in their environments. As the needs of their customers shift, the skills of their competitors improve, the mood of the public perturbates, the forces of international trade realign, *and the government regulations shift,* these companies tack, revamp, adjust, transform, and adapt. In short, as a whole culture, they innovate [italics added].[5]

What Peters and Waterman are ultimately suggesting is that those companies that truly excel are companies that commit to getting their people plugged into the process, whether in terms of quality control internally or community support externally.

As we have said before, a company that trusts its people to design a good widget, build a good widget, sell a good widget, and service that widget, should equally be willing to trust its people to become ambassadors of goodwill to maintain a receptivity in the community toward the company, its products, and the corporate views on public policy issues of great impact to the company.

Even U.S. tobacco companies, long the nemesis of many who view them as merchants of death, have been able, in an amazing four-year period (1988 to 1992), to obtain community support in 28 states for "smoker's rights legislation" that prohibits employers from banning the right of employees to smoke off the job. Even people who hate the act of smoking and individual smokers engaged in the act publicly are not inclined to deny someone that right in the privacy of their home.

The Quarterback Theory of Management

Consider our view of a theory of management that likens itself to a football team. One person calls the signals. All others move out smartly in accordance with a preset play. And heaven help the person who deviates. This organization's chief knows little about baseball, a game that more clearly resembles how the political system works.

In both baseball and football there is a strategy as well as attempts to alter the course of the game as various situations arise. But there are significant differences between the two sports in terms of what is expected of the individual player.

Football is a game for role players, and people with an extraordinary skill, such as running or blocking or tackling, can be successful and contribute to a well-oiled, 11-person machine. In baseball, each player must be capable of several sets of skills. Each of the 9 can be a hero, helping the entire team offensively or defensively. It is not possible to contribute to success by having only one skill that can be called upon. Everyone must be able to hit, throw, and catch, with the role of the designated hitter being the one exception to that rule.

In the political process in a democracy, any individual can be a hero, either in support of a policy or in opposition to the strategy of the organization. No one has to be confined to a narrow, technical role. In that sense, the political process in America more closely mirrors baseball than football.

Take a situation in Midland, Michigan, that began in the late 1960s. The local power company, Consumers Power, wanted to build a nuclear power plant. What is interesting about this case is the apparent attitude of the local power company.

The Consumers Power management seems to us to have subscribed to the quarterback theory. Their initial approach suggests that the company thought it could just call the signals, and everyone on the team would follow the play book they had designed. They seem to have forgotten that any player in the process can be as effective at spoiling a game plan as any substitute player off the bench who rises to the occasion for that one game.

The player they seem to have ignored was Mary Sinclair. She decided to question the need for the plant, the proposed location, and the safety of its design. The company fought back. The way the company has been positioned by some who have commented on the battle, perhaps wrongfully, is that they say there is no need to try to accommodate a homemaker.

They appear to have questioned her credentials. If so, they may have been right in one sense. Mary Sinclair knew little at the outset except that she was opposed. She hadn't even been to college. But, as the fight continued, over a decade or more, Mary attended school and acquired a bachelor's degree, a master's degree, and her doctorate in environmental science, in order both to learn as much as she could, and, to have the credentials to fight the utility behemoth.

Ultimately, following a 10-year fight, she won. The principal point of her initial argument that the site was flawed was conceded. It was a floodplain area. After spending $4.1 billion, the plant was not built.

Some utility spokespeople remain skeptical as to the impact of her role, pointing to, among other reasons, the decision of Dow Chemical to break its contract to purchase steam from the plant. Still, many journalists give Sinclair the credit for single-handedly preventing the plant from being built through her efforts to discredit the design and to raise questions among her neighbors concerning the need for and the safety of the plant. Among those neighbors was Dow Chemical Company:

> She also has the distinction of being the first Midland resident to publicly challenge Dow Chemical. Back in the 1960s, her arguments against a Dow supported nuclear plant (being built, it turned out, on sinking swampland) led to the plant being shut down.[6]

The company not only lost the battle, they helped create a general who even today remains active in the environmental fights in that area of the country. More recently, the mid-70-year-old activist has been at the forefront to prevent Consumers Power from using 100-ton concrete-and-steel storage casks to store nuclear waste, "Dr. Sinclair's third time on the leading edge of efforts to stop nuclear power—and her second stand against Consumers Power."[7]

It could have been handled differently. Studies show that electric utilities that have bent over backward to become engaged in the community have usually had far less opposition and far more cooperation from the public they serve. The ability of companies to minimize opposition can usually be traced to the fact that because of their involvement in the community they have built a foundation of trust. They enjoy that rare organizational image of a company being open to the community and to views that differ from their own attitudes on issues.

The quarterback theory is one of absolute control. It assumes that an organization's chief can control all elements of any process, both internal and external, just by declaring intentions. It manifests itself in a number of ways, often as noninvolvement that obscures the CEO's or CAE's fear of failure or rejection.

As one corporate public affairs person responding to our survey told us:

> A CEO doesn't get there by being involved in conflict. They are the quintessential 'man in the gray flannel suit' who can deal with internal politics, but doesn't know how to fight in the external political world. They've had no natural exposure to conflict—hence

their aversion to conflict in the public arena is due to very little experience in any milieu.

They assume that the political system is *overtly* confrontational. They are not in the business of asking for volunteers. They like the hierarchical model, similar to football in which everyone moves in accordance with the commands of the quarterback. Soccer is the new yuppie sport.

(Parenthetically, it should be noted that the yuppie group sees soccer, like baseball, as a sport in which all players must use similar skills and in which each may receive the psychic rewards that come from having an equal role in the process of helping the team to win. That concept in sports is what the "young, upwardly mobile, educated élite" would want for their children, to be able to succeed them. American football will remain the blue-collar, assembly-line, lunch-bucket crowd's sport as one that appeals to order, discipline, and sameness.)

But chief executive officers of organizations, be they corporate, not for profit, or associations, are not likely to admit that they will not be engaged because they are wimps, or afraid to lose, or unwilling to match wits with a homemaker from Midland, Michigan. No, when such senior executives refuse to visibly participate outside a controlled environment in public affairs or to become truly engaged in the process of public policy formation, they usually trot out one or more of a long series of elaborate excuses that serve to mask their real fear of fighting. The nine most popular excuses include:

- Politics is dirty
- "Fix-it" mentality
- Ideological purity
- We can win the battle (but lose the war)
- Our ox is not being gored
- Groupthink
- Arrogance: They'll never get us
- What warning signs?
- It's self-serving

Politics Is Dirty

Another often-heard excuse for avoiding the challenge of allocating time and energy to advocating for an issue in the democratic process is that politics is dirty and engaging in it tarnishes the participant. This is a glib response to that charge, but it is hard for us to believe that the level of operating standards in public affairs is any lower than for any other corporate activity. To the contrary, we believe that the ongoing media scrutiny and government lobbying and election laws keep public affairs more on the up and up.

And the experience of those who work in the political process is very clear. There is a saying among lobbyists and legislators that "you only have one chance to lie." It means that your word is your bond and that any transgression leads to a diminution of the person's or organization's ability to function successfully in public affairs.

Generally, those who think politics is dirty also avoid engagement in the policy process at the local level. Either they will do nothing at all, seeking remedies through lobbyists in the state capitol or in Washington without ever selling their case at the local level, as advised by Tip O'Neill; or they will practice the art of avoidance behavior by hiring telemarketing specialists to produce the appearance of local support.

The art of telemarketing as a lobbying tool will be discussed in Chap. 8 with a view toward exploring the right and the wrong way to proceed. In either event it represents for some organizations a "quick-and-dirty" way to win a battle at the local level without any true engagement or involvement. (The emphasis, at times, is on the word *dirty*, an appellation most often used by those who have lost.)

Organizations that refuse to become engaged at the local level run the risk of ultimately losing their issues because voters feel more and more alienated. Equally, there are groups that remain engaged perpetually, losing a battle sometimes but more often winning the war of public support. The teachers, we believe, represent one such group.

The teachers stay in close touch with parents and school committees and make sure that their interests are presented not as selfish interests but as interests that will help further the education of the children. The teachers have a powerful lobby at the city, county, state, and national levels, to be sure. But it is at the local level that they have won most of their battles, gaining support among those most affected by the quality of the educational system.

Beyond that, the education unions have encouraged and taught their members how to mount and sustain winning election efforts, all with positive results. Around the country local school boards themselves often include teachers and principals from the community who have gotten themselves elected. They present themselves to the voters as knowledgeable, and their election is tantamount to an endorsement by the community.

This acknowledgement of the political clout of the teachers in no way endorses the educational system they run. Many view it as an unholy mess. But having gained the power to remain in control, in large measure by becoming engaged at the local level, they have established a trust factor among voters who may be saying about the teachers, perhaps, "This is the best we can expect."

The Fix-It Mentality

The fear of fighting manifests itself most often in the fix-it mentality. It comes from an operational mode in which chief executives, choosing not to get engaged in public issues, always leave the solution to others. When there's a problem, get someone else to take care of it.

It is often a corollary to the "politics is dirty" adage, especially when those making that charge are the ones who are both standing in the way of change and in control of the process, and those proposing changes appear to be winning. For those who are opposed to change do lend credence to the notion that with just the right people acting in Washington, or a state capital, or in a big-city political venue, one can, in fact, "fix it." In some, particularly short-term, situations, they appear to be right.[8]

Usually those situations involve issues that, to the press and public at large, are minor, the players involved few in number, and the potential for escalation minimal. In such situations, having the problem solved swiftly with little or no fuss is certainly preferable. That's what good lobbyists do most successfully—solve problems quietly before they become raging public issues.

The opportunity to fix it can more comfortably exist when the proposition is a negative one. That is, when one wants to prevent a government action. It particularly suits those CEOs or CAEs who are unable to articulate what they are for but who know exactly what they are against. They just want to move product. They don't want to change anything about the comfortable world to which they've become accustomed.

But two questions arise: How does one know there will be no backlash; and, if one gets in the habit of noninvolvement in minor issues, how does one prepare adequately for handling major crises when they erupt?

To our way of thinking, the fix-it mentality is a two-edged sword. As long as issues can be handled with minimal fuss, the fact that the problem is "fixed" reinforces the executive's view that that is the best way to proceed. The defect of that process is that even when it is successful, it may leave the company in no better position than it was before to meet the next problem on its own.

That said, a good opportunity to "fix it" often exists when the proposition is a negative one, that is, when one wishes to prevent an action from occurring. One notable example is the junk-bond lobby, which appears to have succeeded in avoiding any change in the law that would have eliminated or sharply curtailed the right of businesses to deduct interest payments. Their success was chronicled in a Knight-Ridder News Service series by Donald Bartlett and James Steele entitled *America, What Went Wrong?*

> In Washington, where 11,000 organizations are lobbying Congress, there is an adage: "Successful lobbies are measured by the legislation they stop, not by the laws they get passed."
>
> By that yardstick, the Alliance for Capital Access[9] is phenomenally successful.
>
> Let's watch the Alliance in action in 1985, the year it stopped a big one. At the time, pressure was building on Congress to do something about the wave of takeovers, leveraged buy outs, and mergers sweeping America.
>
> Describing itself as an organization of high-yield bond users, the Alliance was in reality a Washington lobby for Michael R. Milken, Drexel Burnham Lambert Inc.'s junk bond chief.
>
> Over the next few years, the Alliance became one of the capital's most successful lobbies—wining and dining lawmakers, passing out checks to House members and senators to make speeches, testifying before congressional committees, and extolling the virtues of junk bonds.
>
> In the end, its success could be measured by a simple standard:
>
> Congress never enacted legislation that scaled back the deductibility for interest on corporate debt—the engine that had driven the junk bond movement. The Alliance was so successful in turning back every attempt to curb the deductibility of interest on corporate borrowing that in September [1991] it disbanded, its job done.
>
> So how goes the economic renaissance built on junk bonds?
>
> Four savings and loan associations that contributed thousands of dollars to the Alliance lobbying blitz are insolvent and have been seized by federal regulators. And another large group of Alliance member companies has sought protection from the U.S. Bankruptcy Court. The reason: inability to generate sufficient profits to cover the high debt service of their junk bonds.[10]

But—and this is key—what worked for junk bonds may not work for a company that depends on the community for its support. That support may be for a rate increase, as with a utility, or for the purchase of one's products as with a consumer product company. It may not work for an organization that needs broad support for changing laws and regulations that affect the way the political process unfolds.

Environmental groups, civil rights groups, consumer organizations, to name a few, cannot call or rely on one or more individuals to "fix it."

Nor can groups get a quick fix when they are facing a well-organized, determined coalition in opposition to their purpose. No one truly felt that their individual ox was being gored by the junk bond group. Or, if they did, they had no position around which to rally.

The same is true for gun control. While an overwhelming majority of Americans today support some form of gun control (according to some surveys, 90 percent), their lack of personal involvement in the fight or an organizational structure to which they'll commit their time, money, and sweat means that the die-hard National Rifle Association (NRA) types and the manufacturers of firearms will continue to carry the day. In contrast, the NRA is one of the most well-managed grassroots operations in the United States, as its congressional contributions underscore.

As *The Wall Street Journal* reported in November 1992:

> In preparation for a Clinton victory, the National Rifle Association invested heavily in the House, and estimates it picked up 30 additional votes against future gun-control legislation that the new president has said he will support. Filings with the Federal Election Commission show the NRA put more than $1.64 million into contributions and independent expenditures in congressional races this year.[11]

Beyond all else, however, there remains one additional problem with the fix-it mentality: What happens if you bring in decision maker's buddy to fix it and then that elected official is defeated? Playing the "who-knows-whom" game in Washington—and other government halls of power—is a great inside-the-beltway pastime. However, the outsider's strength comes from the grassroots, from engagement with constituent groups that can ultimately have more power and more persuasiveness than any individual lobbyist.

Ideological Purity

This reason for nonengagement with others is more often the reason cited by the not-for-profit groups. Three come to mind—Planned Parenthood, the Equal Rights Amendment advocates, and *The Real Paper*.

Until 1984, the prochoice group had never lost a referendum. Then, came Colorado. The ballot measure presented to Colorado voters was quite simple. If passed, it would prevent the state from using any public funds in support of abortions. It passed. And for a very good reason as our postelection analysis showed. The prolife group was able to convince a slim majority of voters that, while most Coloradans might support the right of a woman to choose an abortion, they also felt that they should not have to pay for someone else's abortion.

For the first time, the prolife group had found a wedge. It was the economic argument. The campaign hammered away at it while the campaign manager got the fringe activists to keep their unborn fetuses under wraps, or at least confined to the assembly halls and churches of those who fervently believed that abortion is murder.

Ed Grefe was one of the consultants retained to analyze the Colorado campaign and be part of a half-day presentation to Faye Wattleton and other senior members of the Planned Parenthood organization in New York in 1985. His sponsors were staff members who understood that there might be a chink in the armor of the prochoice group's approach. He believed and suggested that the group consider presenting its own economic argument, to wit, what does it cost society to take care of unwanted children, the babies born with AIDS or drug dependencies that no one wanted to adopt?

But following his presentation, Wattleton objected. From Ed's perspective, she challenged his proposal, saying, in effect, he was asking Planned Parenthood to calculate the cost of unwanted children, something she felt they should never do.

Ed sensed that she believed her organization's position to be clear. Namely, that people should support Planned Parenthood's position because it is the right of every woman to make up her own mind. Ed came away from his presentation with the impression that Waddleton was outraged by his proposals. He sensed she thought his ideas bordered on being disgusting.

That could be. But in our view the Equal Rights advocates suffered, ultimately, from the same adherence to ideological purity. Despite warnings from a number of consultants that the entire issue should be framed in economic terms, the coalition of women driving the campaign refused.

We were part of that group urging some of the Equal Rights Coalition leaders in Washington to frame an additional message that would be as compelling to a professional woman as to one whose lack of education had forced her to accept a menial task: namely, equal pay for equal work and equal opportunity for advancement. The Phyllis Schlaflys of the opposition prevailed because they could trumpet the inclusion of lifestyle rights that were anathema to many women as being the sole purpose of the amendment.

Finally, in addressing the issue of ideological purity, there is the story of *The Real Paper,* an alternative paper in Boston. Shortly after the paper was purchased by a group of well-intentioned liberals, they were faced with an effort on the part of their employees to organize the paper. Not wanting to be on the wrong side politically, they did not fight the organizing effort and, as a result, ended up with a very strong union, a difficult contract, and continuing problems. The competitor newspaper, *The Phoenix*, unencumbered by ideological pressures, successfully resisted efforts to organize.

The Phoenix survived. But, like the ERA, *The Real Paper* died because of ideological purity. Prochoice will survive. But taxpayers will pay heed to the prolife argument of not having to pay for someone else's decision to abort until such time as the prochoice group counters with powerful economic arguments to the contrary.

We Can Win the Battle
(But Lose the War)

There are a number of classic cases of what appears to be unyielding organizational arrogance in which the group won the battle but lost the war. None seems more graphic than the case of Nestlè and the American manufacturers of infant food formula. They are lumped together because, while the story begins with what some viewed as the Nestlè Company's apparent intransigence, it ends with their competitors' being slightly tainted with the same brush in the minds of many (despite the fact that they stayed on the sidelines thinking, erroneously, that only the Nestlè ox was being gored).

The battle began in the late 1970s and continued into the early 1980s. It started when Nestlè decided to sue a Swiss activist group that had printed a pamphlet called *Nestlè Kills Babies* in which the group accused Nestlè of what they believed to be unsavory marketing techniques in developing nations.[12] The group was little known, its pamphlet of limited circulation. Hence, the impact of the group's charges, many analysts contend, would have been nil had Nestlè not overreacted. But, like General Motors before it, Nestlè decided to play hardball.

General Motors, it will be recalled, for years was the company that created the phenomenon known as Ralph Nader, an unknown author of a little sold book entitled *Unsafe At Any Speed*. GM reportedly hired detectives to follow Ralph, and the rest, as they say, is history.[13] When news of GM's tactics became public, the book became a best-seller, the author a movement icon, and GM's management approach at the time, some suggest in hindsight, merely the harbinger of some equally astute decisions regarding the marketing of their automobiles over a period of years.

Nestlè accomplished much of the same for its efforts. The company won its suit. But that legal victory led to Nestlè's losing the political war. The suit made an obscure periodical and its authors famous. But beyond that, the charges of the article, having become front-page news as a consequence of the lawsuit, became the basis for a seven-year international boycott of the company's products. It also led to a vote by 117 nations in the World Health Organization (WHO) approving a set of guidelines for member nations to adopt concerning the marketing of infant food formula worldwide.

The controversy has two sides. Nestlè admits that it overreacted to the publication, but given its history of what many believe to have been solid corporate citizenship in developing countries, it is understandable that the company was stunned. Perhaps, as a company spokesperson told us, had the company been more attuned to the process of handling issues, the lawsuit might not have occurred, nor, said he, the blurring of the issue by opponents less interested in the scientific facts being presented by Nestlè than in making headlines concerning the number of alleged infant deaths. Nestlè supported the adoption of the guidelines by WHO and made a commitment to honor the code in principal. That said, some have a different view of what followed.

> After the World Health Organization's adoption in 1981 of a formal code for marketing infant food formula in developing nations, Nestlè began a slow series of concessions in its practices. However, led by a nationwide coalition [in the United States] called INFACT, the boycott continued. It wasn't until 1984 that company representatives and INFACT sat down together for the negotiations that finally ended this controversy. INFACT termed this settlement a major victory, praised Nestlè for its cooperation, and urged consumers to again purchase the company's products.[14]

In 1988, Action for Corporate Responsibility reinstituted the boycott saying that Nestlè had not lived up to its agreement. The company believes that it has done so, and many credible sources support Nestlè.[15]

During the bulk of the controversy, Nestlè was alone. As Nestlè confronted the issue, *none* of the American companies rose to its defense, assuming, as one spokesperson from a rival company told us, they would pick up market share at Nestlè's expense. What the American producers didn't realize until late in the game was that the American homemakers would equally condemn all manufacturers of infant food formula. The industry as a whole suffered a sales dip as shoppers voted along with the World Health Organization in the only way they knew how, by ceasing to buy any infant food formula regardless of the manufacturer.

Much of the damage has been repaired by Nestlè and their American counterparts. But there remains the use of the phrase "Nestlè-like" as a historical perspective on what not to do. As a company spokesperson acknowledged, having once been subjected to screaming headlines concerning the lawsuit, the boycott, and the logically inaccurate premise (based on actual data) concerning the number of babies who allegedly died as a consequence of using infant food formula, the company continues to suffer as an example for what went wrong rather than as an example of how one's good deeds in terms of dealing with the issue are worth emulating.

It has been a costly war for Nestlè, one that might have been avoided had they chosen to walk away from the first battle instead of becoming engaged. To the extent that they won the battle and lost the war, we have an example worth considering before reacting to criticism.

Our Ox Is Not Being Gored

The Nestlè tale, as we have said, is one of winning the battle but losing the war. The infant food formula issue, in terms of how it was addressed by others in the industry, is also an example of avoiding involvement when one's ox is not being gored. It may sound like a good strategy, especially when one hopes to pick up market share at the expense of the company under attack. But, it can backfire.

It is important to distinguish between a situation in which a company is being attacked because it is accused of being a bad company and a situation in which a company is being attacked because of the way in which it makes or markets a product. Even in the initial situation one must exercise caution, for an entire industry can be tainted and suffer. If anything, one should be doubly cautious if a competitor is under attack for some practice that is found to be questionable. It may turn out that all companies in the industry have identical or comparable practices.

For if the process is essentially the same for all companies, those who choose to stand by hoping to pick up the pieces may find their names also crocheted into the shawl-list of those who should be guillotined when the revolution comes and legal or political redress is at hand. There are issues, like the infant food formula marketing issue, that affect all manufacturers, and all must respond.

In one situation, engineers from Boeing and Lockheed joined in with their brethren from McDonnell Douglas when that company's DC-10s were plagued with air-worthiness problems. The builders of the 747s and L-1011s knew that the public was being frightened away from air travel and that touting their aircraft as being safer was a sure way to sabotage the entire industry.

"A good rule of thumb," said one vice president of a pharmaceutical company, "is what I call the 'Vidal Sassoon Rule' which means that if my competitor looks good, I look good; and, if he looks bad, probably I look bad also, or at least I have the potential of looking bad."

More often than not, it is a desire for market share that causes a smaller company to try to raise an issue. For years, as the tobacco industry fought the tar and nicotine content battle, the leaders in the industry, among them Philip Morris, argued that the marketing battles among the companies should be limited to which cigarette delivers less tar and/or nicotine.

Then, Brown & Williamson, one of the smaller companies, broke ranks. In what appeared to be an attempt to gain market share, the company launched a new brand with a message that claimed its new cigarette had a filter that delivered less harmful gases. Whether they gained market share or not, they raised a new issue with which the industry had to contend.

Ironically, when the shoe was on the other foot and Philip Morris became the owner of the smallest soft drink company, 7-Up, it adopted the same tactic. In order to try and gain market share by knocking out Coca-Cola and Pepsi, 7-Up began discussing the amount of caffeine in the colas, noting that 7-Up had none. Similarly, smaller manufacturers of computers were the first to try and exploit the video display terminal issue, ballyhooing their screens as having solved the problem and suggesting, by inference, that IBM had not.

No doubt market initiatives will continue to tempt executives to raise political issues as a way of gaining share. Our view is that such tactics usually backfire. But the fact that such attempts are made periodically means that trade associations in particular have to remind members that usually when one member's ox is gored, everyone gets smeared.

Groupthink

Discussing a role for trade associations in terms of keeping various members from tearing one another apart in the marketplace by raising a political issue leads to another problem by which companies practice avoidance. We call it "groupthink." Let the association do it.

There is merit to the association's marshalling the resources of all its members in order to deal with a political issue. In fact, it may be preferable in a number of situations. But even the associations will acknowledge that there is a need for each individual member to get involved by developing support for the industry's position at the grassroots level. For associations cannot always activate the best, most effective assets of member companies, that is, employees, vendors, suppliers, or stockholders.

That said, we find a number of executives using the need for a group approach as a way to avoid doing anything. In fact, we often find that these executives are with smaller companies. They know that the rule under which trade associations often operate is by consensus and that as long as they find some seemingly important reason for objecting, their solo veto is sufficient to prevent anything from happening. They mask their fear of involvement by raising objections that can never be answered in a satisfactory way. It is only a delaying tactic, one that frustrates an industry response, but it is effective.

When this occurs, it is the more courageous corporation, or members of the professional group, who will break ranks. They form new coalitions and proceed with the understanding that while what they do may not benefit all, it must be done.

Arrogance: They'll Never Get Us

There are organizations that operate as though they live on another planet, one where their actions will never be questioned. One example is Mars, Incorporated. Tracing the company approach to public affairs begins in 1986 when one of the early investigative stories first surfaced in *Regardie's* magazine. It vividly recounted the company's legendary penchant for anonymity:

> Calls to the company elicit less information than calls to the Central Intelligence Agency, which is located just two miles away.
> "Who is the president of Mars?" a caller asks.
> "'I'm sorry, I can't give out the names of our associates,'" a receptionist replies.
> Click.
> Welcome to the world of Mars, a mysterious place where secrecy is a prized asset.
> John Mars and Forrest Mars, Jr., the two brothers who run the company, are as secretive about their business practices as they are about themselves.
> The brothers are convinced that the government is out to do them in by banning some aspect of their business.
> The company wide paranoia generated by the brothers reached its apogee [when a group of] eleventh- and twelfth-graders at a private school in Atlanta wrote to Mars to request information on M&M's. They were researching the origins of famous food brands.

Though other companies responded to similar requests by sending the students illustrated booklets or even free samples and bumper stickers, Mars offered the kids nothing but a cold shoulder.

At another company, such bad press might have led to the replacement of the entire public relations department. At Mars, [said] a company spokesman, "they crawled back under the rock," becoming even more determined not to talk to the press.[16]

A subsequent piece in *Fortune* in 1988 added to the story and noted that the company's approach to public affairs might foreshadow an equally poor judgment in all aspects of business:

Mars Inc. is the black hole of the packaged goods universe—so powerful and large that it influences all the other objects in its system, yet so secretive and dense that not so much as a lumen of information ever emanates from the dark center of the company in McLean, Virginia.

Mars' unique culture may be melting in the hands of the company's co-presidents, Forrest, Jr., and John Mars, whose slightly nutty leadership seems to lack vision.

[Under the brothers' domain,] according to former and current employees, the two have taken one aspect of Mars' culture, egalitarianism, to a new level: They treat everyone like vassals.

[Under Forrest Sr.] the company also became phobic about publicity. Mars executives are forbidden to have their pictures taken for publications. In an embarrassing and costly mistake, the company refused to permit M&M's to appear in the hit movie *E.T. The Extra-Terrestrial*. Hershey gladly stepped in, and a star was born in Reese's Pieces.

Now that storied culture is eating its young.[17]

Nothing had changed by 1992, when a piece in *The Washington Post Magazine* noted:

On the planet Mars . . . [employees are expected to follow] The Five Principles of Mars—a bible of corporate rectitude inspired by Forrest Senior's unyielding quest for perfection.

The fifth principle, and probably the one closest to the brothers' hearts, is Freedom: "We need freedom to shape our future; we need profit to remain free." What this really means, however, is privacy—in every facet of business. But the privacy issue extends beyond business decisions to the company's public relations—or lack of them. If Mars doesn't have to communicate with the world, it won't.[18]

It all sounds like a corporate executive's dream come true.[19] Yet, such a low- or no-profile approach to public affairs can possibly lead to what some might term major screwups.

Take the case of the Princeton Dental Resource Center. This group was sending dentists a newsletter that reportedly claimed that chocolate was a cavity fighter. As the story broke, it was learned that Mars was a principal funding source for the group.

As noted in *The New York Times*:

> For two years now, thousands of dentists have received newsletters from the Princeton Dental Resource Center with current reports on dental health and fighting cavities. And the center has asked the dentists to pass them on to their patients.
>
> The newsletters have some unexpected advice—including bulletins of good news for chocolate lovers. One issue reports that eating chocolate may be as beneficial as an apple a day.
>
> "So next time you snack on your favorite chocolate bar or bowl of peanuts," the newsletter said, "remember—if enjoyed in moderation they can be good-tasting and might even inhibit cavities."
>
> Most dental researchers say there are gaping holes in the chocolate theory. Moreover, many dentists who distributed the newsletter did not know that the Princeton group was financed by a candy company, M&M/Mars. The publication makes no mention of the connection. And researchers and consumer experts are angry.
>
> "This sounds like the most brazen way of doing things that I have ever heard of," said Michael Jacobson, executive director of the Center for Science in the Public Interest, a consumer advocacy group.
>
> Among others who vigorously disagree with the newsletter's report on chocolate's potential anticavity power is the scientist on whose report it was largely based. Dr. Lawrence Wolinsky of the University of California at Los Angeles said his work had been mischaracterized.
>
> Samuel Ostrow, a spokesman for the Princeton Dental Resource Center, denies that there was a mischaracterization of Dr. Wolinsky's study. And Hans Fiuczynski, director of external relations for the M&M/Mars division of Mars, Inc., rejected any suggestion that the company tried to influence the publications.
>
> Mr. Fiuczynski said Mars established the Princeton center in Princeton, N.J., in 1987 as a private foundation. He added that Mars had contributed about $1 million annually to the group, a figure that represented at least 90 percent of its financing. Mr. Fiuczynski said Mars was concerned that placing its name on the group's publications might deter other companies from contributing to it."[20]

That response could be compared with the statement, "I once smoked marijuana, but I didn't inhale it."

What Warning Signs?

There is a kind of groupthink among certain organizational heads that presumes that no one is communicating with one another except themselves. We recall a conversation with a CEO of a major corporation who said he was not interested in having us do an employee survey to find out what they knew about the issues facing the company or what they were prepared to do to help the company if asked to do so.

"I don't want to ask the employees their opinion on anything."

"Why not?"

"Well, suppose they tell me about a problem with the company that I am not prepared or willing to address. If I don't know about it, I don't have to do anything about it."

"True. But, if you're not asking, their local politician is doing so, and he may introduce legislation that would force you to solve the problem. Wouldn't it be better to know what the problem is before it festers beyond a point of being able to solve it amicably?"

Thus early warning signs are ignored. Management hopes, ostrich-like, that any problems that surface will just go away. Or that solutions to problems that won't apply to them or alter their way of operating. One such issue is privacy.

Whether it's credit information, personal habits, or telephone numbers, there is a growing consensus, among both lawyers and politicians, that no one, least of all an employer, has a right to invade our privacy. Yet companies continue to ignore this basic right and the signs of mounting frustration that something must be done to prevent unwarranted invasions of privacy.

A report entitled "Firms Use Spying to Silence Critics" in *The Los Angeles Times* summarized the issue and its consequences:

> Vans with blacked out windows. Midnight garbage thefts. Video cameras in the ceiling. Microphones in overhead sprinklers.
> These are not just the trappings of cop and spy capers anymore.
> Companies are hiring private investigators for a variety of legitimate purposes: to plug leaks of sensitive documents, stop competitor spying, root out drug abuse or employee theft.
> Lately, however, headlines suggest that such black-bag operations are also being turned to more unsavory uses: silencing critics, intimidating whistle-blowers or thwarting union organizers.
> The irony is that companies that use private spying campaigns against critics run the risk of being found out. And when that happens, the embarrassment and public relations damage may exceed the perceived threat that promoted the spying in the first place.[21]

For some companies, their involvement in such unsavory practices seems to be an about-face from a previously held position of trusting their people. One such company so accused recently was Procter & Gamble.

In the time prior to 1982 when Peters and Waterman were writing their tome on those companies deemed worthy of emulation by virtue of having the very best business practices, Procter & Gamble was one they noted as being among that select group that *"view themselves as an extended family."*[22]

Something must have gone awry between the publication of their book in 1982 and the decision to subpoena records of long-distance telephone calls made into and out of a *Wall Street Journal* reporter's phone. For even in the best of families, there is occasionally the messy divorce, and P&G's actions have netted itself a position near the bottom in our survey of who is doing good-to-poor public affairs.

As reported on when it was discovered:

> Procter & Gamble Co., apparently angered over a story in the *Wall Street Journal,* asked Cincinnati law enforcement officials in July to subpoena records of long-distance telephone calls through Cincinnati Bell into and out of a Journal reporter's Pittsburgh home.
> The goal: to identify the reporter's sources, the Journal reported. When the investigation came to light, it was called off."[23]

Procter & Gamble admitted it had erred, according to the Associated Press, and quoted from a letter that company chairman Edwin L. Artzt sent to all employees in which he said:

> "This has been an embarrassing experience for the company and a difficult time for our employees. We made an error in judgment."[24]

But the damage was done. In a similar case Dow Chemical has waged a long-running campaign to reestablish itself as one of the corporate good guys, but it still suffers from a tainted image among those people who recall vividly that during the Vietnam War, Dow Chemical was the manufacturer of napalm and Agent Orange. The foul odor of a corporate policy gone awry can linger for decades. The recovery of a lost reputation can take generations to achieve.

In all of these excuses there resides not only a sense of fear but also a few illusions. One may be that the stockholders are happy. That may be true. But at a time when grassroots pressure is being applied to major institutional investors, especially union- and state-owned pension funds, it would behoove the prudent CEO to not assume that a good price-earnings ratio is sufficient to keep stockholders happy. They may also demand that community concerns be addressed.

A second illusion may be that within the corporate competitive environment, one truly has "control," or conversely, that in the political environment, one has "no control." Certainly, those companies whose products and pricing are more sensitive to the reactions of consumers should be aware very early on of any backlash that can result from a political issue. And in the chapters to come we will demonstrate how any organization can gain some measure of control over the evolution of issues in the public arena.

It's Self-Serving

Suffice it to say at this point that one final excuse for noninvolvement remains: Involvement in public affairs should be avoided because one will be viewed as self-serving. It is easily dismissed when we point to one of the gurus of organization, and no corporate friend, Saul Alinsky.

In his *Rules for Radicals,* Alinsky states bluntly:

> The myth of altruism as a motivating factor in our behavior could arise and survive only in a society bundled in the sterile gauze of New England puritanism and Protestant morality and tied together with the ribbons of Madison Avenue public relations. It is one of the classic American fairy tales.[25]

In fact, ". . . it appears shameful to admit that we operate on the basis of naked self-interest, so we desperately try to reconcile every shift of circumstances that is to our self-interest in terms of a broad moral justification or rationalization."[26]

What Alinsky concludes is that our system works when there is participation and all parties reach out to one another to achieve solutions. How organizations successfully reach out covers the balance of our book. But a couple of guiding principles include Alinsky's view—"If I had to define a free and open society in one word, the word would be 'compromise'"[27]—and the view of a former General Electric CEO, Reginald H. Jones. Jones was quoted in 1974 as saying:

> Our natural constituency is the middle class that not only invests in, but works in and buys from the corporation. . . . We'll have to win our constituency issue-by-issue, like any successful politician.

To which Peters and Waterman add:

> Our excellent companies appear to do their way into strategies, not vice versa, . . . [including] building awareness, broadening political support, overcoming opposition, managing coalitions.[28]

So, we end up with the question: Why do public affairs our way?

Ask Pacific Gas & Electric (PG&E). For years they were viewed by some environmentalists with suspicion. Today, according to *Garbage* magazine writer Art Kleiner, "The company has become trusted by its former enemies." They did it by taking the lead in forming "The California Collaborative," a coalition of 15 groups that "included not just utilities and environmental groups, but rate payers and community-action advocates as well (known for their fierce battles to keep rates down, especially for low-income customers.)"[29]

PG&E did a 180-degree shift in the way they approached public affairs. As a consequence, they have not only been rated among top public affairs executives as one of the best public affairs programs in the country, they have also gained an even more important accolade, the trust of their customers and those who actively opposed them for years. The number of cases in litigation has been sharply reduced, and they have gained public support for increased rates. Their new approach has become a textbook example for others to follow.

Pacific Gas & Electric not only took the risk of community involvement, of reaching out to supposed enemies, of becoming engaged in the community, they also organized themselves around ideas—ideas about the environment and ideas about coalitions, without there being a specific hot issue on which to focus. They decided to become engaged at the very earliest stage of the life cycle of an issue. And, as a consequence, they are reaping the benefits we believe any organization can enjoy from shedding their pattern of avoidance and becoming engaged.

How? The process begins with a plan.

Notes

1. Leonard Laster, "Physicians, Heal Thyselves," *The Washington Post National Weekly Edition,* September 21–27, 1992, p. 24.

2. Thomas J. Peters and Robert H. Waterman, Jr., *In Search of Excellence: Lessons from America's Best-Run Companies,* HarperCollins, New York, 1982, p. 29. (Copyright © 1982 by Thomas J. Peters and Robert H. Waterman, is Reprinted by permission of HarperCollins Publishers, Inc.)

3. Ibid., p. 236.

4. "Identity Crisis Leaves Bush Tagged Great Leader or Wimp," last of five-part series by Knight-Ridder News Service, *The Record,* October 1, 1992, p. A-12.

5. Peters and Waterman, *In Search of Excellence,* p. 12.

6. Art Kleiner, "The Three Faces of Dow," *Garbage,* vol. III, no. 4, July/August 1991, p. 58.

7. Matthew L. Wald, "Battling Nuclear Waste in Michigan," *The New York Times*, December 8, 1992, p. D1.

8. There are times when a crisis erupts and there is little more that one can do except to try to get the problem resolved as quickly as possible. When an organization finds itself in such a situation, there are two excellent references we recommend. The first focuses on the crisis situation and presents a checklist based on its title, *How to Win in Washington* (Basil Blackwell, Cambridge, Mass., 1989), by two veteran public affairs practitioners and Capitol Hill observers, Ernest Wittenberg and Elisabeth Wittenberg. In the second book, *Lobbying and Government Relations* (Quorum Books, New York, 1989), Charles S. Mack provides a detailed description of how to organize that function in a most effective manner. Mack draws on his 25-plus years' experience in the field.

9. Attempts to reach the Alliance for Capital Access to obtain their reaction to the Knight-Ridder piece have been unsuccessful.

10. Donald L. Bartlett and James B. Steele, "Junk-Bond Lobby Wines, Dines, Wins and the Middle Class Picks Up the Tab," *The Record*, last of nine articles entitled "America, What Went Wrong?" Knight-Ridder News Service, November 1, 1991, pp. A1–A14.

11. David Rogers and Jackie Calmes, "New Faces of '93: Shake-Up of Congress Produces Coalition of Women, Minorities; Moderate Gain," *The Wall Street Journal*, November 5, 1991, pp. A1 and A13. (Reprinted by permission of *The Wall Street Journal*, © 1991, Dow Jones & Company, Inc., All Rights Reserved Worldwide.)

12. Steven D. Lydenberg, Alice Tepper Marlin, Sean O'Brine Strub, and the Council on Economic Priorities, *Rating America's Corporate Conscience*, Addison-Wesley, Reading, Mass., p. 150.

13. Simon Beck, "Out of Retirement, David in Rematch with Goliath," *South China Morning Post*, August 8, 1993, p. 5.

14. Lydenberg, Marlin, Strub, and the Council on Economic Priorities, *Rating America's Corporate Conscience*, p. 151.

15. Two groups have given the company high praise: the Muskie Audit Commission, established by Nestlè to monitor its compliance with the WHO guidelines and address its handling of any complaints, and the Methodist Task Force, established by that church's hierarchy to review all Nestlè internal documents to determine whether or not the Methodists should join the boycott. The company has adopted strict guidelines in accordance with the WHO directive and applies them universally, despite being compelled to do so in only the 14 WHO nations that have bothered to ratify the organization's guidelines.

16. Ronald Kessler, "Candy From Strangers, Inside the Sweet World of the Mars Family," *Regardie's* magazine, August 1986, pp. 82 ff.

17. Reed Abelson, "Uncovering Mars," *Fortune*, September 26, 1988, pp. 98 ff. (Reprinted by permission of *The Wall Street Journal*, © 1988, Dow Jones & Company, Inc., All Rights Reserved Worldwide.)

18. Joel Glenn Brenner, "Planet of the M&M's," *The Washington Post Magazine,* April 12, 1992, p. W11.

19. In fairness to Mars, the authors contacted the company to inquire about Mars's reaction to the various articles. Since the articles were less than flattering, we assumed that Mars would give us their spin on each of the articles mentioned. Our inquiry was returned by a person who said the call had been referred to her, that she did some work for Mars, and had been asked to respond on behalf of the company. While this person declined to be named, she did say that "if the company does not like an article, it doesn't bother them. They did participate to an extent and were pleased with the piece in *The Washington Post.* But the company is in business to make quality products and chooses not to spend its time responding to inquiries. It won't even help on a book on the confectionary industry to be published by Random House."

   Questioned about *The New York Times* article on the Princeton Dental Resource Center, the spokesperson suggested we call the center directly. Our inquiry to that group, including our reference to getting their reaction or additional spin on the article, was ignored. A promised return phone call for further comment on the episode regarding candy as a possible inhibitor of cavities never materialized.

20. Barry Meier, "Dubious Theory: Chocolate a Cavity Fighter," *The New York Times,* April 15, 1992, Sec. A, p. 1. (Copyright 1992 by The New York Times Company. Reprinted by permission.)

21. Patrick Lee, "Firms Use Spying to Silence Critics," *The Los Angeles Times,* December 26, 1991, Part D, p. 1.

22. Peters and Waterman, *In Search of Excellence,* p. 261.

23. Lee, op. cit.

24. Associated Press, "P&G Says It Erred in Tracing Phone Calls," September 9, 1991, BC cycle.

25. Saul D. Alinsky, *Rules for Radicals,* Vintage Books, New York, 1971, p. 53.

26. Ibid., p. 55.

27. Ibid., p. 59.

28. Peters and Waterman, *In Search of Excellence,* p. 74.

29. Art Kleiner, "The End of the Official Future," *Garbage,* March/April 1992, p. 55 ff.

PART 2

Get Set

Getting What Ducks in What Rows

3
Strategic Planning for Public Affairs

It's too dangerous to do public affairs in a company that doesn't know what it wants to do.
CAREN WILCOX
Former Director of Government Relations, Hershey Foods Corporation

In our opinion, there are a lot of organizations that appear as though they don't know what they want to do when it comes to the public policy or public affairs arena. That's too bad. For in the future, it is our belief that the key to dealing effectively with public policy issues will be based—as it has been in large measure in the 1990s—on being able to objectively evaluate each strategic resource available to the organization in order to tactically use the appropriate tools in the most cost-effective manner.

An organization begins the process of determining what it wants to do by developing a strategic plan for public affairs. That means candidly assembling a lot of internal and external information. The purpose is to define how the organization is currently prepared to deal with issues at this moment in time.

The data one needs should certainly include an evaluation of the organization over the past 5 to 10 years in terms of its ability to deal effectively with issues. This would include an assessment of what governments at which levels are entertaining proposals whose cost could hurt or help the entity, and by how much; a review of opportunities lost; and a cataloging of the entity's resources and assets at the local, national, and, if applicable, global levels.

At the same time, it is necessary to become familiar with the process and begin plotting the life cycle of an issue. For example, you might well be reading this book because you have been through a public affairs crisis or you are in the midst of one. If so, you understand the difficulty of that experience, the difficulty of being in a position of reacting to a problem that has already exploded.

Successful public affairs requires that you become involved in a problem long before it has exploded into public consciousness. One approach is *adaptive* rather than *reactive*. That means adopting an operational mode, or approach to the process, that is geared toward long-term success rather than short-sighted victory, one that includes multiple contingency options.

Establishing an Adaptive Mode

Top-down, control-freak organizations tend to operate in the *reactive* mode, for example, to the latest series of news stories. In that mode or approach, any plan that includes public relations or public affairs is best defined as what the corporation is *against* rather than what it favors. Whenever something happens in the external environment that management does not like, they react against it without any thought as to whether they could be part of a solution instead of being perceived as part of the problem.

Dealing in a *reactive* mode may have worked to a degree in the less complex, more centralized world of the 1950s, 1960s, and 1970s when organizations interested in affecting public decision making gravitated toward the fix-it mentality described in the previous chapter: Something needed to be done; a decision had to be reversed, a piece of legislation had to be sidetracked, a key bureaucrat had to hear the other side of the story.

Whatever it was, the organization, private or nonprofit, could recruit a Washington-based or state capital–based hired gun to try to solve the problem. Whether the fix-it man (and it was, and is, almost always a man) was successful or not, the organization had little choice but to go this route.

Today, things have changed somewhat. Good lobbyists still play an essential role. But more often they are generalists directing an army rather than single spear carriers. For not only are the important decisions being made closer and closer to the grassroots and away from Washington, but there are fix-it people on all sides, running around and often canceling each other out.

Today, by the time a solution to an organization's problem has turned into a piece of legislation, management may still win a battle or two, but they've already lost the war. If the proposal is inimical to the organization, it's all over when they file a bill because the organization is then *reacting* to someone else's agenda rather than setting their own.

A purely *reactive* mode is, in our judgment, doomed to failure in the long term partly because the organization is playing by someone else's script or game plan. For the organization appears to do little more than constantly *oppose* change, much like the minority party in the Congress of the United States is often charged with doing. There is no creative alternative, nothing to be *for* around which a majority of people can rally.

In addition, when organizations in the community are pitted against one another and operate only in the reactive mode of what they oppose, the situation is ripe for festering hostility. Both sides may then draw upon huge armies of grassroots activists merely to defeat what their opponents propose. But the cost can be extraordinarily expensive both in terms of the dollars and human resources expended, and the result is often political impasse and issue gridlock. Certainly the abortion issue falls into this category.

In sharp contrast are those organizations that are moving toward an *adaptive* approach to public affairs. They begin with a strategic plan. Their planning reflects both an understanding of how issues evolve as well as what are truly the bottom-line essentials of the organization. They also acknowledge it is not only possible, but perhaps even necessary, to have a more positive program in mind for a grassroots coalition, especially if one is to sustain the ardor and continued involvement of the coalition.

Some call this approach *proactive.* Yet, as we have reviewed successful corporate and organizational public affairs programs, we have come to believe that the operative word should be *adaptive.* For many organizations operating under the *proactive* banner are not necessarily willing to accommodate opposing views. Their *proactive* stance is simply one of having organized resistance in place before the crisis occurs.

But, proactive or, our preference, adaptive, the public affairs programs we found in our quest to be truly excellent have an operational mentality that is a far cry from the traditional *reactive* mode. For in sharp contrast to those who believe that confrontation is the best way to deal with ideas stand a number of the outstanding programs mentioned in our survey of senior public affairs executives—among them Hershey Foods Corporation and ARCO.

The Hershey philosophy is to be willing to look at new ideas and to adopt them voluntarily if they make sense rather than be forced. This corporate culture finds its roots in the business philosophy espoused by the company's founder, Milton Hershey. Many of his actions prove the point, but none so dramatically as his decision, during the Depression, to hire those out of work to help construct major facilities in the town that bears his and the company's name.

To many who have worked with the company, such a novel approach to public affairs at first appears incongruent, its headquarters tucked away in an idyllic setting in the middle of Pennsylvania. One would think that its people would be removed from the formation of novel ideas on a daily basis. But it may be because Hershey's people make time to reflect on ideas—rather than waiting so long that they are forced to react—that they have been more responsive to trends than other organizations.

Take the issue of nutritional labeling that arose from consumers' interest in knowing what was in the food they were eating. It first arose as an issue in the late 1960s and early 1970s. It started as an idea posited by those who believed we would all eat more intelligently if we knew the contents of the processed foods we were purchasing.

It evolved into an issue as consumer groups began discussing the need for nutritional labeling. Members of Congress began to introduce bills compelling it. And clearly, there was a cost to be borne for the manufacturers of processed food.

The late Harold S. Mohler, then CEO of Hershey Foods Corporation (HFC), decided it would be more responsive to proceed voluntarily with the labeling rather than wait and be forced to do so. He held meetings with his corporate staff. The scientific people at Hershey supported labeling. They had held informal discussions with the Food and Drug Administration and concluded that it was the right thing to do. HFC's marketing department suggested a go-slow approach.

But, as Mohler and others at Hershey saw the idea of nutritional labeling being floated, they realized that it was inevitable, that it was a good thing, and that rather than invest in holding off as long as possible, they would take the initiative, becoming the first candy maker to put nutritional labeling on their products and thereby identifying themselves as a candid and consumer-oriented company.

The Hershey Foods decision to include nutritional information on their products occurred some 20 years before Congress passed the Nutrition Labeling and Education Act in 1990, forcing the recalcitrant companies to comply. The company had adapted to an issue in a way that was best for everyone.

Mohler had foresight. Hershey Foods Corporation was the first to put sugar labeling on its products even though the labeling requirements only called for carbohydrates. They were also the first to include sodium labeling.

The philosophy that guided the company's decision to proceed was quite simple: If it's the right thing to do for the consumer, then it's the right thing to do for the company without being forced to do so. It is an attitude that has put them in good stead in a number of situations, one in particular that helped them immensely in a major grassroots battle later on.

The adaptive mode is not unique to Hershey. ARCO has had a responsive corporate culture that can be traced to a time when the company's management included the late Thornton Bradshaw. "Bradshaw brought a dimension to the day-to-day operation of ARCO which caused the company to increase its involvement in community activities," says Ken Dickerson, senior vice president of external affairs.

> In his view if a company were not involved politically—and by politically he meant the entire public policy formation process—it was not involved at all. He was ahead of his time in terms of his willingness to adjust to legitimate community concerns.

Dickerson points to the construction of the pipeline in Alaska, still the largest private pipeline in the world. While some of the companies in the funding coalition for the pipeline were prepared to confront anyone who objected to the way in which the pipeline was being built, Bradshaw both urged and agreed to community-based environmental oversight committees, a precursor for those now being demanded legislatively in the oversight of the Valdez cleanup.

Bradshaw's view, like that of Mohler's, was that if the course of action being proposed was in the best interests of all concerned, then it was in the best interests of the company to be responsive to those community concerns. He set the stage for an ARCO management style that, to this day, remains responsive to the public demand for environmental quality.

Lodwrick M. Cook, chairman of the board of ARCO, embraced that style and expanded upon it, leading a team that insists on understanding and being responsive to trends. At a very early stage they picked up on the rumblings in the community that said it was surely possible to create a fuel for automobiles and trucks that would put fewer hydrocarbon emissions in the air.

Noted Dickerson, "Lod knew that the public was demanding fuels that would burn cleaner and instead of fighting the public view, he decided to develop an alternative fuel that would meet the environmental needs of the community."

ARCO responded in an adaptive way by becoming the first oil company to offer a gasoline, one that would reduce smog-forming potential by 37 percent and toxic emissions by 47 percent. The company then went so far as to offer its competitors the formula for the new fuel at no charge.

Their actions not only met with a positive response from the powerful Southern California Air Quality Control Commission, it also reaped a salutary response from the environmentally conscious consumers. But, the real payoff has been bottom-line benefits at the pump. ARCO sales increased in areas where the clean fuel was sold.

In a state that, standing alone, would be the tenth largest country in the world, and which is the third largest user of gasoline (behind only the United States itself and what was once the U.S.S.R.), ARCO has a very impressive 20 percent market share. And while ARCO executives cannot prove that their proconsumer, proenvironment public policy approach to the way they do business has anything to do with their success, they do believe that in a market as environmentally sensitive as California, it certainly has not hurt.

Hershey Foods and ARCO have perceived a link between politics or public policy and bottom-line strategic planning. So, too, has General Mills Restaurants, Inc. We have sat in on corporate planning sessions in which the addition of salt-free items to their menus was being discussed a full year before the issue hit the cover of *Time*. Joe Lee, at the time the CEO of the then restaurant group, and now executive vice president of the parent company, built his division from a single Red Lobster unit to over 1000 restaurants by, in part, sensing trends and building on them.

Other companies have recognized the need to adapt to the environmental movement. These are the companies that looked at the environmental movement not as a threat to their existence but as an opportunity for growth. In doing so, they have adapted to the "greening" of America and have taken it into account in their strategic planning process, according to Jacqueline Scerbinski. Writing in *The Journal of Business Strategy*, she notes:

> The environmental movement has received a divided reaction from strategists who are formulating plans for consumer goods companies.
>
> One group seeks to placate the "greens." The other is retargeting its strategic product development programs to meet the needs of environmentally concerned consumers. Proactive executives from both camps see an opportunity to develop new products and repo-

sition old ones. In addition, they anticipate the benefit of an improved corporate image.

Perceptive planning and marketing executives foresee a legal environment that will prohibit the sale of nonrecyclable and non-biodegradable consumer goods. Thus, they are repositioning their companies to take advantage of new consumer attitudes. Rather than be frustrated by legal constraints, they are using them to their advantage.[1]

Not all companies are following those discussed by Scerbinski. They have not recognized the cycle, the fact that the "greening" culture has arrived—especially with the election of Vice President Gore—nor the need to develop an adaptive strategy. They would prefer to fight regardless of the cost.

For example, the idea that there should be a ban on nonbiodegradable packaging products surfaced in the mid-1970s. Many in the producing and user industries chose to ignore the idea or to believe that by fighting these proposals, the issue would recede. At one meeting of the Single Service Institute addressed by one of the authors in the early 1980s, the group felt that it had turned back the threat by defeating a proposal in committee in Oregon.

We mentioned to the trade group, which represents those who make and those who use such products as single-serving plastic dinnerware, that the same proposal had been made by backbenchers in both the British Parliament and the European Parliament, a suggestion that the idea was taking root as a trend. From our perspective, the executives in attendance chose to reject our suggestion.

In the case of the European Parliament, we felt the trade group failed to heed an important warning, since those elected to the European Parliament at that time were destined to demand and to obtain real power one day. No politician will forever be elected and sit powerless.

Like those who sat in the Congresses that were ruled by our own Articles of Confederation before 1789, members of the European Parliament are destined to become a power to reckon with. That day is almost upon us if it has not, in fact, already arrived, a point we shall return to in Chap. 9. Many groups and individual organizations are blind to early issue development, which means that the same issue is apt to be a source of contention over a long period of time in this country.

For example, the plastics industry and its various trade groups—including the successor to the Single Service Institute, the Food Service and Packaging Institute—continue to have major battles with no end in sight. Industry battles in Suffolk County, Long Island, beginning in 1989, and in the state of Massachusetts in 1992, suggest that after more than a decade, the idea is not near completion of its cycle. Its time will come, especially to those who react and confront rather than adapt and co-opt.

No less proof exists than the fact that at least 20 states now have procurement guidelines for the acquisition of recycled materials, 9 have mandatory deposit laws, and 4 have passed solid-waste legislation. In addition, a Clinton administration executive order calls for the federal government to purchase paper with recycled content. Nonbiodegradable packaging will be severely restricted at some point.

These facts, prompted Scerbinski, a former executive with the Federated and May department stores, to urge organizational planners to adopt "an anticipatory response [in order to identify] new products and [reposition] old ones for the environmentally conscious consumer of the 1990s. These consumers are already seeking recycled paper products, cloth diapers, organic baby food, natural cosmetics, and nontoxic household cleaning products."[2]

In our judgment, some companies like Hershey, ARCO, and General Mills Restaurants, Inc., seem to respond to environmental concerns as opportunities while some appear to treat such concerns as threats. It appears to us, as outside observers, that those organizations who view external issues as threats see little, if any, connection between strategic planning and the public affairs or political process. That failure, in our judgment, causes a disconnect that makes it difficult, if not at times impossible, to perceive any connection between what is being planned in, say, Houston, and possibly miscued, for example, in Alaska.

It may be due to an excessive dependence on legal advice. In a thoughtful piece for the *Public Relations Journal*, attorney Douglas Cooper contrasted the approach of the lawyer and the public relations or public affairs counselor:

> It is in words and their application that the inherent tension between lawyers and public relations consultants is expressed. Every word used to persuade the public is a word which may be used to persuade a judge.
> That's why the attorney will often insist that his client remain *publicly* silent in a crisis. Words are to be used only in the controlled environment of the litigation procedure. *From the attorney's point of view, if the case is won, it does not matter what the public thinks* [italics added].[3]

Whatever the reason, a failure to be guided by an *adaptive* planning approach could engender not only miscalculations in public affairs but also, we believe, tip off miscalculations in other areas of the organization as well. In short, it may suggest an organizational culture with deeper problems.

In the area of external affairs generally, we believe that organizations with a public affairs dimension in their strategic planning process usually take into account two trends: The first is instant replay; the second, the new populism in media response. Both buttress the populism that has been a key part of community protest, especially when the issue appears to be a lack of concern by some big guy for the little guy.

Instant replay allows sportscasters and political analysts to remind the public continuously of what happened and what was said. What is done or said can be played back over and over again as images good and bad get cemented.

The new populism in media says that no candidate is to be trusted unless he or she has appeared before the new public interlocutors, Larry King et al., and answered both the questions of the hosts and those who call in with questions. Populism insists upon an egalitarian accountability.

With that in mind, one can say that such trends have been ignored if the chief executive officer—either in person or in virtual control—is not present at the scene of a disaster from the outset. The CEO may be seen actually lifting bales or simply directing traffic from some accessible command post, but the chief executive is visibly there, involved in the scene and accounted for, when an event that could affect human life or the environment is unfolding. When people are hurting, they want to know that their concerns are shared by those in a position to rectify them.

These trends appear to us to have been overlooked in two situations. One involves Exxon, the other Sears, Roebuck.

Prior to the Exxon Valdez disaster, two other oil companies had dealt with oil spills, ARCO in Port Angelus, Washington, and Ashland Oil Company in Pittsburgh, in such a forthright manner as to have the local press and public officials singing their praises, a reflection of local public opinion as well. In short, there had been success stories a company could emulate and the press could point to that made some people question why Exxon seemed to have ignored what now appears, in retrospect, to be an obvious way of handling a disaster. It's not as though the methods were untried. They had been proven in the midst of a crisis.

More recent events could suggest to an outsider that Exxon still chooses to ignore what other organizations have learned is the more prudent course, at least from the standpoint of a public affairs approach to a populist uprising. Alaska fishermen made the point in August 1993.

Believing that the Valdez spill had led to a dearth of salmon and a weak run of herring, some 60 boats blockaded the approach to the Trans-Alaska pipeline for two days, preventing oil tankers from reaching their destination. Their goal was a meeting with Exxon about their pending lawsuits over the 1989 incident. They got a hearing, but not from Exxon.

Exxon officials, who had refused to meet with the protesters, issued
a statement saying no link had been established between this year's
low return of pink salmon and the spill.[4]

In contrast, the fishermen agreed

to lift the blockade after Interior Secretary Bruce Babbitt [met with
them] and promised more help for the recovery effort. [In addition,] British Petroleum and Arco met with the protesters, as did
Gov. Walter J. Hickel, who invited Mr. Babbitt.
   "I think it's outrageous that an American company with the size
and sophistication of the Exxon company doesn't have the will to
sit down and talk with a bunch of fishermen on this sound," Mr.
Babbitt said.[5]

In fairness, an Exxon spokesman pointed out to us that, at the time
of the blockade, the company was engaged in a major civil suit with
the fishermen due for trial in mid-1994. The company did not wish to
engage in a dialogue that appeared to be an effort on the part of the
fishermen to obtain a settlement prior to the court date.

That said, few would argue that while the company has done an
outstanding job cleaning up the area—so good that the on-scene coor-
dinator for the government has signed off on their effort—their public
handling has left itself open to criticism. As one public relations practitioner put it: It would appear that "the classic example of how not to
do things was the Exxon Valdez oil spill. Stonewalling, arrogance,
denial—Exxon did it all."

But, Exxon's expensive mistake turned out to be a free and important lesson for other large corporations, according to [Sacramento
public relations consultant Stephen] Hopcraft. "Exxon should get
credit for teaching other corporations what not to do."[6]

Again, in fairness to the company, they have cleaned up the area.
That says something positive. But there remains the view that the public handling of the crisis left much to be desired. The company
spokesperson with whom we discussed the spill and its aftermath conceded that the company has never addressed the subject of how well
or how poorly it handled it from a public affairs standpoint: "While it
is a fair question to raise, each person's view of what we did or did not
do is truly subjective."

That is true. But, when appearance is reality, sometimes being
viewed as legally correct and publicly questionable may lead one to
win the battle, but lose the war.

That may have occurred at Sears, Roebuck. Once considered the
barometer for judging truly dependable service, the company was

accused in California and New Jersey of kiting charges for auto repairs. What made matters worse was its initial response.

> Sears' first response to accusations was to call them politically motivated and to deny any fraud. It accused the California department of trying to gain support at a time when it was threatened by severe budget cuts. Using lawyers as its primary spokesmen, it held to that position for several days as the crisis intensified and spread.[7]

Subsequently, the chairman of Sears—while denying any liability or intentional wrongdoing—apologized in a paid advertisement[8] and arranged for an equitable resolution of all 19 automotive class action suits. Apologies from the chairman and the launch of a comprehensive program to standardize auto repair practice are nice. But, had there been a public affairs involvement in the strategic planning process of the company, one would hope that a question would have been raised about putting mechanics in a position where they may have felt the need to use unseemly tactics to boost sales.

An astute observer of trends among Americans would have noted their growing distrust of service people, particularly those who work on cars, and at the very least, wondered aloud, "You know, sting operations, in general, have become popular of late among law enforcement agencies, and, in particular, for checking out price gouging among auto mechanics." Or, at the very best, suggested a wiser course of action for making up the losses Sears faced from other operations with the observation, "Wouldn't we be better off rebuilding consumer trust and confidence in the Sears name?"

Thus, one could argue that an *adaptive* public affairs approach to the strategic planning process at Sears might have engendered the company's alliance with 41 attorneys general to deal with auto repair services *before* the problem arose. That said, the Sears effort seems to have restored the trust that venerable institution has earned over its 100-plus years in business.

Ignoring the role of public affairs in the organizational planning cycle, we believe, can have a direct, measurable impact on the bottom-line profitability of a company. This is certainly true in a consumer product or service company such as Sears. Some may rebound, but many never seem to regain the trust and confidence they once held. It may not affect Exxon directly as oil companies, generally, do not consider themselves consumer product companies, and they seem not to have suffered at the pump.

A consumer product company is one that depends on both the choice *and* the *discretion* of the customer. One can choose to buy or not to buy a car or any of the number of products sold by Sears. Once one decides to make a purchase, the next decision is from whom. Gasoline doesn't work that way. We have to buy gasoline. And, as we shall explore momentarily, only a few oil companies behave as consumer product companies. As some critics have contended, Exxon and a few others choose to remain aloof as manufacturers of a product we cannot avoid purchasing.

The problem for such companies and organizations, as we perceive it, is the operative word *control,* as in a belief that they can choose to ignore any part of an equation they cannot control. Left to chance, one surmises, is that definition of the environment which includes both the community's view of how the organization should function and the political response to that view. Leaving the public and the political view to chance suggests a failure at strategic planning, a failure of apparently not knowing what it is the organization wishes to accomplish.

Developing a Strategic
Public Affairs Plan

To be adaptive requires a strategic public affairs plan that is geared to protecting and enhancing the receptivity of the environment for your goods, services, ideas, or interests. A strategic public affairs plan must clarify the processes and values that are going to give life to the plan. It must be inextricable from the strategic plan for the organization as a whole and updated annually.

Few successful organizations operate without some sort of a strategic business plan, and a few appear to have public affairs strategic plans. Yet, in the corporate world, such business plans usually refer to those items that can be projected and for which the numbers can be crunched. These include financial projections, sales projections, new product entries, production trends—all items that can be analyzed objectively. They represent the foundation for bank loans and investment portfolios. They also represent what the corporate "bean counters" are convinced they can control.

Going "in search of excellence," Peters and Waterman suggested that the truly great companies today had abandoned as myopic the "management theories of the first sixty years of this century [which] did not worry about the environment, competition, the marketplace, or anything else external to the organization." Starting around "1960, theorists began to acknowledge that internal organization dynamics were shaped by external events."[9]

Yet, a cover-to-cover reading of this important and challenging work reveals little, if any, interest in public affairs or public relations. A reader comes away with the notion that by "the environment," Peters and Waterman are using an equally myopic definition, one limited to an external world over which the corporation believes it can exercise almost complete control, namely, its marketplace.

In fact, few, if any, management theorists or consultants, or business schools for that matter, focus on the integration of public affairs into the strategic planning process. They seem to respond with alacrity to trends of a technological nature, yet shy away from sociopolitical trends. Again, we view this responsive chord toward trends of a technological nature as trends over which one can exercise some control.

Management consultants seemingly would rather deal with technological trends than sociopolitical trends for another reason. The former, they believe, lend themselves to quantifiable answers framed by questions with a positive slant about the future that begin, "What if we *do* . . . ," as in "what if we *do* expand plant capacity, open a new sales territory, venture into a new market? What can we expect in terms of a return on our investment?" In contrast, they seem to view the latter as nonquantifiable, thus dismissing attempts to answer the discomforting questions that try to project the impact of the more negative "what if we *don't* . . . " side of the coin.

Thus, they ignore such questions as, "What if we *don't* build an alliance with our employees, open opportunities for women or minorities, establish a meaningful dialogue with the communities in which we operate, maintain an involvement in the process that demonstrates that we are open to change if everyone benefits instead of constantly appearing intransigent to customer opinions?" Beyond that, they also ignore the ultimate question, "What if we don't appraise our community relationships *honestly*, to monitor and anticipate moods, attitudes, trends in public opinion about us as an organization?"

One reason may be that the evolution and impact of public policy issues do not fit neatly into the quarterly planning cycles so favored by investors. Another may be that the management feels insecure in the issue resolution process because they believe they lack any control over the outcome of the situation. Our guess, too, is that they often dismiss public policy issues as externalities easily dispensed with by a fix-it lobbyist, a thought no senior manager today should hold.

Yes, everyone will respond once they have been ordered by law to do so. But, what we are talking about is the difference between organizations that lead rather than follow, that participate rather than react. Organizations that understand that, while control in the sense of dictating the eventual outcome of an issue may not be possible, control in the sense of being an active participant in and helping to shape the resolution of that issue is not only possible but also in the best interests of the organization.

Analyzing Issues

To be a player requires, as Caren Wilcox suggested at the outset, a strategic plan that includes a review of issues facing the organization, short and long term, their economic impact, and contingency options for the organization's involvement. In order to make such a plan work, you need to understand issues in three critical dimensions:

1. Their life cycle
2. Their relationship to your organization's purpose
3. Their ecosocial measurement

The integration of public affairs into the strategic planning process begins with two decisions: The first is to undertake an analysis of both where the organization is in the evolutionary process of issue resolution; the second, to measure the true impact of any issue that may impact upon the organization. Does the issue truly matter? If so, by how much and to whom? The process starts with *issue tracking*, which means, in short, determining where in the evolutionary process are those issues that truly have bottom-line impact.

Understanding the Life Cycle of an Issue

In the world of public affairs, issues start as ideas and follow a four-stage life cycle (see Fig. 3-1): They begin as isolated general concepts, perhaps from an academic; they then gather momentum as *trends*, as others pick up on the idea, apply it to different situations, and write about it in popular publications. They next turn into *issues* that become part of the conversation among people in and around government.

From the issue stage they quickly become *legislation*, bills whose mere existence requires that attention be focused. Finally, after the bill becomes law, there is the *regulatory* process, which is expensive, time-consuming, adversarial, and, often, a defensive operation. Regulations themselves spawn ideas that start the whole process over again.

The idea that sets in motion a trend may be a good idea. It may be a bad idea. It may be neutral, depending upon one's viewpoint or degree of involvement. In some instances, the trend is set in motion through a series of seemingly unrelated "ouches" let out by people who believe they've been hurt in some way.

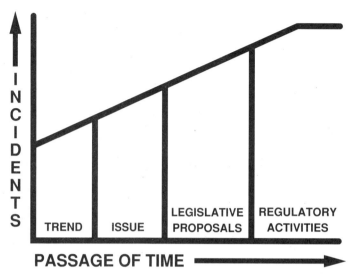

Figure 3-1. Life cycle of an issue.

Take, as an example, the issue of the potential harmful effect of sitting in front of a video display terminal all day, the VDT issue. Its launch as an issue was preceded by a trend in which many people were raising questions about the impact of technology, initially in the home, and the possible impact of electromagnetic fields, or radiation, on health. The ideas expressed by those raising questions included concerns about the effect of radiation exposure on people's health from sitting too close to a color television set or from being in the kitchen when food was prepared by microwaves.

No one denied that an electromagnetic field was established by these devices. Even earlier questions concerning the use of x-rays had led to the abandonment of machines one could look through to see if shoes fit properly. We also knew that such magnetic fields emanated from the common light bulb.

The question to which no one knew the answer, as the ideas were being discussed in their incipient-trend stage, was what levels of radiation could we tolerate in the use of everyday appliances. With no answers, but abundant speculation, pop science found a breeding ground of ignorance and fear in the new technology ripe for believing in the worst that could occur.

The home was one place. At least there, one had a choice. People could *choose* whether to buy a color television or a microwave oven. Outside the home, people had some choice. They could, for example, question a dentist as to the necessity of frequent mouth x-rays. The explosion of the trend into an issue for manufacturers of computers occurred when people found themselves in their place of work *forced* to deal with technology they feared. In their place of employment, people felt trapped. The video display terminal allowed them to vent their frustration.

The VDT issue first surfaced in 1977 when two copy writers for *The New York Times* were told by their ophthalmologist, Milton Zaret, that the cataracts they had developed had been caused by working at a computer and having their eyes exposed to the radiation emanating from the video display terminal. In an interview, Dr. Zaret told us he had begun believing that there was a connection between cataracts and VDTs as early as the mid-1960s.

His theory was heralded in many press accounts as if he were an expert, and he was even asked to present his views in testimony before a congressional committee studying the issue chaired by then Representative Al Gore. It took years, as we shall recount shortly, before the industry eventually succeeded in having Dr. Zaret's views discounted by a court.

Meanwhile, "Zaret's contention that microwaves cause a unique form of cataracts and the VDTs were the probable cause of the eye problems reported by the *Times* copy editors, was the basis of a union action filed by The Newspaper Guild of New York. The Guild subsequently lost the case, partly because of the findings by the National Institute for Occupational Safety and Health that the machines were not hazardous." Very few people know those findings exist.[10]

Subsequently, other ophthalmologists reported "that Zaret's theory is considered erroneous because the type of cataract Zaret described is not unique to people exposed to microwave radiation."[11]

Many suspect that Zaret had read the same articles that had been written about microwaves and color TVs and was at pains to explain the cataracts. He may have based his conclusion on the assumption that the cataracts were due to the only new variable to have entered the life of the journalist, the video display terminal.

But, as the suit was thrown out, initially little more was thought of the issue. But, more "ouches" were about to be heard.

Almost simultaneously in Canada, Denmark, and the United Kingdom, women began to claim that their pregnancy had been terminated prematurely due, in the judgment of their obstetrician, to sitting in front of a video display terminal all day long during their pregnancy. In Toronto, Canada, the issue was elaborated by three female employees of the *Toronto Star*. Whether they were prompted by the newspaper guild is not certain, but most observers give the unions credit for raising the issue worldwide.

What made Canada the focal point of the debate was that it was also the first place in which the second stage of the VDT issue surfaced. The issue that had begun as an idea concerning the possible harmful effects of radiation in the home, that had set in motion a trend which raised questions about the impact of new technology on our basic health, now gained the added momentum of proposals for rectifying the apparent wrong. The unions called for laws either banning VDTs outright or severely limiting their use by workers to a very few hours in total and to a very few minutes per hour without a break.

It is usually at this point, when an organization calculates the impact of the proposal on its operation, that the trend moves to the issue stage. For the basic difference between a trend and an issue is its impact on the organization. An issue will definitely cost the organization money.

In this case the impact could have measurable impact, not just upon the manufacturers of computers but also upon their customers, virtually every business in the world. If, as the unions said, the health risks were real, a company might have to have twice the number of employees to get a task done in a normal eight hours that one shift of people now performed, which would mean losing the anticipated productivity gains from having the same crew work on a single eight-hour shift. That would mean that the new technology would not only cost more in terms of either requiring additional people to achieve the same benefits forecast with computers or less efficiency with the same people, it would also mean, ipso facto, that there would be no savings from the new technology in any event.

Worse, some heretofore nonunion companies would possibly become organized, this time by so-called pink-collar workers, that is, clerical workers who had traditionally resisted joining a union. The fact that people were being made to use a device they did not like, considered impersonal, and, in many instances, viewed as job threatening was cause enough for grumbling. They were now being persuaded that the health scare gave them reason for being represented. The unions saw this opening and seized upon it.

The unions also saw the VDT issue as peculiar to women since men, at that time, were loathe to touch a computer, considering it nothing more than a faster, fancier typewriter. That the pink-collar worker could be organized, that proposed work rules might lower productivity, and that the use of computers themselves might be restricted all added up to one obvious fact: The cost of resolving the VDT issue could be enormous.

It took until 1993 for the industry to finally successfully challenge Zaret's assumptions. In the case of *Hayes et al. v. Raytheon Co.*, the chief

U.S. district judge, James B. Moran, ruled that Zaret's testimony was inadmissible.

> After scrutinizing Dr. Zaret's deposition and affidavit to find evidence or information about his methodology we are left with very little.
>
> Dr. Zaret's general statements that the injuries were caused by radiant emissions are not enough to establish sound methodology. The doctor does not point us to scientific studies, data, or research in support of his theory. Dr. Zaret's opinion that the facts of this case fit his own unsupported, unproven hypothesis does not establish a reliable methodology and, therefore, the testimony is inadmissible.[12]

The industry's efforts to combat the VDT issue have gradually borne moderate success. Major scientific research continues to support their position. Its major trade group, the Center for Office Technology, is headed by Dennis McIntosh, an executive schooled both in grassroots coalition building and in developing a substantiated case.

Among other documents it has assembled is one that should put to rest the claim that pregnant women are affected by sitting in front of a video display terminal:

> The U.S. Centers for Disease Control investigated the clusters [of miscarriages] and concluded that the background rate of miscarriage in the population is such that the clusters could have occurred entirely by chance.
>
> The National Institute of Occupational Safety and Health (NIOSH) decided to investigate miscarriage rates among telephone operators who worked with VDTs. NIOSH compared miscarriage rates in birth among more than 300 directory assistance operators who used VDTs, with the miscarriage rate of more than 400 long distance operators, who used a telephone console without a VDT. In its 1991 report NIOSH concluded that: "The use of VDTs was not associated with an increased risk of spontaneous abortion."

The point worth noting here is that there were early warning signs, not only from the questions being raised about technology in general but also about the introduction of the new technology into the workplace. These early warning signs included consumer reaction to microwave ovens and color televisions. There was a demand for safety guarantees. But in the workplace, no one was worrying about how to introduce the new technology.

Sales presentations were being made at the senior management and board levels about the great savings that would accrue if the company would computerize. What impact the new technology would have on working conditions, staff morale, and employee acceptance were either not considered or considered and dismissed.

We recall a scene at a now-defunct *Fortune* 500 company that was headquartered in Connecticut. Clerical people had Wang computers in front of them on their desk and a typewriter on their sideboard. No one was using the Wang system. They were all typing letters and reports on their typewriters. Perhaps, the same lack of attention to trends in employee relations carried over into the marketplace where the company was taken over and dismantled.

The point that we wish to discuss here and impress upon organizational planners is the need for early on trend and issue analysis.

Consider two trends currently in vogue: one, that people are voluntarily eating fewer calories, and two, that in the United States the population is aging. For an organization such as a manufacturer of steel, neither trend may have much consequence. They might change the menu of the employee dining room. They may have to make some adjustments in their retirement package. But the bottom line of their business is probably not affected so that neither trend is an issue for them.

But if the company makes candy, both trends are issues. They may need to redesign their product, perhaps produce a "light" candy bar. They may need to market it differently, perhaps showing seniors enjoying life more with a nutritious candy snack. In either event, they may have to deal with nutritionally conscious buyers for whom the idea of knowing more about what they eat can lead to calls for nutritional labeling, an added cost as packaging must be changed.

A good public affairs operation will pick up the early warning signs, the ideas that launch trends which, if ignored, frame the early emergence of an issue. Such an operation will then posit scenarios in which the issue may lead to legislation if the issue promoters are positing the need for legislative redress, or suggest new ways of doing things to avoid legislation.

Oftentimes the early warning sign is pending legislation or issue resolution in a different industry. The fact, for example, that tobacco products are prohibited from advertising on television and radio is a precedent that can be repeated if other products are deemed harmful. It may even be the emergence of legislative proposals in early warning jurisdictions, countries, states, or cities that historically have responded to a call for political action.

Sounds simple enough, but not only do too few organizations follow this prescription, they also often dismiss as irrelevant the role of public affairs in achieving long-range business success. One reason is attitude. There is an arrogance among the senior officers of some organizations that they, Perot-like, can do as they choose and suffer no consequences. Issue tracking is meaningless if the attitude within the company is arrogant or reactive.

Those organizations that tend to succeed in public affairs do so initially, in our observation, because they have a strategic plan that includes a public affairs dimension. But they also succeed because they are managed by individuals who recognize that issues do evolve and that the American ethic ultimately favors compromise, two facts that favor an approach to public affairs that is nonconfrontational. Such organizations have a corporate culture that has an adaptive mode of operating, an approach to the process of public issue involvement that enables them to measure the impact of an issue in order to weigh how to adapt to its outcome.

Measuring the Impact of an Issue

Too often organizations fail in their quest for achieving a specific goal because they have too many issues. Their effort gets diffused. In contrast, by keeping one's eye focused on those issues with bottom-line accountability, it is possible for an organization to achieve its objective.

To begin, there are two ways of evaluating the impact of an issue. The first way is to distinguish among issues as those which are truly *critical* to the bottom line of the organization, those we could deem *tangential* to the purpose of the organization, or those a group may wish to become involved in for some purpose other than simply to protect their bottom-line interest. This last group we call *lateral* issues.

Second, such analysis should also include a distinction among issues in terms of whether they are purely *economic*, purely *moral*, or issues that we call *ecomoral*. By "economic," we mean fiscal and monetary issues; by "moral," that broad range of social, and at times religious, issues.

The two types of issues are not the same, as the Republicans who bowed to the religious-moral-social conservative right discovered when Bush and Quayle lost the fiscal-monetary-economic conservative right whose beacon of enlightenment included a brand of conservatism that was also socially libertarian.

There are issues with no economic impact, issues with minimal economic impact, and issues in which an artificial set of economic facts are introduced in order to cloud over what may be the winning moral aspect of the issue. The genuine ecomoral issue can be played either way, a fact that often works to the advantage of whichever side ultimately controls the ground rules for the debate. Since so many issues tend to fall into this category, with demonstrable success depending on how an organization gains control, a large part of Chap. 5 will be devoted to an understanding of the ecomoral issue.

What is important here, when considering the life cycle of issues and developing a process for adapting to the change such issues may foreshadow, is that this categorization of issues allows us to distinguish among issues that go to questions of survival, that is those which are essential to groups and organizations, and those which are significant but not at the heart of things.

Critical issues are survival issues. Lateral and tangential issues can be of interest to the organization but are not tied to its survival. Each requires attention, but the approaches ought to be very different.

A critical issue can be economic. Jobs are a critical issue. Wages are a critical issue, especially to those who believe they are being treated inequitably. A union is often in this situation. For members of the black community, farm laborers, women, and other groups that feel dispossessed, income is a critical issue.

Prohibiting or restricting the use of a product or changing the way it is marketed or packaged can be a critical issue for a manufacturer. A proposal to shut down an existing plant in which either jobs are at stake or alternative means of production will cost considerably more is a proposal that is economic in nature. The issue can be measured in real dollar terms.

A critical issue can be moral, that is, with no economic tie involved. Prayer in school is a critical issue for the true believer. Gun control for devotees of the Second Amendment to the Constitution is a matter of right, in our sense a moral critical issue. Rarely mentioned in the gun control issue is the fact that its opponents include those to whom the issue is both economic and critical, the gun manufacturers.

The critical moral concern raised by supporters of the Brady bill lose out to those for whom the dollars at stake are key. It helps the gun manufacturers to have the camouflage of a constitutionally righteous group of hunters manning the barricades. It also helps that, despite their products being the cause of some $14 to $18 billion annually in gun injuries, as some experts have suggested, no antitobacco type of antigun lobby has emerged.[13]

One reason suggested by seasoned observers is that, unlike the tobacco industry that can play hardball with anyone, the gun nuts prefer to play spitball. It's effective, but hardly a general strategy worth emulating.

A lateral issue is one that may be used for a number of purposes. It may become the issue worth discussing when the critical issue is so heated that no discussion can take place.

If, for example, a legislator is particularly opposed to the position of an organization on one of its critical issues, the organization may decide to become involved in an issue of great concern to the legislator but of little or no concern to the organization, simply to open a dialogue. Lateral issues may be the only way in which an organization can begin to build a coalition of people who may need to be neutralized even if there is no way to solicit them as adherents.

A lateral issue may be one in which there is opportunity to build goodwill among important groups. Many corporations got behind the passage of the civil rights bill in 1991 in part because they believed it was the right thing to do. The fact that it would help them cement their relationship with a black consumer group or black employees was a possible benefit to their effort.

But it would be hard to prove that passage of the bill truly represented the bottom-line, survival need of a critical nature. The same can be said for the 80-plus chief executive officers who, by year end 1992, had signed on as supporters of the National Leadership Coalition on AIDS. They have recognized the need to exert leadership in dealing with the worst scourge of several centuries and to commit themselves proudly to the notion that they are straight, but not narrow.

Tangential issues should be part of any public affairs analysis for the simple reason that their conclusion may present a harbinger of things to come. But, generally, other than being noted as part of the issue landscape, they may be dismissed.

The evaluation of an issue must begin with how much it will cost the organization if its proponents succeed. What we have seen too often is a reaction by organizations to issues that adopt either the Nancy Reagan slogan "Just say no" or General Custer's final command before leaving for Little Bighorn: "Do nothing 'till I return."

That response may win a temporary reprieve from the intensity of the effort, but if there is truly in motion a trend among the public that calls for remedial action, the better-run companies appear to be those that can adapt to the changes rather than attempt to resist forever.

Adaptation does not mean capitulation. It means seizing the initiative to be part of the public dialogue and rallying support for a solution that is mutually beneficial for the organization and the public at large. It means sensing trends and getting out ahead of them and, by so doing, having an impact on their outcome at a far earlier stage than those who wait to react to the legislative proposals (see Fig. 3-2).

Rallying support will depend on framing the message in a way that builds on either a high moral ground or a low-cost ground, or a combination of the two depending on timing and creativity, a process we will enlarge upon in Chap. 5. Suffice it to say now that the success of that endeavor begins with establishing a mechanism for monitoring trends and adapting them into the long-range planning cycle of the organization. It next requires the identification and involvement of the key players.

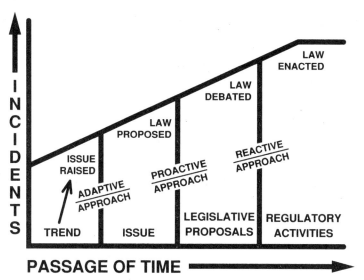

Figure 3-2. Three approaches to public affairs.

Notes

1. Jacqueline S. Scerbinski, "Consumers and the Environment: A Focus on Five Products," *The Journal of Business Strategy*, September/October 1991, pp. 44 ff. (© Sept./Oct. 1991, *Journal of Business Strategy*, Faulkner & Gray Publishers, New York, N.Y. Reprinted with Permission.)

2. Ibid.

3. Douglas A. Cooper, "CEO Must Weigh Legal and Public Relations Approaches," *Public Relations Journal*, January 1992, p. 40.]

4. Associated Press, "Alaska Fishermen Blockade Tankers," *The New York Times*, August 23, 1993, p. A8.

5. Ibid.

6. Rick Rodriguez, "A Better Way to Fix Corporate Screw-Ups," *Sacramento Bee*, July 3, 1993, p. A2. (Copyright, *The Sacramento Bee*, 1993)

7. Richard W. Stevenson, "Sears Ducks, Then Tries to Cover," *The New York Times*, June 17, 1992, p. D1.

8. Entitled "An Open Letter to Sears Customers," the ad signed by Ed Brennan said, "With over 2 million automotive customers serviced last year in California alone, mistakes have occurred. However, Sears wants you to know that we would never intentionally violate the trust customers have shown in our company for 105 years."

9. Peters and Waterman, *In Search of Excellence*, HarperCollins, New York, 1982, p. 91. (Copyright © 1982 by Thomas J. Peters and Robert H. Waterman, Jr. Reprinted by permission of HarperCollins Publishers, Inc.)

```

10. Mike Clancy, "Regional News," United Press International, March 31, 1981, BC cycle.

11. Christopher Winans, "Microwave Transmissions: Do Biological Effects Pose Health Threats?" United Press International, August 7, 1981, BC cycle.

12. Jay Judge, "'Lacking Sound Methodology,' Expert's Opinion is Barred," *Chicago Daily Law Bulletin*, March 9, 1993.

    Dr. Zaret told us in an interview that he is unaware of the case, that he never examined Carol Hayes and was not a part of the proceedings. He stands by his belief that there is a cause-and-effect relationship between cataracts being caused as an effect of sitting in front of a video display terminal regardless of what the court said.

13. Mary Elizabeth DeAngelis, "Biting the Bullet: How Crime Drives Up the Cost of Medical Care," Knight-Ridder Newspapers, *The Record*, March 14, 1993, p. RO-1.]
```

4

Working with Your Authorizing Environment

The Internals and the Externals

In previous chapters we have discussed how all issues are local in the sense that what drives emerging issues is how they affect people in their daily lives, how organizations often fail to deal with an issue because of their own fear of involvement in the public policy process, and how that fear manifests itself often in organizations' choosing to ignore early signs that a problem is just over the horizon, therefore being forced to react to crisis rather than adapt to conditions as they emerge.

These failures—to appreciate that all issues are local, to overcome the fear of fighting, to attack an issue before it becomes a crisis—are what enables public affairs and public relations experts to make a living. What those consultants sell is crisis management.

What we are selling are ideas that will prevent crises from occurring, or reduce their severity when they do arise. What we are proposing is a more strategic approach, the need for organizations to devote resources every day to creating a public affairs environment that is favorable to their objectives.

The first element of a strategic approach is the idea that no individual can do it alone, and no organization can either. We live in an interdependent world. In the long haul, no company can sell its goods and services, or win approval for its public policy positions, without the understanding and support, or at least the acquiescence, of lots of people inside *and* outside the company.

In effect, a particular, interested world from both inside and outside the organization needs to *authorize* the organization to do its work for it to succeed. That's why our friends at Harvard's Kennedy School of Government call this the *authorizing environment*. The authorizing environment consists of two worlds, the internal environment and the external environment.

We think about the people in the authorizing environment in two ways. First, how close are they to the heart of the organization? For this, we divide people into four categories: family, friends, strangers, and foes. Second, we think of some of the most important characters in the external environment in terms of their role.

In particular, we think of the interested external environment for any organization as consisting of three primary sets of characters: the press; the policy-makers and policy shapers, including especially the politicians; and the provocateurs, including interest and advocacy groups.

Our basic premise is that any organization must have, over time, a continuing relationship with its authorizing environment, both internal and external, in order to be successful in public affairs and in attaining their primary objectives.

As we have discussed before, organizations are too often unwilling to invest in these relationships because they continue to cling to the idea that they can solve their public affairs problems when the problems arise. This may have been true 20 or 30 years ago, but it is rarely true in today's fast-moving competitive world of instant communications.

Even when it does work, it is only a short-run solution. After a crisis has been solved with a fix-it response, the organization is no better off than it was before the crisis occurred. It has not solved the problem that led to the crisis. It is no less likely to be confronted with a crisis in the future, and it has no recourse, other than going back to the fix-it person, when the next one comes along.

We believe that the basis for the fix-it solution to public policy problems stems from three erroneous process views. The first is choosing to see the world of public opinion as a "we-they" duality rather than an orchestra with many different instruments. The second is assuming that there is a never-changing, predictable, static quality to the body politic. This belief holds that there are a handful of decision makers, a few more activists, and a slightly larger group that is informed; but that the overwhelming majority of people, three out of four or more, make up the great uninvolved, and uninvolvable, mass. (Ross Perot, in our opinion, may have dislodged that narrow top-down view during his 1992 campaign.)

Finally, there is a fundamental misunderstanding that one can build a successful outreach to any of the key external groups, be it press, pols, or the opinion leadership of advocacy groups, without first doing the hard work of building awareness and support internally. If many employees in a manufacturing company first hear of a new product when the advertising campaign is launched, or if, in a not-for-profit setting, employees and volunteers first learn of a new program or initiative from newspaper accounts, you know that the organization has not paid enough attention to those closest to home. Some day they will pay a price for not having done so.

Starting with Family
and Friends

The initial profile of public opinion on most issues is a bell-shaped curve. As the chart in Fig. 4-1 suggests, those who should stand with you at the outset, the group we refer to as "family" and "friends," may represent anywhere from 1 to 10 percent of the public; while the foes, those provocateurs who oppose you and who are equally emotional and committed to the opposite view, begin with 1 to 10 percent of the public's support and possible involvement.

What that leaves is a great number of people who either do not know about your issue, or who may not care very much about your issue, or whose reaction to it may be based on nothing more than the perspective expressed by your foes. We call this group "strangers" because their involvement in the issue at the outset is little or none.

Generally, most of the key characters in the external environment—the press, the pols, and the public opinion shapers who lead many community groups—are initially in the group of strangers. This group also includes most ordinary citizens whose opinions are often molded by what the press, pols, and public opinion shapers end up thinking about your issue.

Conventional wisdom in the world of public affairs has been to divide this universe among saints, sinners, and savables. This view suggests that those who support the organization are saints, those who oppose it are sinners, and those who are "up for grabs" between the opposing camps on an issue are, until proven otherwise, savable. While the three S's are both alliterative and an easy shorthand, our preference for placing various constituent groups in one of four cate-

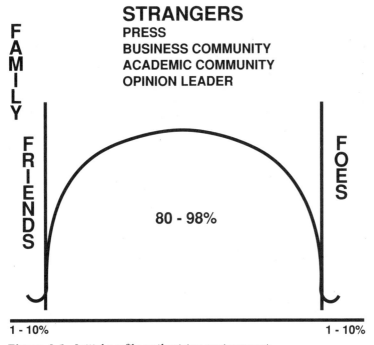

Figure 4-1. Initial profile-authorizing environment.

gories—family, friends, strangers, and foes—is based on our belief that the three S's do not go far enough.

It may seem semantic to divide the potential saints into family and friends, especially since, with a properly directed effort, the two groups ideally merge into the family of saints. But the distinction between family and friends is crucial, for there is a fundamental difference in how to engage each group; their motivation for becoming involved in your issue is usually vastly different.

In the corporate world, family are those people, such as employees and stockholders (and, often, their close relatives), whose livelihoods depend on the organization's success. They have the greatest stake and the strongest interest, particularly if the issue faced by the organization affects either jobs or profitability or both. They share, or should share, an *emotional* commitment to the organization. We say "should share" because management cannot assume all employees are committed, that they even understand, let alone support the company's view.

In not-for-profit organizations, the family includes those who feel most directly that the issue is one that affects them personally. Their emotional commitment is based on a belief that their cause will either protect the status quo they cherish or change the present conditions they view as hostile to their health or hearth.

Such not-for-profit groups count among their family those who contribute to the organization—as most donors tend to share an emotional commitment—but it also includes those who get involved in the envelope stuffing, the local branch organizing, and the recruitment process. However, as we shall examine momentarily, donors are not always, or at least not immediately, family.

Family, in a nutshell, are those people who are most directly *involved* in the organization for whom the emotional tie is, or should be, firmly fixed. They feel the impact of the issue.

Friends are those people who have connections that are not so direct, such as customers and vendors of corporations. Friends have the potential of becoming emotionally connected to the organization, but their initial tie is purely an *economic,* or in the case of not-for-profits, perhaps an *intellectual* or *moral,* commitment.

In that sense, for the not-for-profit groups, friends may be donors who have *invested* in the organization but who have not yet become emotionally involved. And just as a customer or vendor in a corporate structure may not have the same degree of commitment as an employee or stockholder, so too a contributor may not have the same commitment to a not-for-profit group as someone for whom the stakes are personal and for whom the investment of time and talent is equal to or greater than any dollars given.

A lot of people write checks to assuage their consciences. They think that they need do no more and prefer it that way. It's one reason many churches have redefined tithing or stewardship. In the new definition, parishioners are asked to contribute time and talent as well as treasure, a concept of becoming involved that, as we will see, is being applied in other situations.

In fact, there are lots of reasons why people invest in not-for-profit groups without becoming involved. They may philosophically agree with the precepts of the organization. Someone who is involved in a group to protect wildlife habitats may also contribute to a program to save the whales but not become involved in any organizational efforts. Someone who has a friend or a member of their family who has died from AIDS may contribute to an educational or research program to deal with that dreaded plague, yet never carry a banner in a parade or become involved in a protest movement to ban discrimination against gay people.

Similarly, in the political world, those who have a liberal bent to their social agenda may be more inclined, as a consequence, to contribute to liberal candidates and causes. They may even vote for someone of similar temperament, but they may decline a more active role in a campaign. There is a kinship to the cause, but it is a step shy of involvement, one critical distinction between friend and family.

Friends may be motivated to invest because there is a potential quid pro quo. It is assumed by many that such reasoning is common in the world of politics. Someone, perhaps a job hunter or a lobbyist, wants a job or contract or just access in return for their contribution.

But such quid pro quo exists in the not-for-profit world as well. It occurs when a donor to one cause expects the person who solicited the contribution to, in turn, pony up a like sum to the donor's favorite charity when the time comes for the roles to be reversed.

We know of at least one major corporation that tracks all requests for contributions to its chief executive officer in terms of those to whom he says yes and those to whom he sends regrets. When the chief executive then agrees to chair a fund-raiser for a cause in which he has an interest, he turns to those to whom he has said yes. It is a process not lost on those who argue that corporate contributions should be part of a strategic approach to public affairs.

Another motivation in the not-for-profit world is what we call "psychological patronage." While it is true that $100,000 donors to political campaigns may want something in return, the more likely motivation is that they want to be invited to special briefings or to a weekend at Camp David. In the nonpolitical world, it may simply be a sense of noblesse oblige or the sense that the donor is part of a rather exclusive group capable of helping the local arts or action group, wanting to see and be seen at all the "right" functions in the community.

People whose motivation is anything short of true love may be willing contributors but not necessarily willing to man the barricades when crunch time comes. Their motivation may have less to do with the cause than with who asked them to contribute. This may be particularly true when the donor has given in response to "sand-bagging," whereby the guy at the top of the contributor ladder has the power to force those below to give or get hurt, a situation as likely to occur in a political action committee solicitation as in one for the United Way. Often when the boss asks, the so-called generous response can be termed "generous" only in fact, not in spirit.

The willingness of such noninvolved donors to do more than write a check may be nil. They may have simply said to themselves, as they contributed a modest sum to some group whose purpose is to feed the hungry or provide athletic outlets for the physically impaired, "There, but for the grace of God, go I."

The fact that they contributed may sound sufficient to them, but it may not be enough for you in some critical situations in which people putting themselves on the line may be more important than their financial support. In addition, personal involvement often significantly increases the financial commitment.

It is why we think friends are an important but distinct category in the process of analyzing people in the internal side of the authorizing environment. There is the potential for taking them from a place of having given dollars or having an economic interest to a place of committing themselves, but it requires real work and often means overcoming considerable resistance.

Corporations are only just beginning to realize the connections between economic commitment and emotional commitments. For years, the corporate community has been busy organizing political action committees, or PACs.

They have been reasonably successful in these efforts. Large amounts have been raised and contributed to political campaigns. But the sums raised and the percentage of employee participation per corporate political *action* committee among companies that have *no* political *education* program pales in comparison to those corporations and not-for-profit organizations that have employee or volunteer political education programs.

The difference is that political education programs give rise to direct employee-volunteer involvement in the political process. And that involvement has led to an enormous difference—as much as a 100 percent increase in one corporation—in the numbers of dollars raised and the percent of donors contributing to those PACs.

As Neil Sclipcea, president of the National Fund-Raising Center in Washington, D.C., puts it:

> It's important to remember that successful fund raising is generated by issues or candidates and an organized constituency. So, in a political campaign, be it for a candidate or—in the case of initiative and referenda—a cause, our primary goal is to first get people *involved*, to have them become part of the decision-making process that develops the structure for the entire campaign effort.
>
> Involvement precedes investment. Because involvement leads volunteers not simply to contribute, but to contribute far larger sums than those not involved, and to contribute more frequently. Asking people to give before they get involved may generate a few bucks, but the payoff is a pittance in comparison. With the emotional issues most organizations contend with, it should be fairly easy for PACs to raise huge sums if they have a program for employee/volunteer education and involvement.

Sclipcea knows his business. Considered by many as one of the foremost fund-raisers in the country, he teaches the courses on the subject at The Graduate School of Political Management at The George Washington University.[1] His ideas have also taken hold in the newly emerging democracies in Eastern Europe and South America as fledgling political parties in many countries have sought his counsel on how to structure a fund-raising program.

Politicians have long understood this notion. As one told us recently:

> You can give me $1,000. That helps. But stimulate a number of your employees to volunteer for my campaign and, following my election, I'll remember those who stuffed envelopes or walked precincts in my behalf long after I've filed the report on the contribution from your PAC. The volunteers are real names and faces. The dollars are lost in a report of hundreds of thousands of dollars.

Clearly identifying and mobilizing the family first is essential. They are involved. They care. They have jobs on the line or their health at risk, or their feelings about an issue are so overpowering they have lost any logic to their love (or hate—but that's a different problem for an organization to confront, a different set of problems to overcome than we are prepared to deal with in this book).

The commitment of family is emotional. They are the first group one must deal with in terms of organizing. Once involved, family are the best ambassadors, not only for reaching out to the friends but more importantly for reaching out to the strangers as well. Without their wholehearted endorsement and involvement, the process of reaching out to others becomes far more difficult.

But you cannot take family involvement for granted. Even though their stakes are direct and their commitment is emotional, they have to be engaged. They have to be asked. This is a point of political organization often overlooked in the corporate world, and occasionally in the not-for-profit world as well.

We know of situations in which companies have run major advertising campaigns on television ballyhooing their environmental record. Yet, employee surveys reveal major questions about the corporate commitment to the environment among their employees.

During the Watergate fiasco, we saw one survey in which the employees questioned the company's credibility because their Washington lobbyist had gone to jail. Employee skepticism, based sometimes on fact but just as often on ignorance and a lack of internal communication, turns the company's first line of support into the first line of failure. Employee *support,* on the other hand, is a powerful resource in combating outside opponents, even the media.

In the early 1980s, the Coors Brewing Company received the media inquiry that everyone dreads: Mike Wallace called to say that *60 Minutes* wanted to do a segment on the company.

When the *60 Minutes* call came, the company was locked in a struggle for survival. They had been boycotted by virtually every known interest group, having been accused of being antiunion, anti-Hispanic, antiblack, antiwomen, antigay, antiwhatever. Their share of the market had plummeted. In each new market they entered, they were met with a storm of demonstrators. CBS assumed they had one of their made-to-order exposés.

But throughout this period Coors management had kept in close touch with their employees, constantly communicating with them, listening to their grievances, discussing the bad national publicity the company was receiving, and explaining their side of the story. As a result, when Wallace called, the company felt confident about their employees. Their employees were, metaphorically, ready to lay down their bodies for the corporate cause.

Management decided to let it all hang out. They gave CBS virtually free reign of their headquarters. While the outside world had one thing to say about the company, it was an entirely different story internally. The company knew that and took a chance.

They opened their doors, their books, and their file cabinets. They gave Wallace complete access to their employees. And, as Wallace later admitted, it was the first time in the history of the show in which he and his producers had let it be known where they could be reached if anyone wanted to speak and *no one called.* For Wallace, *that singular act* of nonaggression by the employees stunned him.

The result was something close to a puff piece, an unheard of event for *60 Minutes,* and an image coup of historic proportions for Coors at a time when they needed it badly. It marked the beginning of the end of the downward slide. Coors started back on the road of public acceptance as both a good brew and a good company.

Moving on to Strangers

The Coors story is a good bridge to discussing the category we call "strangers." Strangers neither know you nor care about you or your issue. They are comfortable not getting involved since they have no known interest, and they may even benefit in some way from your misfortune, for example, more market competition leading to lower consumer prices.

Those who more often than not elect to remain aloof from your issue include community leaders, opinion influencers, and Jane and John Q.

Public. They include the groups usually referred to in the saying, "politics makes strange bedfellows." Those who might profit from your discomfort can include one's competitors in the marketplace, but it can also include those politicians who see your discomfort as a way of enhancing their base of support, and media types interested in boosting circulation or winning the ratings game.

The willingness of such groups—be it community leadership, the public generally, the press, or the pols—to get involved on your side in the evolution of an issue will be based on the possibility that they share, or should share, an *intellectual* commitment to the issue and, until proven otherwise, should be placed in the savable category as potential allies.

We have numerous examples in which the likeliest of strangers have become allies. We have read of environmentalists aligned with the military and air-quality advocates endorsing initiatives of oil companies. We know of editors suffering from emphysema who have written editorials in support of the tobacco industry's right to market its products to an adult audience. And in a case we shall examine later in the section on coalition building that works, there were clergy engaged on the same side of an issue as candy manufacturers.

Those who might ordinarily sit on the sidelines and stay uninvolved can include groups that are organized for specific economic purposes, such as a business organization or trade union. They can include groups that are organized to deal with specific social issues such as the National Rifle Association or the National Organization for Women.

They can also include groups that can be identified by some obvious demarcation of interest, such as farmers or blacks or seniors. Each may have one or more issues for which its primary audience is its own family of supporters, a group that may not initially see their own stake in the outcome of your organization's issue.

Strangers are important because they represent the third party, those who, if they can be convinced to become involved, offer to the uncommitted community an endorsement that is seen as pure. The views expressed by family and friends in the discourse can be challenged as self-serving.

But if academicians, other business leaders, community-based groups, and respected opinion leaders side with you, the issue begins the process of resolution in your favor. It becomes even more dramatic if members of the public not aligned with anyone or any organization, a group so often ignored, step forward to endorse your position.

Dismissing your argument as self-serving can be made by anyone at any time. It can be leveled against corporate interests. But it can also be leveled against many do-gooder organizations. It can often sting and do damage. The charge of being self-serving can be partially blunted by the advocacy of a large group of employees or organization's members. After all, if those most involved don't care, why should outsiders? The self-serving charge is a given. It begins to fade rapidly when strangers to the issue become involved on your side.

That third-party endorsement, that elimination of the self-serving obstacle, is essential if the strangers in the most important outside roles are to be brought on board in support of your issue. For these are the strangers who could profit from your troubles if they are not sympathetic.

They include the press; the policy makers, especially the politicians; and, the provocateurs, including the Influentials in a community who lead the interest and advocacy groups, either as de facto leaders, as executive directors, chief executive officers, and the like, or as spiritual leaders, the writers of books and articles. We tend too often to think of provocateurs as only those who oppose us, failing to appreciate that, like the term *self-serving*, it is a term that can and should be applied to anyone who can *provoke* action on either side by virtue of his or her position within the community. All three are important because they can influence the failure or success of any issue.

The importance of the press, the policy-makers, and the provocateurs can be measured not only in the influence they can wield but also in the numbers of people they can reach. As many as 80 or even 90 percent of the public may be uninvolved in your issues, but most of them are reached by the activities of the press, pols, and provocateurs.

Dealing with Press, Pols, and Provocateurs

The first principle of successfully engaging with the press, pols, and provocateurs is to realize that they are different from you, but that they, too, have a legitimate role to play in the world of public affairs. Respecting their role and the pressures under which they are operating is important in creating an attitude on your part that opens up the possibility of a working alliance.

Your attitude will inevitably affect your behavior. It is a we-they world in the sense that you are more concerned with your issue than anyone else, but success comes to those who accept those differences and work with them rather than shut them out.

In our research we often found that those who viewed the outside world as hostile also tended to be equally suspicious about their family and friends. Those who fail to understand that the fate of their issue lies with the community are usually suffering from the same fear of fighting that makes them hesitate to open up to those who would be most committed emotionally and economically.

They seem incapable of understanding that standing alone they could well lose and that in building a coalition of people and groups who will support them, they might win more than the immediate issue itself. For while some consultants would suggest that it is a crisis-driven mode that requires an instant-response mechanism, we believe coalition building is a process that, allowed to percolate, establishes credibility on many levels.

Respecting their role goes hand in hand with the next principle: understanding their culture. The character of the media, of politics, and of advocacy are all different from one another and different from your organization, and knowing each of them on their own terms, as well as you know your own, is essential.

Here's an example of what we mean. The role of the press is to report a story. The story is *their* story, even if it is about you. And it is called a "story" because it is like a story, with a plot and a story line, good guys and bad guys, and a beginning, middle, and end. It is extremely unlikely that a good story for the press will be the same as the way you would write it if you were doing it yourself.

So while you are part of the story, even central to it, it is not your story. The press needs your help to make the story a good story from their perspective, but a good story from their perspective will not be one that is your version of reality. But if you do not help the press to write the story, then your version of reality will not influence it at all.

To take another example, understanding the role and culture of the politician means knowing that the merits of the argument are a necessary but not sufficient condition for support. In the political world, the rule is that once you've convinced the politician on the merits, you need to make it easy for him or her to do what you want done. "You've convinced me, now force me." The pol needs to hear from the constituents before the support can be solidified.

Dealing with the media and the political community is a subject we will revisit on several occasions. For our purposes here, the point is that moving out from friends and family requires engagement with external characters whose cooperation you need in order to succeed. The press, pols, and provocateurs are important, but they are not naturally on your side. Connecting with them requires being able to understand how the world looks from their point of view and using that perspective to make connections, find shared interests, and work on the common ground.

Saul Alinsky, in the prologue to his book *Rules for Radicals,* states the first principle of advocacy best when he says:

> As an organizer I start from where the world is, as it is, not as I would like it to be. That means working in the system. My "thing," if I want to organize, is solid communication with the people in the community. This failure of many . . . to understand the art of communication has been disastrous. Even the most elementary grasp of the fundamental idea that one communicates within the experience of his audience—and gives full respect to the other's values—would have ruled out attacks on the American flag.[2]

What Alinsky means is that to build bridges so that your issue can win requires an understanding of where the potential allies among the group of strangers are coming from in terms of their intellectual ability to embrace your issue. It requires, therefore, as we discussed in the previous chapter, an understanding of the differences among issues that are critical to your organization, those that are tangential, and, most particularly, those that are lateral.

For while the lateral issues are not critical to your organization, they may well be critical to a stranger to your issues with whom you want to build a relationship. And one begins the process of bringing strangers on board for their support of your issue by first building a bridge of involvement in what is important to them.

Building Bridges to the External Authorizing Environment

Let us consider a few examples. One involves a politician who came to terms with his antitobacco views when he needed the tobacco industry's help with a project of critical importance to his town. Two others include examples of major corporations taking on significant involvement in solving community issues as part of their public outreach efforts, and doing so by working shoulder to shoulder with community activists. A final example is one of former antagonists realizing that they could compromise on a plan in which each benefits.

When Ed Koch was a member of Congress, it is believed that he introduced more antitobacco legislation than any other member at that time. He was not a friend of the tobacco industry. However, when he became mayor of New York City, he was faced, suddenly, with a bankrupt city. He needed a bailout, a loan from the federal government requiring congressional approval.

While some in Congress were sympathetic, a large block of votes from the South appeared headed for disapproving the loan. Most of their constituents had little regard for New York City, viewing it the modern Babylon or Sodom. Koch appealed for help to Philip Morris, headquartered in New York.

The company's lobbyists went to see tobacco state legislators on behalf of the city. The city's bailout bill passed the Congress, and for several years no antismoking bills surfaced in either the city council or in Albany. Could be that the result was incidental, and certainly no discussion ever took place between the company and the mayor, but, for a time at least, there was a modicum of harmony on the issue.

The two examples of corporate involvement with community activists come from Los Angeles. They each involve efforts at reform—of the local education system and the local police. They were written up in *The Los Angeles Times.*

> The two efforts—to impose more civilian control over the Police Department . . . and to rehabilitate an ailing school system—have thrust the business community into the forefront of local politics. But its role is decidedly different from the days when secretive committees handpicked public officials and set public policy agendas in private clubs.
>
> Today's executives are trying to transform their concerns into popular causes by opening their doors to old antagonists, including labor organizers and civil rights advocates.
>
> It adds up to a tacit admission that private elites do not believe that they can win on their own anymore in Los Angeles and that coalition-building is the order of the day even for those at the top who used to shy away from the hurly-burly of street politics.
>
> Dominated as they are by members of the downtown Establishment, the two campaigns for school reform and police restructuring have a surprisingly populist flavor.
>
> Men such as lawyer, Warren Christopher, the former U.S. Deputy [now] Secretary of State; Robert E. Wycoff, [then] president of Atlantic Richfield, and Roy Anderson, chairman emeritus of Lockheed, are opting for the tactics of grass-roots activists, getting their message out to churches and synagogues, participating in debates and presiding over raucous public meetings.
>
> The corporate architects of the two campaigns are gambling that if they take their case to the public they can build a majority around common goals and values—even in a city as divided as this one is by culture, language, income and geography.
>
> The campaigns to change the school district and the Police Department operate independently from one another. But they have much in common. Both are trying to force formidable bureaucracies, the educational system and the Police Department, to become more accountable to the citizenry.
>
> The school reform movement, led by the private, nonprofit Los Angeles Educational Alliance for Restructuring Now (LEARN), contends that education will improve only if the teachers union, the Los Angeles Unified School District's central administration, and

the state Department of Education relinquish to parents, teachers and principals much of their power over school finances, curricula, hiring and firing.

LEARN's stated purpose is to decentralize the school district, making individual schools the master of their own fate and vastly expanding the power of principals, teachers and parents.

The decentralization plan is to be worked out by the LEARN board in partnership with the seven task forces, which besides teachers and other school district employees, include parents and the leaders of civic and neighborhood groups.

Once a plan is adopted, it will be up to LEARN participants to win public support and approval from the school board and lawmakers in Sacramento.

Veteran legislator Mike Roos, a former state assemblyman, was hired to shepherd the LEARN reforms through whatever political minefields lie between Bunker Hill and Sacramento.

[So far the campaigns] have impressed people with their ability to reach out to groups as diverse as the Southern Christian Leadership Conference, Industrial Areas Foundation, UTLA, Mexican-American Legal Defense and Education Fund, and the Gay and Lesbian Community Service Center.

As yet unproven is the ability of these new coalitions to win over the unaffiliated majority—those parents and voters who are primarily concerned with having good schools and safe neighborhoods.[3]

The LA coalitions may not succeed in winning over the unaffiliated majority to the reforms sought. But, by simply being part of the activist groups attempting to improve the quality of the schools and the policing of neighborhoods, those corporations that did get involved have secured a tie to a group of strangers that might possibly not have occurred had they remained passive and uninvolved. The net result may be that former strangers will be friends when an issue of importance to the corporation surfaces.

The final example, one of antagonists getting inside one another's head and coming at an agreed upon solution by starting, in part, from a priority of their opponent's agenda, was written about recently. A report from *The New York Times* cites a case of antagonists coming together to achieve a solution in which everyone benefits.

The story involves the rice farmers of California. Historically, they angered environmentalists in two ways. First, they flooded their fields, using up scarce water, according to critics. Then, they burned the stubble left over from the previous season's crop in order to get ready for the new planting, creating still another environmental problem.

But it will be different this winter. More and more farmers, with the blessing of state and Federal water officials and environmentalists alike, will get rid of their stubble not with fire but with water, flooding their fields to rot the remaining straw.

That this is happening is the result of an extraordinary truce in the environmental wars. Under the truce, the farmers get an environmentally benign way to clear their fields and relief from bad publicity and the environmentalists get new wetlands for migrating waterfowl. Everybody, it seems, wins.

Most notable among the environmentalists [supporting the accord] was Marc Reisner, who in 1986 wrote *Cadillac Desert,* a history of water use and misuse in the West, and has long accused rice farmers of wasting Government-subsidized water by growing a monsoon crop in the desert that is California.

But Mr. Reisner now calls the rice growers "the most progressive" of California's agricultural interests on environmental issues. "I am in the awkward position of being pals with my former enemies," he said.

The participants in the project, called the Ricelands Habitat Venture, are the Nature Conservancy, the California Rice Industry Association, Ducks Unlimited, the National Audubon Society, the California Waterfowl Association, and Mr. Reisner. Under the plan, the fields are to be flooded from December through February, a time when they are fallow anyway and when the birds come south for the winter.

Conservationists have long talked about cooperating with their opponents in industry and agriculture to reverse environmental degradation, but the rice truce is one of the few successes.

[A spokesman for the Federal Bureau of Reclamation] called the truce a "fabulous marriage" in which economic and environmental values alike are promoted, at little financial cost.

What makes the rice project so unusual is that it allows the rice farmers, who have been criticized by Mr. Reisner and others for using too much water, to use even more.

Among the benefits cited: "the 300 pounds an acre of grain left after the harvest provides ideal food for migrating birds . . . [and] the flooded fields will add to the region's capacity to store water during the wet months without building costly dams and reservoirs."

Douglas P. Wheeler, California secretary for resources, said the program may serve as a national model for resolving environmental conflicts. "This has made allies out of former enemies. It is a model we have not seen before in which each of the participants can be so well rewarded."[4]

Beginning the process by walking a mile in the other person's shoes sounds simple, but in practice it takes more patience than organizations have. Such organizations fail to see that in the big-picture policy game, Americans tend to come down on the side of compromise and civility.

The average person is put off by stridency on either side of an issue and sees no reason why contentious groups cannot find a way to work things out regardless of the inherently contradictory views espoused at the outset of the conflict. Getting to the point where both sides can come away winners requires both a willingness to see the conflict from the opponent's viewpoint and a candor that is often lacking.

The Role of Candor

A second principle, one that follows from the first of coming at one's issues from the viewpoint of understanding where the other person's position is coming from, is complete candor and honesty. It is a principle more often ignored than followed, and ultimately, to the detriment of the cause.

For reasons we are unable to fathom, except as part of the fear of fighting syndrome, some organizations feel they must hide their involvement in outreach efforts to groups in the community. They begin by saying that they don't want people to find out that they are involved in funding the efforts to help them on their issue. Guess what. It's always found out.

Organizations that choose to operate in such a clandestine manner try to fund third-party efforts to organize strangers, efforts designed to demonstrate community support both to impress politicians as well as to obtain editorial support. Yet, they'll try to mask their involvement fearing that knowledge of their support will somehow make the effort less credible. Guess again. They do lose credibility. Not from their obvious interest in the issue, as they would wish to believe, but from the revelation of their behind-the-scenes subterfuge.

It's a lesson some organizations find out the hard way. As *The New York Times* reported:

> It looked like a consumer organization, and it seemed to spring up spontaneously to fight a provision of the pending budget bill that it said would condemn poor people to inferior medical care.
> The group, calling itself the Coalition for Equal Access to Medicines, is an unusual union of poor people, minority members and public health advocates, but it did not come together effortlessly. It was created and financed by another interest group, one with perhaps the biggest stake in the outcome: the prescription drug industry.
> The group's aim [was] to kill provisions of the deficit-reduction bill that would encourage states to establish lists of approved Medicaid drugs. If a drug was not on the list, called a formulary, Medicaid would generally not pay for it.[5]

According to the *Times* piece, the Coalition for Equal Access to Medicines was the brainchild of APCO Associates, a branch of the GCI Group, the public relations division of Grey Advertising, Inc. It was financed by the Pharmaceutical Manufacturers Association. It failed in its attempt to delete formularies from the deficit-reduction bill passed by the Congress. One reason may have been that:

> Members of Congress who follow drug issues said they were unaware of the industry's involvement in the coalition, which describes itself as "an ad hoc volunteer organization."[6]

The point to be made is that there is a constituency that will rally to support virtually any cause. What is required for credibility is above-board honesty about who's involved, who's funding the effort—who it is, in short, who cares enough to get the effort rolling. Failure to reveal from the outset may result in a loss. At the very least, it results in an embarrassment that is unnecessary and counterproductive.

Such candor is essential if there is to be any hope of sustaining support among one's family and friends. It is equally essential if there is to be any hope of winning over a skeptical press, an initially disinterested group of strangers, and an uneasy group of politicians. If ever a provocateur for the opposition is given a tool with which to defeat your side of an issue, it is when it becomes known that you are moving forward in a less than candid way.

Two examples come to mind in terms of how *not* to structure an outreach program. They include the Baby Bells and the major league sports organizations. The Baby Bells have been involved in an effort to obtain permission to sell advertising as part of their fiber optics electronic information services. The major league sports organizations have been trying to gain public support for their opposition of legalized betting on their games.

The story about how the Baby Bells tried to hide their involvement in a public outreach effort was reported on in *The Washington Post*. But both the *Post* story and the effort by the major league sports organizations came to light as a result of phone bank operations that told more about the two groups' efforts to conceal their involvement than it did about the issues themselves. What it revealed is that there is a major difference between true *grass*roots movements and what we might call *Astroturf* organizations.

According to the *Post* story, the Baby Bells helped underwrite a so-called grassroots organization, Small Businesses for Advertising Choice (SBAC). But SBAC

> does not disclose that connection unless pressed.
> The SBAC's origins are difficult to trace. Its stationery letterheads

don't disclose all sponsors. Its canvassers across the country don't identify backers. And some of its members assume the group is funded solely by small businesses and do not know how it was organized.

Gene Kimmelman, legislative director for the CFA [Consumers Federation of America], said the SBAC "is an effort to deceive small businesses into supporting the corporate interests of the Bell companies."

The SBAC was put together by the Washington-based consulting firm ABRH Consulting, Inc., which has organized other groups around major telecommunications issues.

Even small businesses organizations that have signed on as members of the SBAC aren't always sure about the group's organization and funding.

The Greater Falls Church Chamber of Commerce, for example, is listed as an organizational member but neither the president nor executive director knew much about the SBAC.

Terry Neese, who is one of the honorary co-chairmen of the SBAC, never heard of ABRH Consulting and wasn't certain who was funding the group.[7]

In the sports world, the fumbling effort by the major leagues came to light when one of the authors received a phone call from a woman who said she represented the Coalition Against Sports Betting in New Jersey.[8] One of the problems initially was getting the story straight as to exactly what the caller wanted done.

She hardly spoke English. Or, if English was her native tongue, one assumes that her verbal skills were so bad that she had probably not made it past grammar school, if that. In reading her script, for example, she kept referring to the problem of sports betting as one that would "rise" taxes on the poor. Surely, the scriptwriter wrote "raise."

When she asked if she could patch the call through to the local state senator, she referred to him as "Senator Cardall," not "Senator Cardinale." She also felt it important to patch through the people she spoke with as she said it was time for the "legislation" to act, not the "legislature."

Trying to find out if there was legislation pending about which one should be concerned, the question was asked:

"Is there a bill pending?"

"No, honey," she replied, "this won't cost you nuthin'."

Her lack of education and articulation aside, it was the inability to answer questions about who she worked for or where she was calling from, and why she was doing what she was doing that raised questions. For it's possible, even laudable, to hire less than coherent people, given the cause.

When asked to name her employer or where she worked, she put us on hold, then came back to say she had just moved to the area and did not know the location of the place she was calling from. Asking to speak to a supervisor led to a dial tone as the call was disconnected.

We subsequently tracked down and interviewed the head of the telemarketing organization that was hired by the professional sports organizations to build their grassroots coalition. His attitude was cavalier to say the least.

He explained that his employees were trained to get someone whose emotion at the moment supported his client's cause. A quick response could be patched through to a legislator's office, and the telemarketer could be paid. He was paid by the call, not by the conviction of the caller.

It mattered not at all to him that his employees had no responses for inquiries such as ours. As he said, "It costs me too much to have my people sit and discuss the issue with anyone beyond a simple 'do you understand the issue from our perspective and will you do something to help us, *now*.' This is aimed at getting an emotional response. I want them on and off the phone. She should have hung up on you earlier than she did."

So much for integrity in the formation of a broad-based coalition.

In sharp contrast to this Astroturf approach, there are many examples of corporations and organizations developing true grassroots support in support of an issue. One that comes to mind is a fledgling effort that may well benefit the pharmaceutical industry.

In some ways it is a model for the type of coalition we are advocating when confronting a major public policy issue. The organization is called Americans for Medical Progress Education Foundation.

Launched in 1991, it is the brainchild of Leon C. Hirsch, president and chief executive officer of the United States Surgical Corporation. Hirsch, unlike some chief executive officers, is not afraid of tackling an issue, especially when it affects his industry. Nor is he reticent about his personal involvement.

The group Hirsch is putting together has an uphill battle. The judgment on whether they will succeed or not is still out. But they have begun in the right way, which alone makes their case worth noting.

The issue Hirsch is concerned about is the use of animals in research. It is a tough issue because few Americans want to think about how pharmaceutical companies prove the efficacy of miracle drugs nor about how a company like U.S. Surgical develops and trains surgeons on new surgical techniques. We all want to benefit from the drugs and to find ways to limit the invasiveness of traditional surgery, but those who object to the use of animals in research have grabbed center stage with the brilliant, though misleading, phrase, "animal rights."

The people actively opposing the use of animals in any kind of research seem to fall into two groups. One, People for Ethical Treatment of Animals (PETA), has raised many valid concerns. There should be some dignity to the way in which the research is performed. But a splinter group, one that PETA denies having any responsibility for, has a program that is as radical, as vicious, and as criminal as the most extreme elements of the antiabortion brigade.

These folks break into laboratories, set free the animals that are there, and burn the notes of the researcher. They express no qualms about disrupting and destroying the research work in progress. Much of this research includes investigations into the causes, and possible cures, for some of humankind's deadliest diseases. That includes cancer and AIDS to name but two.

In the view of Leon Hirsch, such tactics must be countered. Toward that end, he provided the initial funding for the establishment of Americans for Medical Progress (AMP). His financial and personal involvement has been noted from the very beginning. His mission has been clearly stated from the outset.

But unlike the coalitions put together by the Baby Bells or the professional major league groups, each member of AMP's board of directors has been fully informed as to Mr. Hirsch's involvement and the purpose of the group, which is "to spearhead the effort to educate American opinion leaders and citizens about the necessity of animal research if new cures are to be found." That board of directors includes theologians from the major denominations as well as medical researchers from preeminent institutions.

One theologian-board member is the Rt. Reverend John H. Burt, D.D., Episcopal Bishop of Ohio, Retired. Prior to joining the board of Americans for Medical Progress, he had been part of a group conducting an ethical study of the genetic research revolution at the Texas Medical Center. He had also participated in two major conferences dealing with the subject. He felt that

> too few people were aware of the preponderant number of great breakthroughs in surgery and medicine that had been made as a consequence of genetic studies conducted on animals, mostly rodents, some primates, and dogs abandoned and scheduled to be put to death in a pound.
>
> For example, through research on animals, a method was discovered which allows a surgeon to now remove a gall bladder without making an incision. This new procedure not only avoids the potentially harmful side effects of surgery, it also provides the patient with a great savings by enabling the person to go in for the procedure in morning and be back at home that night. Without animals, there would have been no way to discover the procedure or train the surgeons who first began using it on humans.

It seemed as though there ought to be a group of people—that included the public, people in religious life who had studied the issue, and medical researchers—educating others to the fact that human beings are more precious than animals and that some animal experimentation is necessary if medical science is to advance.

Bishop Burt's willingness to talk about his involvement signals a major difference with those groups that purport to have a board that, on investigation, knows little about the purpose of the group or the promoters of the effort. He even admitted that his four children had given the news of his involvement a "frosty reception. But, as I began to educate them as to the benefits that humans have received from such research, such as vaccines to prevent polio, they began to realize that there was a second side to the story that had been clouded over by those opposed to such research."

In 1992, Americans for Medical Progress launched a series of television spots and full-page newspaper ads. Part of the effort was aimed at getting publicity, part at confronting decision makers with an alternative view, and part at recruiting donors. The response from the public to date has been most promising. Contributions are beginning to sustain the growth of the group, and it is hoped that the membership will begin providing legislators with a more reasoned position on the use of animals in medical research.

Whether the Americans for Medical Progress Educational Foundation succeeds only time will tell. But it has already gained credibility in its launch, a credibility that will enable it to continue to attract strangers to its cause who intellectually accept the medical and theological arguments put forward by the foundation's board.

Certainly, the United States Surgical Corporation could have opted to handle its issue like the Baby Bells and the major league sports organizations. U.S. Surgical could have hidden its involvement and hired quick-fix consultants. The company might still have won short-run victories doing it that way. But they would have risked public embarrassment and the loss of the goodwill earned from coalition partners. There would have been no lasting impact on the war, even if they had won the battle. We're betting AMP will win the war.

Notes

1. The Graduate School of Political Management at The George Washington University in Washington, D.C., was founded in 1988. It offers a unique graduate program in the nation's capital to those who would be political campaign managers, lobbyists, elected officials, journalists, government

relations executives, pollsters, media consultants, and a host of other developing specialized occupations in politics.

2. Saul D. Alinsky, *Rules for Radicals,* Random House, New York, 1971, pp. xviii and xix.

3. Frank Clifford, "Corporate Suites Become Arena for Activist Politics," *The Los Angeles Times,* April 6, 1992, pp. A-1 and A-20. (Copyright 1992 *The Los Angeles Times.* Reprinted by permission.)

4. Robert Reinhold, "Environmental Truce Clears Smoke in Rice Fields," *The New York Times,* December 12, 1992, p. L-8.

5. Robert Pear, "Drug Industry Musters a Coalition to Oppose a Change in Medicaid," *The New York Times,* July 7, 1993, p. A-1. (Copyright 1992/1993 by *The New York Times* Company. Reprinted by permission.)

6. Ibid. In the same *New York Times* article it was noted that "APCO employees refused to discuss their work for the Pharmaceutical Manufacturers Association." Our call to APCO to discuss the *NYT* article was never returned, but we did learn from other sources a few fresh facts.

    For one, the spin on the story came after the reporter spoke to someone at the pharmaceutical association. Whether it was a fair spin is debatable.

    For another, APCO has guided the creation of a number of coalitions that tend to be created in the way we recommend. In another chapter, we will discuss one stellar example. That this one received the negative treatment it did may speak more to our suggestion for more candor at the outset when the coalition is being formed.

7. Cindy Skrzycki, "Companies Adopt Grass-Roots Lobbying Tactics to Push Programs," *The Washington Post,* February 3, 1992, p. A-6. Our attempt to get a reaction to the *Post* article was unsuccessful. There was no telephone listing for the SBAC; and, while the person we spoke with at ABRH Consulting said she would get someone to call us with a rebuttal, no callback ever came.

8. There was no listing in the telephone directory for any such coalition at the time we attempted to discuss this call. Nor were we successful in getting any of the spokespeople for various major league organizations to discuss the coalition.

PART 3

Go

How to Do It

5
Framing
the Message

There is nothing more important for success in public affairs than framing the message. Defining the problem is the first step in attacking it. At the beginning of most challenges in public affairs, the problem is undefined or unclear to most people. Most problems have very different ways of being defined. And the way a problem is defined is critical.

It is critical because the problem definition should determine how the message is framed. And the way the message is framed will determine who falls into the community of interested people and how those people will understand what you are talking about.

Problem definitions not only help define who is the interested community, they contain the seeds of solutions. The way the message is framed, the way the problem is defined, will determine who becomes interested, will create the range of possible solutions, and will even signal what is success.

Here is an example of what we mean. For years, a debate waged about whether alcoholism was a disease or a crime. The fight was between law enforcement people and social welfare people. The consequences were enormous. Would people go to jail? Or get help?

If alcoholism is a disease, then the public will be sympathetic to the afflicted individuals, the medical community will be interested, and cured patients will be measures of success. If it is a crime, then the public will be less sympathetic to the individuals involved, the criminal justice and law enforcement communities will be interested, and punishment-rehabilitation will be measures of success.

Then along came MADD, Mothers Against Drunk Driving. They began to redefine the problem a third way, as a matter of individual accountability. That definition gives rise to a whole new set of laws and procedures and new interested parties, such as bartenders, who now may be criminally liable for serving someone who is underage or has had too much to drink. None of these definitions are inherently right or wrong, but whichever one controls at a particular moment will affect public policy decisions around the issue.

There are a few basic rules for framing a winning message in any public affairs battle: Get there early, be candid and credible, and never be defensive.

The first rule is *get there early*. It is relatively easy to frame the way an issue is going to be understood if you are the first one trying to do that piece of work. Changing a message that is already out there is much more difficult, though not impossible (for example, MADD).

That is why some politicians, particularly relatively unknown ones, often spend a lot of money on television advertising very early in the campaign. If few people have a clear sense of the candidate, the first sharp image is likely to be a defining one. On the other hand, if that image is not the one you want to stick, you then have to find a way to make people doubt their own understanding, question themselves in effect, and then reconstruct a new and different idea.

The second rule is *be candid and credible*. A message that is not credible will not define the issue. For example, look at George Bush's troubles in 1992. He never learned the lesson of Lyndon Johnson's withdrawal from the 1968 reelection campaign. It was not that Johnson had failed to stop, or win, the Vietnam War. It was that he had misled the American people. Johnson's term ended with a crisis in credibility.

Ditto Bush. We recall his standing with Clarence Thomas in front of his home in Kennebunkport, Maine, and trying to get all of us to believe that "race had nothing to do with my selection of Judge Thomas." Few of us believed him, based on our own life experience, whatever our opinion of Thomas.

Worse, right up to election eve, Bush kept insisting that there was no recession and, that if there had been one, we were on our way to recovery. But there were too many people struggling to make ends meet, too many people out of jobs, too many companies cutting back and laying people off. Our personal experience and general perception simply made it impossible to accept Bush's message.

Bush's argument about the recession sounded a lot like the way some lawyers argue in their briefs. "My client is innocent, but if the jury decides he is guilty, then he is guilty of a lesser crime than the one with which he is charged." It is called "arguing in the alternative."

Sometimes messages don't work in public affairs because their authors forget what forum they are in. Each environment has qualities and values that determine what are acceptable forms of argument. Arguing in the alternative works in a courtroom but not in the arena of public opinion.

Forty-page position papers work in academia but not in public deliberation. Technical language adds credibility in an environment of experts but loses credibility in a world of intelligent laypeople. There are several reasons that groups, like politicians, choose to enter the political fray devoid of candor.

For example, lawyers representing the tobacco industry have been able, so far, to successfully defend against the charge that their clients' products caused cancer in any particular plaintiff. No physician or scientist has been able to prove to the satisfaction of the legal standard of certainty that there was a cause-and-effect link between having smoked and a specific disease. And increasingly, juries challenge individual responsibility, asking the plaintiff, in effect, If you knowingly use a product for x decades, how can you now claim compensation?

To convict the tobacco companies of a crime, or even to make them civilly liable for a death, requires a very high level of certainty. For a criminal conviction, it has to be beyond a reasonable doubt. And that is a very hard standard to meet when lots of people who have never smoked suffer from the same disease that killed the smoker.

But this lack of adequate proof in a courtroom has no weight in the court of public opinion or even in the life insurance industry. The tobacco industry is smart not to raise the causality argument in their public campaigns. No one would believe them, even if they trotted out the same experts who were so effective on their behalf in court. And the scientists who create reasonable doubt in their testimony in a case are not effective if they try to weigh in against the actuarial tables that show that people who smoke generally live shorter lives.

The point is that while some arguments may work in a courtroom or in actuarial tables, the public accepts the fact that smoking and smokers lead less healthy lives, and a political campaign resting on the contrary assumption would fail. Similarly, when a President says that race has no bearing on his selection of a judicial appointment while standing beside a black man whom he is nominating to fill a seat vacated by a black man, we wince. Think how different it would have been if he had said that he was pleased to nominate a person of color.

Advertising is another example of the nature of the environment affecting the credibility of the argument. In the United States we have grown accustomed to hyperbole in advertising. We are not offended, at least not consciously, when someone tells us that a product is "the best." Saying that is simply that copywriter's job.

We know that the celebrity endorser is saying it's "the best" because he or she is paid to do so, and we don't seem to care whether or not the celebrity actually uses the product even if he or she should. We don't even hold those who carry the advertising responsible for its content. Subconsciously at least, we dismiss the excessive claims as pure fluff.

Because we don't trust advertising enough, it a questionable medium for making thoughtful, substantive arguments about public issues. It almost signals weakness. Advertising may be effective in public affairs not in a dialogue but when you are simply seeking recognition. In product advertising, people tend to discount subconsciously half or more of the claim when advertising is presenting a positive image of a product.

But there are situations in which recognition, not credibility, is the issue. Then, advertisers follow the rule of bombardment. They repeat the name often enough so that people will think about the product, a key step toward the sale. Often the most offensive ad is the most successful because people remember the name and try the product.

In a situation in which no public consciousness exists, such as in a new product introduction or in which there is a public view that what exists can surely be improved, the claims made by the advertiser remain pretty much unchallenged. If the claim proves to be true once the product is tried, advertising can reinforce the message or belief structure.

But the image of advertising makes it part of the problem when it is used to change a strongly held perception, whether it is about the joys of owning an Edsel or the thrill of having a nuclear power plant in the neighborhood. Advertising fails as a medium for trying to disprove a negative that has already taken hold.

It does more to reinforce the negative than to change it because advertising has so little credibility on the authenticity of its claims. That is why single full-page ads explaining how the pharmaceutical industry is not making unreasonable profits or double-truck ads explaining how IBM, in the early 1990s, was not falling apart can reinforce the negative without ever turning around anyone's view.

This leads to the third rule about framing the message: *Never be defensive.*

Whenever you find yourself in a defensive posture in a public affairs dialogue, you know that you have allowed the other side to define the conversation. The challenge is to reframe it. There are three possible responses: You can join the argument, you can redefine the argument, or you can acknowledge the error in some way.

Joining the argument concedes the framing challenge and reinforces the opponent's claim. By screaming "taint so," you will remind people of the argument against you and reinforce it because no one will be impressed by your making the counterclaim. Your saying "taint so" makes people think "tis."

Redefining the argument is tougher than defining it in the first place, but it at least responds in a way that gets the conversation where you have a chance. Instead of saying "taint so," you are saying, "here's a different way of looking at it." Then you might be able to have a dialogue about what is the right way of thinking about the issue.

But often the most powerful response is to agree with your opponent, acknowledge the arguments, or offer the critical information even before it is articulated against you. Here's an example of doing it right.

Ashland's Spill

Saturday, January 2, 1988. At 5:02 p.m. a 4-million-gallon storage tank, located just outside of Pittsburgh, Pennsylvania, and owned by Ashland Oil, collapsed while being filled, releasing 3.9 million gallons of diesel fuel. The fuel surged over containment dikes onto the surrounding properties, creating the first major oil pollution accident for Ashland in its 64-year history. Nearly three-quarters of a million gallons of oil had spilled into the Monongahela River by sundown, threatening the drinking water supply of communities in Pennsylvania, Ohio, and West Virginia.

By the morning of Tuesday, January 5, when John Hall, chief executive officer and chairman of the board of Ashland Oil prepared to address the media at a press conference in Pittsburgh, some 15,000 residents of the Pittsburgh area were without fresh water. The press was full of stories about problems in the construction of the tank.

Reporters also wanted to press Hall on early reports from Ashland that had downplayed the potential damage from the spill. Ashland's outside legal counsel had urged caution in dealing with the media. They were concerned about the effect of any statements on future liability for the company from damage or injuries related to the spill. But Hall framed the issue in human, as well as, candid terms:

> "I want to apologize to the people of the Pittsburgh area for the inconvenience they have experienced as a result of this incident," Hall said at the outset. "The company expects to pay the cost of the cleanup and reimburse the appropriate government agencies for reasonable expenses they have incurred in connection with this incident."[1]

Hall and his fellow executives reiterated that message during more than 1000 meetings with press, elected and appointed officials, and the general public over the ensuing weeks. They acknowledged the company's errors in both the permitting and testing process in the installation of the tank, and repeated over and over again their intention to be at the forefront of all efforts to make right what had gone wrong. Their effort was guided throughout by what Hall termed "the decision to take responsibility for the incident."[2]

Their actions reinforced their words. As Dan Lacy, Ashland's vice president for corporate communications, noted:

> We tried to assess the damage done to various agencies and wrote out a check immediately, representing twenty percent of the amount, and sending it with a note attached that this was a down payment with the balance to come once the full sum of the problem had been assessed. We even went door-to-door giving people $200 with the same message. This is to help you now. Let us know if you suffered greater damages.

According to Lacy,

> The honesty of Hall's decision to bring out bad facts, take responsibility for the spill, and reimburse people for reasonable costs associated with it resulted in about 10 days of stories on John Hall's honesty and the company's candor rather than on the bad information previously released by the company [in the first few hours following the spill]. These [positive] stories in turn increased Ashland's credibility in the eyes of the public.

Noted the *Huntington [West Virginia] Herald Dispatch:* "We can't help but say well done to John Hall, Ashland's no-nonsense chairman and chief executive officer." To which the *Louisville Courier Journal* added: "By taking the risk to say that Ashland held itself accountable for what happened, Hall joined Lee Iaccoca and very few top executives in America who can now speak for their companies and know they will be listened to with respect by the press and the public."

Hall was candid, nondefensive, and reasonably early. Candor is refreshing. It adds to credibility. But it is not a sometime thing. Notes Ashland's Lacy:

> I believe it is possible to build a bank account of goodwill in the community . . . but that bank account [creates] a level of expectation, one in which the community assumes you will act honestly and responsibly. This is different than that traditional corporate culture which is to deny accountability for one's corporate actions.

Elections are the most visible example of public dialogue around public affairs, and they offer some sound clues for people in the corporate and nonprofit sectors who are engaged in dialogues on public policy issues that are similar but usually less dramatic and less well publicized. Americans tend to vote for a candidate primarily based on trust, rather than whether or not they think the candidate is qualified for the office or whether they agree on the issues.

That is why a candidate's credibility becomes an issue in itself in so many campaigns. Destroy the candidate's credibility and you win. But if you watch the dynamics of most campaigns, an alternative or even an addition to attacking credibility is simply putting the candidate on the defensive. Credibility and defensiveness are interconnected. Accuse a candidate of some unsavory act, and any direct response is necessarily defensive.

But elections have lessons that go beyond the get-there early, be-candid-and-credible, and don't-be-defensive triad. They reveal some basic truths about the American character and ethic and thereby teach us something about the content of the message, about what messages will succeed in a public conversation about policy questions.

Resonate with the American Political Ethic

It is easy to forget that the United States was founded upon an innate distrust of government and a basic trust in the individual. It is one of the reasons the Founding Fathers structured the government the way they did, dividing power among three branches and between two separate levels of government. And while most acknowledge some role for government, we as a nation continuously vacillate as to how much government we want.

We may reach out for government in a time of turmoil or disaster, but we quickly return to question how much government should be involved in our lives. Key elements of this American political ethic have implications for both the process of framing the message and the content of that message.

Compromise and Coalitions

The diffusion of power among governmental bodies led John Calhoun in the early nineteenth century to posit the notion that this nation is governed *not* by the majority, as textbooks would suggest, but by what he termed the *rule of the concurrent minority.* What that means is that an issue starts out with only a few supporting the proposition as first articulated and that its acceptance by a majority does not occur until it has been reshaped so that enough identifiable minorities, sufficient in number to become the majority, do not *oppose* the proposition now restated in a new form.

Put another way, it is not a majority made up of those who favor the proposal as much as it is a majority made up of those who do not oppose it. Contrarily, it is easy to defeat a proposal either by convincing various groups that they have a reason to join in opposition, or raising a question as to whether it is worth bothering about, effectively positioning the proponents as a group with a solution in search of a problem.

One of the continuing problems with the Congress in session all year is that, for the money they earn, all Members feel they must "do something" to justify their position. So, they introduce bills. It's good newsletter material, gets them some media exposure, and usually means little. Perhaps, without articulating this thought so poignantly, it is one of the reasons why the public dissatisfaction with the institution of Congress persists and the movement for term limitations seems to have taken hold.

What is basic to the American political ethic here, and applicable to the world of public affairs generally, is that there is a positive value on modifying your position so as to bring more people under the tent or at least to stop them from wandering under the other side's tent. The battle between diametrically opposed positions, therefore, is one of redefining one's position in order to gain either the support of, or the opposition to, the proposal.

Doing so in the legislative arena often requires coming up with a solution that is somewhat less than the original proponents sought. It is the notion that in a system of concurrent minorities, half a loaf is always better than none at all. The lesson is that compromise and coalitions send important signals because they resonate with deep values in the American political ethic.

Here's an example of what we mean. For years, legislators from districts with frequent flooding problems tried to get federal flood insurance proposals through the Congress. They failed repeatedly as, among others, big-city congressional representatives saw no need.

It was not until the early 1970s, following the riots in the Los Angeles area of Watts and those that followed the assassination of Dr. Martin Luther King, Jr., in many metropolitan areas, that the mood changed. The federal Riot Reinsurance Bill passed that included in it the establishment of a federal insurance administrator. Following the riots, the Congress enacted a crime-insurance-cum-flood-insurance bill with a coalition that included members who had been pushing for years for the long-awaited flood insurance.

The luxury of such give-and-take in the legislative arena is not available when it comes to initiatives and referenda where the proposition is written and must be voted up or down without amendment. The give-and-take must occur before the proposition is put into its final form.

Candidates' flexibility is also constrained, albeit by different factors. The dynamics of elections are different from the dynamics of issue deliberation. A candidate can compromise and consort with unlikely allies, but the message is not nearly as unambiguously positive.

We accept our candidates, like our advertising, as unrealistic, and we value consistency and purity in the campaign. It is almost as though we know the winners will be less pure once in office so the more righteous they are in the campaign, the further they can travel down the road after being elected and still be okay. Waffling can be woeful to the candidate if caught in the act.

Distrust of Public Power

Another central element of the American political ethic that has implications for public affairs message framing is that as a people, we believe that those who are governed best are those who are governed least. Unless times are really bad, we seek continuity rather than radical change.

We tend to view with suspicion anyone meddling with the status quo, especially when we fail to see a direct connection between the proposal offered by the meddler and ourselves. When the proposal calls for a new government program, there is immediate resistance, not simply to the possible cost involved but also to the accrual of power by some government agency and to the distribution of benefits if we are not getting what we perceive to be our fair share.

We are also a populist group, preferring an egalitarian approach to our governing process. Yet, while our populism may rise up and demand that all people be treated alike, our sense of Horatio Alger makes us temper our criticism of the financially successful. We cling to the idea that we, too, may one day come to be among that privileged class or, absent our own rise, that our children may achieve such status.

Along with our distrust of government, there is an abiding distrust of those who seek political power. As a nation, we place virtually no group lower in our estimation than politicians, even though we often tend to put those who directly represent us on a pedestal. We may hate Congress, but we keep reelecting our own member of Congress.

In contrast, while we may rail against the abuses of business, we tend to trust success, especially business success. That's one reason why business leaders tend to do well at the polls when they run for office. Initially, there is the view that if they can run a business well, they can run a government.

It doesn't prove true in every case, but the subconscious thought is there: George Romney rebuilt American Motors and then was elected governor of Michigan; James Longley was a successful insurance executive who became governor of Maine; Chuck Percy went from CEO of Bell & Howell to U.S. senator from Illinois; and Ross Perot, of course, went from his business success to a serious third-party campaign for the presidency. All of them used their business acumen as an argument for voting for them.

As focus groups we've conducted underscore, distrust of business is often linked to a suspicion of a behind-the-scenes, business-politics collusion. When things are done in the open, there is the tendency to have greater trust for the business executive. As we have posited and will continue to examine, the primary reason for developing grassroots organizations is to demonstrate that the proposal under consideration not only has broad-based support but it is also not a guise for something else under a collusive arrangement between lobbyists and the organizations they represent.

This distrust of meddling in the status quo has led to another interesting distinction. Political theorists have noted that most democracies change through evolution while ours has made adjustments through revolution. We have been forced to change. And the driving force for change has, more often than not, been economic.

Make the Moral Versus the Economic Argument

On most any issue there are lots of arguments that can be made on either side. Glib people can make most of them as compellingly as they can be made. But all the arguments really boil down to two: the moral and the economic.

Whether it was the group in 1776 railing against unfair taxation, or the Whiskey Rebellion, or movements from labor to civil rights, there is a pattern of proponents pushing both moral and economic arguments with the economic arguments eventually becoming the most compelling.

It may be framed as an onerous burden imposed from abroad—the time of "no taxation without representation"—or as onerous discrimination imposed at home—the current discussion among women and minorities of the "glass ceiling." But the basic wrong that galvanizes people has economic considerations at its core.

As we have mentioned previously, such arguments can be defined strictly in *economic* terms, strictly in *moral* terms, or as a combination *ecomoral* issue. You can begin the process of issue definition by asking who has the high moral ground and who has the low cost ground? The ideal situation is having them both work in your favor.

This does not come about because the high moral ground or the low cost ground is indelibly embedded in one side or the other. On the contrary, there are likely to be high moral ground arguments and low cost ground arguments on both sides. Which one gets there is a matter of timing and creativity.

There are several categories of high moral ground arguments: It's the right thing to do; it mirrors the American ethic; it's supported by good science; it's helpful to those less fortunate than we; and, increasingly, "God told me!" Each of them can be compelling in different contexts. There are only two basic low cost arguments: It will cost you money, or it will cost us money.

Ideally, the argument you make should be a combination of the two. A good example of this will be cited as a case study in the next chapter—the NO-ALCC coalition organized by Hershey Foods Corporation and other candy manufacturers to pass legislation requiring that candy with liquor in it be regulated as liquor and not treated as candy. There was a powerful moral argument, namely, that having candy with liquor in it sold simply as candy in stores would make liquor-laden candy available to children and would lead both to abuse and to the buildup of a taste for liquor.

But there was also a powerful cost argument, in this case a cost to the candy manufacturers who were not going to produce liquor-bearing candy. They had invested an enormous amount of time and money in creating the public understanding that candy was a wholesome and harmless source of sweets and quick energy. All of that would be put at risk if people began to identify candy and liquor together.

While it is best to have both arguments on your side, it is our experience that the good economic argument will beat the good moral argument every time. The fact that the tobacco industry has not, to date, lost a single statewide referendum on the issue of banning smoking in public places offers considerable proof. In referenda on smoking in public places, it is possible for the tobacco industry to win the argument, as they have, by raising the question, "Do the voters really want to pay what it costs to enforce this legislation?"

While the moral arguments were mostly on the side of the antitobacco proponents (there were some on tobacco's side, but they went more to the edge than to the heart of the issue), the opponents effectively used arguments about the cost of actually enforcing and regulating the activity to beat the proposal. Given a choice between what some perceive to be a moral good and what many more perceive to be an economic cost, those who promote the cost argument will generally prevail.

People with a moral commitment to an issue sometimes disdain the economic argument out of a concern that it will somehow tarnish their position. Advocates of birth control and abortion, for example, are hesitant about using cost-saving arguments to advance their goals even if they completely believe in the factual validity of the argument.

It is a shortsighted view, even on as emotional a topic as these, since the people who will be determinative in the end are those on the fence, the ones who have no emotional stake in either side and are looking for other arguments to help them decide. Again, the proof rests with those discussions over public financing of abortion counseling in which the winning prolife argument has been framed, not as a moral certitude but as a question of whether the voter, even a prochoice voter, wishes to pay for someone else's abortion.

If a sufficient number of people or organizations can be identified as sharing the impact of an economic issue and that message gains the upper hand, that coalition usually wins. One of the advantages of the economic argument is that it is unambiguous, a quality not often shared with the social or moral argument.

The same is true for nuclear power when the proposal at hand is to shut down the facility. Despite concerns about nuclear power, in most cases the winning argument is an economic argument: Do customers of the utility want to pay for the shutdown and the added cost of producing electricity with an alternative fuel?

Economic arguments tend to carry the day simply because they do affect people in an objective, measurable, and, as a consequence, far more painful way than any moral argument. For the pain felt by the majority in a moral issue is usually of the subjective, "I-know-how-you-must-feel-(but-really-don't)" variety. And since the "moral" majority really doesn't know how the minority feels, it may impose its views, absent either a leveling economic rejoinder or an equally compelling moral argument such as one's freedom to choose or right to privacy.

Historically it seems clear that we respond to economic issues when they affect us directly, and we will vote our pocketbooks, whether for candidates or for causes, when we are convinced that by doing so we will keep more money in our pockets. You'll note that Bill Clinton, unlike Walter Mondale, talked about tax cuts during the campaign and tax increases after the election. While Clinton said he did not know the depth of the deficit (what *were* his economic advisers telling him during the campaign?), he has traded on the notion that we will keep less money in our pocket if we do not make some basic changes.

When two sides of an issue are being played out exclusively on a moral or social level, each tends to get entrenched with neither ever truly winning. The abortion issue is an example. True believers on the extremes of both sides—those who say never and those who say okay under any circumstances—have seemingly frozen the issue in time.

When the more moderate approach of permitting abortion under such circumstances as rape and incest is added to the debate, a majority favor the middle-of-the-road position. But it is an issue that will never go away for it is not viewed as a pocketbook issue to the most vocal people on either side, who are willing to mount the barricades. The notion of a woman's right to choose, a moral argument like the notion of abortion as murder, leaves no room for compromise and coalition building.

When two sides of an issue appear to be economic, either a similar stalemate results or the winning side is generally able to present its case as being of the greater good for the greatest number. Advocates of controlling auto insurance rates, for example, have argued fairness and have used a number of themes with great success.

These include: the pain of increasing premiums, the general sense that affordable insurance is each individual's right, the horror stories of unjust settlements, and the view favored by the trial lawyers that an accident represents an opportunity that is, lotterylike, tantamount to cashing in the winning ticket. There are both moral and economic elements here.

In an early battle over understanding the role of insurance in our lives—four initiatives in California in 1988—the industry took a reported $80 million loss before realizing that they were losing the argument because they were waging the battle on the wrong terrain. The industry was making lawyerly arguments that were not connecting with the public.

The success of the critics of the insurance industry, particularly in the health insurance and the property and casualty insurance areas, is based on a subconscious belief among Americans that the contract between the insurer and the insured is a social or moral contract. The companies, in sharp contrast, view the insurance policy as just a business or economic contract. One is inviolable, the other negotiable.

Given no convincing economic arguments, the moral or social side of issue can be compelling and winning. But for the large portion of relatively uninvolved people on an issue, a strong economic interest provides a reason to move away from the moral side of the equation. That has now begun to happen with the insurance industry, but only after the industry developed grassroots education programs to counteract the arguments of their opponents.

Another example can be found in the role of Proctor & Gamble in the disposable versus cloth diaper controversy. While only the company's defenders and the environmental activists were leading the debate, momentum built continuously on the side of banning disposable diapers. But when the company began to reach out with economic and convenience arguments to people who began uncommitted, the tide began to turn.

What good public affairs management is all about, at times, is tilting the issue one way or the other in order to gain ground. It may take adding an economic dimension to an otherwise solely social or moral argument in order to both cloud the issue and change its potential outcome. Those seeking to alter the moral persuasiveness of an environmental issue may fund a study that shows that there is a hidden cost that few will wish to bear.

Conversely, an issue that has ambiguous economic ramifications (higher cost to car buyers but savings spread across society from fewer hospital bills) but that appears both reasonable and in the common good can be tilted by a moral or social dimension not acknowledged initially. The seat belt laws are one example.

Despite initial auto industry opposition to the cost, then user resistance to the hassle, the tide of public opinion was clearly swinging in favor of laws requiring the use of seat belts as being in the best interest of all concerned. Enter the NAACP.

The NAACP has begun opposing mandatory seat belts on grounds that are understandable. They view the proposed laws as but one more weapon empowering white police officers to harass black citizens. Many black citizens of our nation have reason to believe that some laws offer the racist police officer or district attorney an excuse to prosecute people of color. A study of citations in Chicago, for example, showed that the enforcement of antismoking ordinances were particularly selective. The overwhelming preponderance of citations were being issued by white cops to black citizens.

Adapt the Message

Thinking strategically about the message and *adapting the message* to the exigencies of the situation are the essential points here. Sticking to a single argument because it is "right" is a danger to be avoided.

One industry that has been particularly adaptive, and therefore worth studying, is the tobacco industry. For whether one likes tobacco or not, their public affairs strategy is often brilliant. The leading company in the industry, by most of our survey respondents, is Philip Morris.

Or, as Steven Mufson pointed out in an article in *The Washington Post Magazine:* Philip Morris "has the Rolls-Royce of public affairs programs. . . ." If Philip Morris is the Rolls-Royce, it comes by that accolade because its management philosophy is one of adaptation wherever possible.

One example of that genius was the convening of an unusual group of academicians a number of years ago. The group included sociologists, anthropologists, and a few philosophical types who pointed out a few "facts" that suggest that the industry will continue to prosper as it has for years.

One reason they noted was that people have been smoking for thousands of years and will probably continue to do so for reasons no one comprehends. That smoking may be cigarettes, pipes, and cigars; it may be the item one President tried but didn't inhale. (Coincidently, according to a few Drug Enforcement Administration officials, when the number of pot imbibers is added to the number of tobacco users, the total number of "smokers" is believed to have risen, not declined in the past 20 years.)

But also worth noting from a public affairs management standpoint is that the industry leaders have been able to constantly reposition the issue in ways that enable them to continue to win. For example, when the antitobacco group talks about the cost of smoking to the health of the smoker, the industry counters with the cost of enforcement.

When the antis then talk about the health costs related to smoking that they say are borne by the community, the industry switches to a civil libertarian social argument. Then, when the antis talk about the civil liberties of the nonsmoker, the industry switches to the privacy issue, emphasizing the "right" to be able to smoke in the privacy of one's home, unencumbered by employer restrictions.

The industry would not prevail if they were without a group of smokers and nonsmokers who believe in the right to smoke. Castigate this group, if you choose, but they represent a significant enough plurality to keep antitobacco advocates from winning in their attempt to eradicate the industry.

Finding and mobilizing a plurality that will support one's side of an issue is the subject of the next chapter. But, as part of a process of framing one's message in order to build a support mechanism for an adaptive strategy, it is also worth mentioning here. Another battle worth noting in this regard is that over the use of cloth diapers versus disposable diapers, which we have mentioned before.

The disposable versus cloth diaper issue is an ecomoral issue over which Proctor & Gamble appears to have gained control. For Proctor & Gamble, it was a critical economic issue, their share of the 17 billion disposable diapers sold annually.

The company's winning strategy was to counter with palatable social arguments eagerly awaited by a customer group that was prone toward the disposable diaper if only P&G could provide solace to their angst. It did. But we're getting ahead of ourselves.

The cloth versus disposable diaper controversy started out as a winner for the environmental groups opposed to disposable diapers. The manufacturers took an initial beating. But because even the most ardent environmentalist, if she is a working mother, is more inclined to convenience over compost, disposable diapers have made a comeback.

As an article in *The New York Times* trumpeted:

> The war over how to cover American baby bottoms has ended in a rout.
>
> Exhausted by their failure to convince parents that the nation's landfills have turned into reeking mountains of disposable diapers, many of the most zealous environmentalists have simply stopped trying.
>
> The signs of surrender are everywhere. Three years ago, 22 states considered taxing or banning disposables. None have ever succeeded.

Noting that "there has never been a more potent symbol of the national conflict between convenience and conservation," the article quotes one expert as to the inherent reason the cloth diaper issue is dead:

> "After all convenience is something we should consider."
>
> It takes only a few brief conversations with harried parents to appreciate the overwhelming freedom that disposable diapers can offer. Even the most aggressively "green" parents seem to have ways to rationalize their use of such an obvious symbol of the throwaway society. Stricken by fear, guilt and conscience, some have even been caught hiding their Pampers when friends come to visit.
>
> "I hate to admit what a chicken I was," writes a confessional Patricia Poore, editor of the quintessentially environmentally correct publication, *Garbage* magazine. Ms. Poore came out of the closet as a user of disposables in [a] current issue.
>
> "It's funny," said Judy Enck, a senior environmental associate at the New York Public Interest Research Group, who is an opponent of cloth diapers and proud of it. "I've seen backlashes before, but I never saw one this powerful."[3]

True. A powerful backlash occurred because of the link forged between the user group for whom disposable diapers represented an important convenience and companies like Proctor & Gamble for whom the disposables represented an economic need. P&G spent millions of dollars framing a message to convince people that what they wanted to do anyway was the right thing to do.

An equally powerful social issue backlash, one with no economic interest, was the quiet revolution among Americans to ignore weather reports in centigrade and road signs in meters, a fact that has weather forecasters no longer giving us the weather report in centigrade and road sign painters no longer bothering to add information in which no one has an interest. If people don't want to give up smoking, or using disposable diapers, or judging the weather in Fahrenheit, they won't.

Do the Lateral Arabesque

While two sides of a moral or social issue can become frozen in their movement, it is possible for the adroit public affairs practitioner to fashion a message that might be called a "lateral arabesque," the political equivalent of the dancer's leap to the side.

The more simple lateral position is to find a middle ground for which both sides can claim a victory. A more complex lateral movement occurs when one side offers a solution that it does not truly want but that it also knows the other side not only does not want but cannot oppose. Such deft maneuvering requires great skill, for the proponent of the offer must be prepared to accept the consequences if the other side suddenly shifts ground and accepts the offer. Let us examine one case.

The case involves a proposal to allow an abandoned building to become a home for 50 MICA adults. The acronym stands for "mentally ill, chemically addicted." The home was to be run by the Quakers. The building was located on First Avenue in the Stuyvesant-Peter Cooper Village area on the east side of Manhattan in New York.

At one time, the building sought by the Quakers had been a warehouse. It had then been rehabilitated into a group of co-op apartments. But the builder ran out of money in the process, and the bank foreclosed. The building targeted for the MICA home was across the street from Epiphany School, an elementary, Catholic school.

The problem started when the community began to realize that they had been given the wrong information about the purpose of the building. Local political leaders had spread the word that the site was to be used for 20, drug-free, homeless AIDS men, not 50 MICAs.

One local politician in particular, intent on getting elected to a newly vacated city council seat, was bent on trying to have the issue two ways—as a sign that she could control what took place in the community and as a sop to the mayor with whom she was trying to curry favor. Her intent was to ram the proposal through local Community Board 6 with little fanfare and even less public involvement.

The reason for the tactic was obvious. The community would probably not have opposed a shelter for drug-free AIDS patients. While the
income level varies, by and large it is a fairly sophisticated and
responsive community.

The neighborhood is home to the largest shelter for homeless men in
New York City and one of the largest women's homeless shelters. It is
also home to a methadone clinic, a drug treatment clinic, and an out-
patient program for habitués. It is not, by any reasonable stretch, a
NIMBY (not-in-my-backyard) community.

A true AIDS hospice for sick people would not have galvanized the
public opposition, but the building afforded little in the way of security, and no one could guarantee that those admitted would not be wandering the streets during the day. Even the proximity to the school was
not, in itself, an issue. Day Top operated a successful drug treatment
facility within a block of the school.

But this proposal, aside from having been misrepresented, was different. Already, parents were distraught about their children's being
accosted by the homeless allowed to roam freely during the day before
heading to their shelter. And residents saw the equation as something
much different—a shelter for some 50 mentally ill people who were
also chemically addicted to crack and other substances. They viewed
50 MICAs as time bombs potentially in the path of their children on
the way to school. Seen in that light, the community desire for a different outcome was understandable.

Two potentially nasty problems confronted those who opposed the
shelter. The first was the Quakers who accused the group of being
homophobic, blue-collar, ignorant whites who were, in addition to the
aforementioned attributes, totally heartless.

The second was ACT-UP, the militant gay activist group that is particularly incensed when it believes AIDS patients are being discrimi-
nated against in some way. A representative of ACT-UP had attended
the preliminary Community Board 6 meeting, and the implied threat
of a major public disturbance had been made clear. The key was to
find a solution that avoided confrontation and got the community off
the hook.

Enter Jim Mahon, an attorney and named partner in the Manhattan
law firm of Richardson & Mahon, P.C., a resident in the community, an
active member of the Epiphany Church, and someone with the scars to
prove that he'd organized a political campaign or two. Within days his
home became the campaign center for a neighborhood effort to deal
with the proposed MICA center.

From the outset Mahon recognized that the threats from ACT-UP to
the community could be real and devastating. They might lead to the

shutdown of the school if even temporarily. Worse, they might force Community Board 6 to accept the proposal, which would fuel an even greater reaction among the neighbors.

Mahon proposed what we would call a "lateral arabesque," a solution that would mute any opposition from the gay community and one that would probably not be accepted by the Quakers. He knew the risks. He explained the strategy and the potential for having to accept an outcome only slightly less palatable *if* the Quakers shifted their grounds. His neighbors swallowed hard and agreed to his plan.

The night of the showdown, to accommodate the 200-plus who demanded access to a room meant for 50 and equipped to handle a normal turnout of 10 to 15, required a change of venue. Even then loudspeakers were needed to carry the proceedings to those not able to enter the hall.

The Quaker representative made their proposal. He also turned on Jim Mahon, as the now designated representative spokesman for the community, accusing him of all the heartless things NIMBYs are charged with, concluding with the charges that the community did not want to take its turn "helping the misfortunate victims of AIDS." He sat down.

Jim rose amidst tension in the air, the representative from ACT-UP appearing ready to pounce, and declared: "On behalf of the community I just want to say that we *welcome* a hospice for victims of AIDS. [Pause]. So long as it is for *children* with AIDS." The applause that followed underscored the community's support.

What Mahon knew is that the Quakers do not work with children. He also knew that ACT-UP was as concerned for children as adults and could not demonstrate against a community willing to take children. What he had gotten the community to agree to was to accept an alternative if the Quakers shifted. They did not. The building stands vacant.

The politician who was pushing for the MICA home, but hiding its true purpose, lost in her bid for the city council by a scant 50 votes. Worse, she, a Democrat, in a Borough that barely knows how to spell the word Republican, lost to a Republican. Jim Mahon was part of the winner's campaign team.

What Mahon, P&G, Philip Morris, and others who tend to win understand is that one must adapt one's message to the situation. A critical part of that adaption process, and the message development process, is to understand that one must marry the problem, not fight it. If Hershey Foods Corporation had presented the liquor in candy issue as one that could potentially hurt Hershey in terms of taxation instead of presenting it as helping children—which, in fact, it did—Hershey would have lost the battle.

The lateral arabesque moves the issue to another place. It is most usable when the issue can be framed either as an economic or as a moral or social issue. A look at a similar issue makes the message framing or message positioning somewhat clearer.

As we noted at the beginning of this chapter, defining whether alcoholism is a disease or a crime often depends on whether the battle is presented on the solution level or on the definition level in terms of how people will understand the question. If the issue is defined as panhandlers' harassing the public and making a mess of public terminals, the reaction is "good riddance." But, if the solution to the problem of alcoholics' freezing to death is presented as shelters, then the reaction is "There, but for the grace of God, go I."

Many of us forty-plus somethings, grew up thinking that if one had "one too many" drinks at a party, we were somehow excused for any kind of conduct, from beating up on one's wife or child to maiming or killing someone on a highway. Mothers Against Drunk Driving (MADD) has turned one's loss of control into personal accountability.

As we have noted before, opponents of gun control have successfully sold the notion that each of us should have the right to physical security and that if such security can only be assured, in our mind, with the presence of a gun in our home, then so be it. We have even been sold the image of the friendly hunter, clearing the woods of an overabundant deer population.

What must turn around such a message is the question of whether sport or personal protection should include assault weapons which, by definition, are used for assault. What is beginning to turn that image around is Jim Brady, wheelchair bound because of the easy access of guns. What will change the National Rifle Association's image of invincibility will be statewide referenda or initiatives in which the majority of voters can decide how extensive a reasonable person's arsenal should be.

It is the fear of the outcome of such a public vote that moves the NRA to forever seek the comfort of the legislatures in which their ability to strike political fear in the hearts of legislators is well documented. By being able to swing 4 or 5 percentage points of a vote in a close election, they keep most legislators in line. Were they to lose statewide in some key states, they would lose their grip.

Waste Management is a huge company in the business of cleaning up environmental problems and helping companies dispose of waste material. Part of the company's challenge is that people often see its role as part of the problem while the company sees itself as providing solutions.

As a *Wall Street Journal* article noted in 1991:

Environmentalists keep attacking Waste Management Inc. And it just keeps getting stronger.

Yet, for all their enmity, environmentalists trying to clean up the trash business have helped Waste Management a lot more than hurt it. The more pressure they have put on the company and the industry, the bigger, stronger and more profitable Waste Management has become.

And its prospects for growth remain impressive. In the 1990s, new federal rules will probably close half the nation's 6,000 garbage dumps and make Waste Management's dumps—all of which already meet the new regulations—even more valuable.[4]

It is one reason the company tries to mollify opponents and to build support in the community in advance of announcing a new project, a process we will deal with in Chap. 6. But their problem is not unique. It is one in which the message has been framed by the opponents and must be shifted, in a lateral way if necessary, just as others have done.

William S. Gibson sums up the process of message development. He is vice president and director of government and public affairs for The Continental Corporation, a leading property and casualty company headquartered in New York. To Gibson,

Real power comes from the economic and political capital you can demonstrate.

Economic capital can mean the number of jobs affected by the decision or the cost to the community in other ways. Political power can be demonstrated in terms of the votes that can be influenced by the decision. But, ultimately, for the economic and political power to work, politicians must see that there is *reasoned* pressure stemming from the inherent rightness of the position you are taking.

Once the right message is framed, the organization must look to developing grassroots understanding of it that can be mobilized in its support.

Notes

1. Anne K. Delehunt, "Ashland Oil Inc.: Trouble at Floreffe (B)," Harvard Business School Case 9-390-018, January 23, 1990. Information released by Ashland Oil, Inc., for reuse by authors.

2. Anne K. Delehunt, "Ashland Oil Inc.: Trouble at Floreffe (D)," Harvard Business School Case N9-390-020, 1989, p. 1. Information released by Ashland Oil, Inc., for reuse by authors.

3. Michael Specter, "Among the Earth Baby Set, Disposable Diapers Are

Back," *The New York Times,* October 23, 1992, p. A-1 and B-2. (Copyright 1992 by *The New York Times* Company. Reprinted by permission.)

4. Jeff Bailey, "Tough Target. Waste Disposal Giant Often Under Attack, Seems to Gain From It," *The Wall Street Journal,* May 1, 1991, p. A-1. (Reprinted by permission of *The Wall Street Journal,* © 1991 Dow Jones & Company, Inc., All Rights Reserved Worldwide.)

6
Mobilizing the Troops

We're reaching out to our people more now than in the past for the simple reason that the issues affecting our business do not affect only those at the top. They affect every employee. And if an issue is going to affect people's paychecks, I think they should have a voice in that issue.

JACK D. REHM
Chairman, President, and CEO
Meredith Corporation

How do you begin thinking about actually mobilizing the troops on your behalf? We begin by asking basic "who" and "what" questions.

First, who are the troops? We have talked before about three groups of people who are key to a successful public affairs program: family, friends, and strangers. As we discussed in Chap. 4, this is the order in which they have to be engaged. The process for engaging each of them is different in some essential elements but it is based on a common set of ideas.

Just to review: Family are those people who have direct personal stakes in the organization. Employees are always family, but family may include others who are closely linked, such as retirees.[1]

Friends are those who have an indirect stake in the survival and success of the organization. Suppliers are usually friends. So are members of a trade association or lobbying group.

Strangers are people who do not have an economic stake but may have an intellectual or philosophical perspective that puts them into alignment with your organization, either over time or on a particular issue.

Second, what are people who join a grassroots organization going to be asked to do? From looking at a great many organizations and grassroots situations, we are convinced that many public affairs programs fall short of the hopes for them because the chief executive officer and the most senior public affairs people in charge ask too little, rather than too much, of the people they seek to engage.

In the formation of a cohesive coalition, those in charge fail to go beyond the level of agreement to participate, to some more significant degree of engagement. We think of the process from agreement to engagement as the five I's: identify, inform, interest, involve, and invest.

A good grassroots public affairs program must first identify the potential participants, then inform them about the opportunity and the issues in a way that sparks their interest. The better programs then go beyond that, seeking more active participation.

The goal of the better programs is to affect the behavior of people, not just their position, to inspire them to do something, not just stand there. And, as you will see, the best of the programs we shall examine in this chapter go beyond involvement to get people to significantly invest not only their time and talent but their money as well in the grassroots effort.

This five-stage process is designed to build a broad-based grassroots organization, which can be mobilized around a particular issue and then, once in place, do the quiet day-to-day work of spreading the word. In this chapter we will discuss a range of examples of mobilization and active engagement of large support groups, providing some models that can be adapted to any organization.

The form of the mobilization and of the resulting grassroots organization may vary. For example, many grassroots organizations are formal and organized, but some are informal, unstructured, and latent, waiting to be put together and spurred into activity around the next hot issue.

A grassroots public affairs effort may or may not include some vestiges of the earlier top-down strategies, such as a key contact program. It may be an opt-in or an opt-out program. The former would require a positive response for the potential volunteer; the latter would be less voluntary, requiring nonparticipants to actively decline getting involved. An organization, whether informal or formal, may be crisis driven and totally reactive, or it may be designed to be more strategic and adaptive.

But all successful grassroots public affairs initiatives seem to share one important quality: Whomever the group includes and however it is structured, it is generated by an organization that has a commitment to emphasizing the development and building of relationships that persist over time, beyond the immediate crisis or opportunity. For the corporate community, that means choosing to develop a relationship with its people, instead of seeing them simply as a means to an end, and with its customers, versus simply making a sale. For the association or not-for-profit organization, it means building involvement with people before seeking an investment.

The Steps toward Mobilization

Building Relationships

Relationship building evolves from a philosophical mindset that views people as critical to the process rather than ancillary or primarily antagonistic. Such organizations see the communications process as one that requires character—honesty with others and a willingness to admit failures and assume responsibility. Some organizations already possess that mindset. Here are some examples.

The speaker was Steve Giovanisci, vice president for public affairs for ARCO. The discussion was about the handling of an oil spill:

> We took the attitude that it was our spill. We did it. We will take care of it. We paid a heavy price, but we followed our basic beliefs and made the situation right.

Giovanisci was discussing the ARCO spill that occurred in Port Angelus, Washington, on December 21, 1985. It was a major spill, the first of its kind. What ARCO would do would be watched closely by its competitors and by the general public.

ARCO's belief system was not born on that pre-Christmas day. Nor is its public affairs commitment limited to crisis management. As we discussed in Chap. 3, the philosophy that guides ARCO's corporate culture had its genesis some two decades prior to the spill when Robert Anderson and Thornton Bradshaw were, respectively, the company's chairman and president. It continues today because of the unflagging support of the company's current chairman, Lodwrick M. Cook.

People within ARCO continue to credit all three individuals for a corporate culture premised on their belief that they and the people of ARCO should be deeply engaged in community activities, both in traditional local improvement programs as well as in the political process that affects those programs. Anderson and Bradshaw may have initiated the process, but it has been institutionalized by Lod Cook who embraced those ideals and developed them even further, creating the model of corporate-community activism others point to today as enviable and exemplary.

Noted Giovanisci:

> It has been our involvement in the community across the board that gives us our credibility when we say anything, whether it is a claim about a new product or our views on what should be done to reduce the deficit, improve education, or clean up the environment. That trust does not come from being glib, nor simply from making a few donations to charitable causes.
>
> It has come about because we work at trying to be an asset to the community, and it has grown because we begin our involvement in the community with an attitude that says we share the community's goals. We see community outreach as another form of communication.
>
> That's different from companies that assume a "we-they" attitude toward the community. They are the same companies that say "no" to some idea if it's going to raise the price of gasoline one or two cents at the pump. We say "yes" if the idea makes sense for the community, one which will provide them with cleaner air, a better lifestyle, a safer environment.
>
> To our way of thinking, if, after evaluating the proposal, we think it's a great idea on balance, one which supports an improvement in the environment at a modest increase in the price, we'll come down on the side of the environment.

The ARCO belief in building relationships with its customers is not unique. There are other companies that share this philosophy. Many were described in the book *The 100 Best Companies to Work for in America*. That study dealt with corporate cultures. Stories we heard during our research suggest that many of these companies would have little difficulty rallying both their troops and the community should they face a public issue.

For example, a neighbor told us recently about her visit to a Nordstrom clothing store. She had just an hour to spare and needed a cocktail dress for an important event. The department she went to had evening wear priced at $500 and up. There were several shoppers looking at what was on display. Our friend explained somewhat anxiously to the lone salesperson that she was in a hurry.

The Nordstrom employee quickly but briefly focused on the problem. She told our customer to forget about the three-dress maximum allowed in the dressing room. Then, between attending to others, she brought several different outfits to the dressing room for our friend to try. None of them appealed to her. Then, just as the hour was ending and she was frantic to leave, she found a cocktail dress on sale that she thought would do. The item had a deep markdown, well below nearly everything else in the department. She bought it.

On the way home our friend was thinking that she had taken up a great deal of the salesperson's time, especially considering that the purchase had been greatly reduced in price. She felt badly that she had, perhaps, abused what she described as a very helpful, very friendly employee. To her surprise, the following day she received a letter in the mail from the salesperson, thanking her for having come by the store, hoping that her purchase was satisfactory, and ending with the hope expressed that our friend call on the employee at any time.

Our friend not only has vowed allegiance to Nordstrom, she has also observed how the Nordstrom approach to relationship building contrasts with the treatment she has received in other department stores. Compare the Nordstrom approach to that of, say, a retail chain whose salespeople are less empathetic or whose salespeople have been caught in a sting operation in which they were accused of kiting charges for automotive repairs.

In the automotive arena, it is easier to understand why some companies have forged ahead of others when one hears such stories as those we were told while looking for examples of companies that are concerned with building relationships. One notable example is Lexus.

The Lexus story took place shortly after a defect was discovered. Most owners assumed that they would be sent a letter telling them about the problem and recommending that they bring in their car during the times the dealership was open. What happened stands in sharp contrast to the handling of such problems by some automobile companies.

Lexus contacted each person individually and indicated that they would pick up their car and return it at a time convenient to the customer. If that meant picking up the car at the end of the workday, the company would do so and guarantee to return it in time for the person to drive their car to work the next morning. When each car was returned, the owners discovered that their car had not only a full tank of gas but also that their car had been washed and vacuumed.

The ARCO approach, whether to cleaning up a spill or providing an environmentally correct gasoline, the Nordstrom approach, and that of Lexus, are based upon building a relationship with the community and one's customers rather than simply making a sale. It is reflected in everything the companies do. It is long term rather than short term. And it is as essential, we believe, for building a great company as it is for creating and sustaining a truly viable grassroots organization.

Our reasoning is quite simple. There are public affairs and public relations consultants who say that the only purpose of a grassroots organization is to have impact on legislative or regulatory proposals. That same group, were it involved in marketing, would claim that the only purpose for going into business is to make sales.

In either instance, we admit that such advice may work in the short term. Grassroots organizations without sustained commitment do win, and companies without a relationship philosophy do make sales. But from our observations, we doubt that success based solely upon winning and selling can be sustained long term in either arena. It is also clear to us that issues arise and fester in the political arena because organizations have focused on the short term rather than the long term.

For the companies that seem to grow, despite economic hardships, are those who base their marketing strategy on creating relationships rather than making sales. And, we suspect, that those who continue to avoid serious public crises—or those who face such issues with the support of their employees and constituent groups—are companies that view their employees as family rather than as a mere business expense, their constituents as friends rather than adversaries with whom they must contend.

Thus, in our judgment, there are at least three types of companies: those we've described whose corporate culture easily lends itself to the creation of a grassroots program; those whose corporate culture may inhibit the growth of a true grassroots organization; and, those who have begun to appreciate that the catalyst of an external political crisis may present an opportunity necessary to change the corporate culture. That change would include both a commitment to deal with community-based issues as well as to build a communications program that may impact favorably in other areas of the organization.

Going beyond the Key Contact Approach

Before proceeding, we should note one very popular type of corporate structure that does not fit any of the models mentioned above. It is called the *key contact approach*. It lends itself to the corporate, top-down mentality. Usually, it works in this way:

Each member of management is assigned one or more legislators or administrators—members of Congress, state legislators, governors, or regulators—with whom they are expected to develop a relationship. The goal is to have, within the company, one member of management assigned as the key contact with someone who has power over the company politically. No doubt such programs work, especially as the pressure for one's involvement in the program is the stick of not having achieved all that was written into one's job description.

There are at least two benefits or values gained from a key contact program: Lacking any predisposition on the part of management to reach out to its troops to have them rally to one's defense, key contact programs are better than nothing; and, occasionally, they become a halfway point, a benchmark of minimal commitment to be expanded if they are not, by themselves, successful.

When it becomes apparent that the key contact effort is insufficient, part of its value may also be that the organization has in place a cadre of managers trained in the process of how to become involved politically. That is only a plus if each manager has a positive attitude and good communications skills in the political arena. Otherwise such managers may be more destructive than helpful to the launch of a grassroots effort, seeing subordinates' involvement as mandatory rather than voluntary.

Moving beyond the limited participation of key contact programs to the more inclusive and broad-based constituency-building efforts, we found three companies in our survey of public affairs people whose corporate culture has sustained the growth of enviable employee grassroots organizations. They were launched and sustain their progress on the notion that building a relationship first with their *family*—that is, their employees—is of critical importance. In our judgment, these programs should be considered models by other organizations that are intent on mobilizing their troops. The three include ARCO, Philip Morris, and Nationwide Insurance.

Then there are programs that build a relationship with groups we define as *friends*. There are several worth mentioning for others to examine. They have all been developed for the purpose of building and maintaining an ongoing outreach to identified external constituents. One program, ARCO's, is an extension of its pioneering efforts to develop its own "family." Others include Continental Insurance, the American Council of Life Insurance, and the Beer Drinkers of America.

Finally, there are programs that seek to build a grassroots program among what we call *strangers,* those who should have an interest and may be so inclined once they understand the issue and its impact upon them. We divide them into three categories. First, there are coalitions organized over a long period in which a relationship is truly developed. We shall explore a few of these examples in this chapter.

Next, there are "inside-the-Beltway" coalitions, Washington-based groups of associations that may or may not speak for their membership but who are able to suggest to the Congress and others that they

represent a grassroots constituency. They are often effective in a legislative situation but rarely sustain a relationship building process that
minimizes future crises.

A third, and often more potent category, are those coalitions of strangers
that spring up, like instant coffee, when the heat of an issue boils up and
brings them into action. Unlike the organizations of family and friends
that are brewed percolator style, such grassroots efforts seem unintended
to have staying power. We will deal more with them in Chap. 8.

In fact, what ultimately keeps the category we call "strangers" separate
from the category we call "friends" is a disinterest by the organization
reaching out to the former to maintain any contact with them beyond
winning the momentary battle at hand. If politics makes strange bedfellows, some view these coalitions, metaphorically, as one-night stands.

This lack of interest in building a relationship with those potential
allies has led to the use of the term *Astroturf* to describe such organizations to distinguish them from the true "grass" of the homegrown
variety. Astroturf fixes fit well into the strategy of those organizations
with a corporate culture that, in our view, operates on a level psychol-
ogists describe clinically as suffering from "classic avoidance behavior." We pointed to them earlier as suffering from a fear of fighting if it
requires direct engagement.

Unable to build a relationship with their own employees or their community, such companies must turn to the appearance of reality. We shall
examine this type of effort, for while they are designed simply for reactive purposes as a defensive weapon, they can be and often are effective.

It is only a pity that the effort expended on the quick fix could not
better be spent over a longer period of time, and at far less cost, on
building a meaningful relationship with heretofore strangers. It is part
of the fix-it mentality that operates perennially in the crisis mode. As
such, we will deal with this third category of coalitions in Chap. 8.

Mobilizing the Family

As stated previously, the distinction between family and friends is crucial, for the difference in how to engage them is fundamental. Family
are those people, such as employees and their close relatives, whose
livelihoods depend on the organization's success. They have—or
should have—the greatest stakes and the strongest interest in the outcome of any external threat, especially one that could lead to job loss.
Thus, their commitment can be emotional.

In that sense, corporations often have a more difficult time mobilizing their family than organizations whose very purpose is emotion
laden. Those committed on one side or the other of prolife and pro-

choice, the National Rifle Association types, those who view every environmental glitch as a catastrophe about to either explode or implode, the Calvinistic prohibitionists who view any pleasure as something to be condemned (or, at the very least, taxed severely), those for whom the art of compromise is akin to devil worship—the notion of catching more flies with sugar than with vinegar repugnant—are already manning the barricades. Stimulating their emotional response requires merely turning the key in the ignition.

For corporations and their trade associations, such instant response is uncommon. Many are in no position to call on their people for help primarily because between management and employees there is a chasm of distrust. They fall into that category referred to in *In Search of Excellence* in which "most organizations, we find, take a negative view of their people. They verbally berate participants for poor performance."[2] •

In such situations, the affected companies or industries may have bigger problems than the subject matter of this book can handle. They should merely heed Peters and Waterman when they note that "the excellent companies have systems that reinforce degrees of winning rather than degrees of losing."[3]

Many commentators have noted that the better-run companies, those for whom people want to work and toward whom customers and the community feel a special adhesion, tend to think of their employees as family. Such "excellent companies appear to do their way into strategies, not vice versa."

They have a way of getting their people involved in broadening political support, overcoming opposition, and managing coalitions.[4] Thus, it is not overtly revealing to note that many of the same qualities that make a company among the better managed and better received are the same qualities that enable those companies to mobilize their employees into an effective and sustainable grassroots organization.

The family concept is critical both to the corporate culture and to the approach to building a grassroots organization. As Chuck Broms, manager of political affairs at ARCO, noted: "Focus groups in California tell us that 50 percent of all employees are suspicious of the message management wants to deliver to the politician. If the employees begin with a negative view, it's very difficult to motivate them to take a voluntary action on behalf of the company."

The ARCO Model

ARCO is the grandaddy of corporate grassroots organizations. Its program started in 1975, during the heyday of the Anderson-Bradshaw regime when employees responded to the clarion call issued by

Bradshaw "to participate in the voluntary, nonpartisan Civic Action Program."

The Philip Morris CIP

A close second, in terms of longevity, is the Civic Involvement Program at Philip Morris. It was launched in 1977 at the urging of the company's then chairman, Joe Cullman 3rd. Both the ARCO and Philip Morris programs, as the progenitors of employee involvement programs, were trumpeted in many articles and books. As Ed Grefe was associated with the formation of the Philip Morris program, he used it as an example of how a company can prepare its people to deal with issues.

The success of the ARCO and Philip Morris programs begat others equally interested in forging alliances with their people. One of the earliest, and now a pacesetter in its own right, was Nationwide Insurance.

Nationwide Insurance Company's CAP

The Nationwide Insurance Civic Action Program, which was started in 1978, is modeled on the ARCO CAP. Jim Lorimer, the vice president for government relations at the time, read about the ARCO program in a *Wall Street Journal* article, flew to ARCO's Los Angeles headquarters, and copied much of what he learned.

As Alan Smith, a government relations officer for Nationwide noted: "He foresaw that the industry would be under attack and that Nationwide needed to develop a grassroots capability. What we built became a pilot program for the rest of the industry to examine and decide whether to buy into or not." Today, the program is considered one of the model programs itself, having added slight variations to adapt it to its own culture.

From the outset the program had as its primary goal to make the people at Nationwide better informed. What remains unique about the program is that it was started at a time when neither the company, nor the industry for that matter, had any serious external issue. Lorimer, in his industry, was ahead of his time.

Nationwide's CAP was greeted initially with some skepticism by employees who thought it would represent Big Brother telling them how to think. Lorimer, and his CAP manager, Amy Showalter, have made certain that such is not only not the case but that the Nationwide CAP remains merely a method for getting both sides of an issue before

Nationwide's people and a process for encouraging them to get involved at a level with which they, the participants, feel comfortable.

Employees and agents are invited to participate. They volunteer by sending in a card. The volunteers are organized into chapters that correspond to the company's 14 regions. A steering committee of from 6 to 25 persons is elected by existing committee members from among the volunteers in that region. Election to the steering committee or selection as chairperson is dependent primarily on the evidence of interest and participation in CAP activities.

The committee develops program ideas for the CAP members for the coming year. These include opportunities to participate in a variety of programs, educational forums, debates, and brown-bag lunches. Some are for discussing techniques, some for issues. Part of the program is also devoted to reinforcing what CAP is all about and what CAP hopes to accomplish and part to reviewing the primary mission of Nationwide and the impact of various issues on the company's ability to accomplish that mission.

But other activities are more purely political. Voter registration drives have signed up some 11,000 new voters over the past 14 years. In addition, there is speaker training, drills on how to make a call to a legislator or write him or her a letter, and information on the importance of being present at hearings at which issues are being debated.

Trips to Washington or a state capital are planned. Discussion subjects that are not insurance related are frowned upon, but no one doubts that the skills acquired as a member of CAP can be put to good use when someone volunteers to help a community group.

Periodically, candidates for office are invited to meet with CAP members. These have included mayoral and gubernatorial debates at the Nationwide auditorium at its headquarters in Columbus, Ohio. Its presidential forums have been eclectic. John Anderson, Jimmy Carter, and Geraldine Ferraro have appeared at Nationwide. In 1992, in addition to both Bush and Clinton, one of their guests was the candidate for the Libertarian Party.

CAP volunteers are also asked to fill out cards that indicate who they know among the political leadership and how well they know that person, what community-based associations they are members of, whether they have ever held office or are active in a political party, and other information that would prove helpful in the development of coalition grassroots activities. Amy Showalter's office keeps the database current, a major chore considering the need for updates following each election cycle.

The names of volunteers willing to work in a campaign are forwarded to that candidate, a particularly powerful message when the candidate is an incumbent legislator seeking reelection. It's a reminder that among the legislator's constituents are many who also happen to be Nationwide employees or agents.

The building of an internal relationship is paramount. It is based on the same philosophy with which Nationwide has grown as a company, namely, that customers want to deal with someone who knows their name and their needs, an approach that is as effective with customers as with employees. Their CAP success speaks for itself.

Today, some 46 percent of Nationwide's 5000 agents and 50 percent of its 15,000 employees are active in the company's CAP. In addition, an effort to reach out to Nationwide's retirees has resulted in a 20 percent response among that group.

As they chart responses to calls for making known CAP members' views on legislative proposals, Nationwide can count on a 30 percent response rate routinely. In one situation, fully 95 percent of their volunteers got involved.

With such a measure of responsiveness, it is little wonder that Showalter says of herself that while she is the titular chair, her primary role is that of "coach and cheerleader, giving them guidance, setting standard, then encouraging them to get out there and do it." Prior to joining Nationwide, she had worked both as a staff member to a legislator and as a lobbyist in Columbus. So she knows and respects the value of grassroots activity from her own experience.

One major key to such success is training. That includes such basics for those selected as CAP chairs as how to handle volunteers, a particularly sensitive subject when the volunteer who "reports" to the CAP chair may be a couple of steps above the chair in the company. A second major key is the reinforcement volunteers get.

Praise comes from all levels: fellow volunteers, managers, and those who administer the CAP itself. At the highest level, an annual dinner in Columbus, attended by the general chairman, John Fisher, and top company officers, signals not only the company's commitment to the program but also the degree to which Nationwide appreciates what its people are doing on behalf of the company.

With the CAP program firmly in place, Showalter has developed a key contact program. That is the reverse of the process that takes place at other organizations, as noted earlier. Her reasoning makes sense:

> Provided it is carefully managed, a key contact program offers an important addition in that key contacts can deal more with policy and substantive issues in the dialogue with political leaders. In contrast, while broad-based grassroots is essential as a tool to support the lobbyists, it offers more in terms of positive public relations with the audience that we need to reach, namely, the policymakers.

She does concur, however, that stand-alone key contact programs are less effective. Beyond that, she also notes that the preponderant number of those who get involved in the political education tend to contribute to the Nationwide Political Action Committee, a fact that underscores the notion that grassroots involvement is the key to success in many aspects of public affairs.

The Informal Approach

Beyond these three companies, there are models of companies that are building a relationship with their employees for the purposes of political action. Some are structured in a formal way, like the three mentioned above, but are limited in their scope of activities. Others are just as intense if unstructured. Before leaving a discussion of reaching out to mobilize one's family, two informal programs that turned up on our survey as worth mentioning are Glaxo Pharmaceutical and the John Hancock Insurance Company—the former in the early and limited stages of development, the latter a testament to the less-structured approach.

The Glaxo Civic Action Network was launched in 1991. The initial purpose was to make employees aware of the political problems facing the pharmaceutical industry and to recruit them into taking part in that industry's legislative response. Spurred on by the Clinton administration and actions of various state legislatures in the area of health policy, some 2800 people, or 43 percent of the company's 6600 employees, have volunteered to become involved. They are being kept abreast of developments and taught such basics as how to write a letter to a legislator.

A computer program lets Glaxo's CAN manager Barbara Tracy know in which legislative district each volunteer lives. The entire effort has been capped off with a major voter registration program that includes information on absentee balloting. Employees who write letters keep Tracy informed, and she, in turn, lets them know the outcome of the legislative efforts and how their representative voted.

Beyond the Civic Action Network, the company has also launched an outreach effort through its sales force. Trained volunteers arrange speaking opportunities in which they present a program entitled "The Value of Medicines," in an effort to explain the value pharmaceutical products represent in the fabric of our society.

The John Hancock Financial Services Company has still another model, one less formal, and in many ways somewhat unique in its less structured, albeit effective approach. John Hancock's program is aimed at making its people politically aware of what's happening in general

rather than simply discussing what's happening in their industry. Its
goal is to build a sense of trust and respect between the company and
its employees, a belief based on experience that the company is being
truthful and unbiased in its presentation of facts about issues.

For example, using the election cycles as focal points, the company
hosts monthly luncheons at which speakers discuss a wide variety of
topics, from the role of the media in politics to the ramifications of a
statewide ballot measure. In addition to the forums, using other communications devices like electronic mail, employees are educated on
issues and challenged to remain on top of issue development through
quizzes about current topics with simple prizes for the winners.

John Hancock uses its own 1200-seat auditorium for some of these
forums, so large numbers of people can and do come. For overflow
audiences, closed-circuit television is provided. Beyond that central
location feature, however, the company has taken the forum concept
on the road, holding events of a similar nature in selected field offices.

The program got its start in 1984. At the time it focused exclusively
on voter registration. Today, it sees employee involvement as critical.
Hancock does not have a formal CAP or CAN program with an established membership. They consider such programs time-consuming
and labor-intensive. Instead, they have perfected a low-key approach
to getting their employees involved, which John Hancock's government relations people, according to the program's director, Jenny
Erickson, refer to as "watering the grassroots."

"Before asking our people to do something," Erickson says,

> we hope we have not only elevated their awareness to a level of
> sophistication that is higher than other companies, but we also
> hope that we have done so in such a way that our employees
> believe we have been objective in our approach to public issues. If
> they trust us—and we believe we continue to build such a relation-
> ship—we are confident they will respond when the need arises.
>
> We don't write our people telling them, in turn, to write a letter
> to some legislator saying they are *against* some action about to be
> taken if Hancock is opposed to that action. Instead, we write a let-
> ter which explains the issue from the company's viewpoint—the
> consequences to the company if a product could not be sold—and
> ask, *if you agree with us* or if this issue concerns you, write a letter.
>
> We know we get more people writing for the company than
> against us because we ask our employees to let us know *if they get a
> response.*

In one such situation we learned about, John Hancock sent some
20,000 letters to its employees asking that they write their legislator
concerning the issue of taxation of employee benefits. The employees

sent back 4000 responses that they had received from legislators. Watering the grassroots can sometimes produce a tidal wave.

The good programs have a number of elements in common. They have support from the chief executive on down. They are voluntary. They have staff support and adequate budgets, the long-range view being that it is cheaper to build a viable grassroots organization than to pay lobbyists and Astroturf organizers at a time of crisis.

They have ways of recognizing those who do good things, thereby not only acknowledging the volunteer but also encouraging others to participate. They try to build an esprit de corps based on trust. And they have one other element in common that is worth mentioning: training.

Training

In tough times, the training budget is an inviting target. Yet it is just those circumstances from which investing in your own people is likely to pay the greatest relative dividends. Everyone in the company is also a democratic citizen and a resident of some community. If they aren't carrying the message, who will be?

But how well prepared are they to exercise their democratic responsibilities or to involve themselves in their communities in a way that is consistent with the ideals and interests of the organization? Even loyal well-intentioned employees will rarely make these connections on their own. And we are talking about even going beyond good citizenship.

Who should be trained in the organization to speak to the press? Does the vice president for public affairs serve as a shield or a facilitator on questions of access down the line? People on the assembly line are always more credible spokespersons than people in sterile corporate offices. Are they ready for that role? Preparing the people inside the group for the responsibility of carrying the message outside the group is indispensable.

Training for the Legislative Arena. Training among the better-run coalitions divides into three distinct parts—legislative, political, and monitoring.

In the legislative arena, volunteers are trained to do things that are needed when a bill is pending or a regulatory ruling is under consideration. This includes how to write a letter, contact a legislator, attend a hearing, or testify, if need be. It is the process of communicating one's view to a legislator or regulator when a bill or ruling is pending. It is the most frequent use of volunteers in any grassroots organization.

The problem is that most people have never written a letter either to a legislator or to an editor. Even fewer have contacted a government official. Having to teach how to compose a letter—keeping it short, direct, nonthreatening, and including a fact as to how the proposal will affect the writer—and where to send it may seem rudimentary. But for those who are new to the process, learning how to do such a simple task raises the comfort level so that people then undertake the activity in a positive way.

Few people appreciate the importance of letters, especially at the state, county, and city legislative levels. Few legislators below the congressional level get more than one or two letters on any subject. Hence, if an organization is able to get many letters sent by volunteers, the issue will be noted by the legislator. Even fewer understand the importance of filling a hearing room merely to demonstrate support for the person making their case.

Testifying is usually thought of in state or congressional terms, but it is equally important for an organization that deals with issues resolved at the village or community level to train its people on how to present a positive message before a city council or village trustee meeting. Most grassroots programs are limited to higher-level legislative involvement.

Training for the Political Arena. In the same way, if an organization is facing an initiative or referendum, getting people to volunteer to become involved in a political campaign must be approached with proper training. Few people volunteer, not because they don't want to do so but because they not only don't know what is expected of them but also because they are often afraid to ask. The reticence is natural. Volunteers often assume that everyone except them knows what it is the person requesting the volunteers is asking.

The good program assumes the volunteers know little or nothing and teaches them what it means to walk a precinct or work a telephone bank or host a coffee klatch. If time is taken to explain, for example, the process by which two people (always a man and a woman) canvass a precinct—where they get their maps, the size of the area they would be expected to cover, the usual time of day, the length of the time commitment, how to tally sheets, how to handle hostile voters, and any other particulars—the number of volunteers willing to undertake this activity will climb dramatically over situations in which it is assumed that everyone in the room knows what "canvassing a precinct" means.

In our experience, volunteers respond with alacrity when they are told in advance what it is they are volunteering to do. Few grassroots programs add this dimension and usually only in situations in which the organization faces referenda or issue initiative campaigns periodically. Our surmise is that the organization would get more of its people helping candidates for office if people knew what to do and were encouraged to participate.

Training on Monitoring. Monitoring is the process that separates the occasional from the true relationship building coalition. It deals with the problem of what to do with the troops when there is nothing to do. For nothing is worse than getting a group of volunteers psyched to get involved then having nothing for them to do. Monitoring is the solution.

By making volunteers aware of the issues affecting the organization and how issues move from one community to another, the training in monitoring begins. Volunteers are encouraged to read their local papers, listen to local radio stations, particularly talk radio, watch local television, and report what is being written or said about the issues that are of concern to the organization.

Acknowledgment of such activities is essential. It reinforces the importance of monitoring especially if it can be said that, as a consequence of the early warning, a potential problem was dealt with expeditiously. Monitoring gives volunteers something specific and important to do.

The better-run programs we discuss have ample training and good materials to follow. But for those pursuing both the process of organizing a grassroots coalition and establishing training programs toward that end, the best source is the Public Affairs Council, located in Washington, D.C. Aside from its well-stocked library of materials used by organizations throughout the country, the council offers many seminars on the subject. In addition, its staff are always on call to help public affairs people figure out how to proceed.

Mobilizing Friends

No less a commitment is required as one moves beyond the organization to the next group of those who should be courted, one's friends.

In the corporate structure, one's friends are those people who have connections that are not so emotional or so direct as employees, stockholders, and retirees. Their primary stake is generally economic.

As we have mentioned, this group includes customers, vendors—advertising agencies, law firms, accountants, suppliers—and the like. Suppliers are often approached for help in a crisis because there is leverage over them. That works as long as there is no competing issue faced by the supplier because the economic connection is clear.

A trade association is a group of friends, being aligned by virtue of a shared economic commitment. They are business associates or competitors who come together to deal with issues that affect each in comparable ways. Like suppliers to a single corporation, however, one problem faced by trade associations is that members of the alliance may have more pressing issues in other arenas.

In addition, one or more members of the association may see either the potential for a competitive advantage on the outcome of some issue, or the association's membership may include members whose outlook even on industry-specific issues is poles apart. For instance, an association that includes "mom-and-pop" shops as well as billion-dollar giants may have difficulty agreeing on many issues affecting the future shape and growth of the industry. An example of this are the single-unit and chain drugstores. Their interests are different enough so that they have formed separate trade associations.

In the not-for-profit association, the same tug between haves and have-nots may force a critical break over issues on which on the surface they would seem to be aligned. The American Association for Retired Persons (AARP) has had this problem in some situations when dealing with health care issues.

The more affluent seniors may not see an identity with their less well off senior brethren. It is one reason for the proliferation of narrower, more limited-membership associations, people or groups willing to work together because they share an economic connection with no important issues or interests dividing them.

Friends are really strangers with whom a relationship has been developed. It should include customers. It should include residents in the communities where the company has its facilities or employs many people. For it is the economic connection, more than the emotional connection, that defines the relationship that should exist between the organization and the potential friends. It only takes more time to figure out that connection and to build a relationship.

Sometimes the connection is around jobs, as in jobs that might be lost in a community due to some governmental action or inaction. Sometimes it is a communion of financial interests. One such situation is the growing rebellion over environmental rules as public officials and private homeowners across the country have begun to question the value of strict and very expensive environmental regulations that sometimes bring very little gain at the margins for enormous cost. Until recently, that fight had been the exclusive prerogative of big business.

Few companies have recognized the need to structure a formal process for reaching out to potential allies. One of them is ARCO. A second is the Continental Insurance Corporation. What is novel about the ARCO and Continental programs is that they represent some of the earliest attempts we have seen at integrating community relations with government relations.

Many corporations have a community relations program. But few have taken the next step of trying to bring those programs together so that they can support each other at every step of the way. ARCO and Continental have charted new ground.

ARCO

The initial thought at ARCO was to develop a primary correspondence list for the chairman, Lodwrick Cook. But that was just the start. What blossomed was a program to identify and maintain an accurate and current list of key people in every community served by ARCO. The Cook list might have been a few hundred or a thousand. As the program evolved, the goal became the development of an external constituency advocacy program.

The idea for the program initially came from Bill Duke. Prior to joining ARCO in 1973, Duke had been both a journalist and executive assistant to U.S. Senator Jacob Javits. He believed that ARCO was, in some ways, like a candidate for political office, always in need of conversation with constituents, communicating its views, winning public support, and reestablishing contact with its key community groups.

Duke had been part of the birth of CAP. But, he felt that the company's support should be broader. He viewed CAP as providing three legs—ARCO's employees, retirees, and royalty owners—to a stool that should have a fourth. The fourth leg of the stool would be opinion leaders and other significant people in the community who might support ARCO in one or more situations were they informed through a communications program aimed at them.

His idea for advocacy is to determine areas of shared interest between the company and various constituencies as a basis on which a dialogue can be started, then create a system for identifying and maintaining contact with those constituencies on a regular basis. His belief is that audiences will respond to messages that are within their scope of experience. This means establishing a dialogue in order to find common denominators.

Duke argued that the company needed to think through who its primary as well as specialized constituencies should be and develop a program for targeting communications to each. Such communications would include being invited to specific ARCO sponsored events and, as appropriate, other outreach activities in which ARCO might seek their opinions and reactions to issues of shared concern between ARCO and the community.

Toni Martinez-Burgoyne was appointed director of external affairs to run the program. She saw other opportunities: developing targeted efforts to groups important to the company, such as Latinos, Asian-Americans, Native-Americans, African-Americans, and women; reaching out to influentials in communities in which the company either had facilities or were considering as potential sites for new facilities; and identifying every public-speaking opportunity in the five primary marketing states for the company's products. The information was not only to be collected but also put on a system where it could be updated for use by ARCO on a regular basis.

For example, she sees this process as part of the spearhead of developing relationships for ARCO in advance, often, of ARCO's moving into a new community:

> It just makes sense. Prior to making a major investment, a company must determine the major components of a community's environment. It is not enough to determine how we shall affect plant and animal life; we must appraise the concerns of the resident human beings there. Early contact with the people and their concerns can often help us avoid conflict and tailor our company's positive entry to that particular society.

From a modest beginning in 1985, ARCO's external affairs constituency system has grown to over 20,000 individuals and 12,000 organizations. It can pinpoint communications to any person or group based on their area of interest, their location, their relationship with the company, if any, and a host of other parameters.

Responses to events and inquiries are added, allowing Toni Martinez-Burgoyne to develop profiles over time on people and groups. Her system also enables the company to plan events and other activities without having to reinvent a list each time and to continuously monitor its effectiveness.

In addition, she is in a position to target speakers for the company by location, type of organization, whether or not the group takes a position on issues, and willingness to welcome a spokesperson from the industry. Some 2000 public-speaking opportunities have been identified. The goal is to position the company so that it can reach out to any group at any time, providing a vital direct supplement to its communications program.[5]

The Continental
Insurance Company

The Continental Insurance Company, like Nationwide Insurance, has been ahead of its time in beginning the process of organizing for community outreach. In the insurance industry, "before one's time" means pre-1988, before California's Prop. 103, the $80 million debacle that got much of the industry thinking about grassroots. Proposition 103 was the initiative that legislated cutting auto insurance rates 20 percent. Continental started its program in 1985, shortly after David Vidal joined the corporation.

Like Bill Duke at ARCO, Vidal, a former reporter for *The New York Times* and a White House Fellow, saw the need to have the capability to target communications to groups within the community who could affect the outcome of issues. He realized early on that his company was part of an industry that had difficulty communicating with the public.

He also knew that Continental's outreach would be limited in another way. Like other insurance companies that do not sell their products directly, Continental has little or no real contact with consumers until after a sale is made. From a public affairs standpoint, such distance can be a nightmare. As Vidal notes:

> The consumers are not our front line. We don't have a relationship with our consumers at the point of transaction when the sale is made, only at the point of service, where the consumer forms an opinion about the company and the industry. There is a structure between us and the consumer. But the consumer doesn't care about our structure. It's a challenge—if we are not part of the end where they buy it, but we are part of the response end when they need us to make a claim or renewal, we can either be in high heaven or up the creek without a paddle.

Vidal's challenge has been to structure a program that will enable the company to build community presence in its primary marketing areas as well as provide community outreach support for the independent agents who sell Continental's policies. His initial goal was to organize the company's contributions program in such a way as to have greater impact on the communities in which the company marketed its property and casualty products. In the process he has developed a system for the company that enables it to target constituent groups, especially those who may either benefit directly from a corporate contribution or who may be included in a company-sponsored activity.

> I have looked at my task as being one in which everything we do which carries our company name, has a value, a perceived worth.

Thus, while those who come in contact with us through one of our programs may not be buyers of our insurance, we hope that they see that they are aligning themselves with quality. For they are buyers of insurance per se.

That approach, one endorsed by the company chairman, Jake Mascotte, has had some measurable impact. During the Democratic National Convention the company hosted two state delegations, Colorado and Hawaii. "Our involvement with the community both before and during the Convention gave us an opportunity to build relationships that helped us immensely when we had to deal with the aftermath of Hurricane Iniki in Hawaii," noted Vidal.

II-CAN

Proposition 103 was a turning point for the insurance industry, albeit an expensive one. One of the lessons learned was that an industrywide grassroots organization with the capability to mount an industry response rapidly, needed to be established.

Chosen to lead that effort was the American Council of Life Insurance (ACLI). That group has responded to the challenge by fashioning not only one of the best post-Prop. 103 efforts in the overall insurance industry—surpassing, in our judgment, efforts among the property and casualty people and the health insurance companies—but also one of the best among trade associations in general.

Called II-CAN, the Insurance Industry's Citizen Action Network has streamlined the process for organizing ACLI's family and friends. Working through its 200 member companies, II-CAN has organized a list of 200,000 employees, agents, and retirees into a formidable grassroots organization that has, since its inception following the California election, proven its effectiveness both in statewide initiatives and in dealing with anti-insurance legislative proposals. It is a model many other trade associations are beginning to emulate.

Beer Drinkers of America

Another national model of organizing friends is the effort of the Beer Drinkers of America (BDA). Started in 1987, it is the brainchild of Bob Nelson, a leading political and public relations practitioner in California.

Nelson's idea was fashioned when he was retained to help defeat some antibeer proposals in New Mexico. Nelson reasoned that the beer drinkers themselves would view taxes on their alcoholic beverage of preference in a dim light. He knew that of the 110 million adult Americans who admit to enjoying alcoholic beverages, fully 80 million of them claimed beer as their only choice. He saw that constituency as an untapped resource and decided to try and rally the beer drinkers in New Mexico to take sides with the industry.

His experiment included several key initiatives. The first was to ask New Mexico beer drinkers to join an organization and to pay $10 annually to be a member. For their $10, members received a quarterly publication (entitled, appropriately, *Heads Up*), a membership card, and regular briefings on proposals to either tax beer or restrict places and times the product could be enjoyed.

With the information on the proposed restrictions would also come information on legislators who represented the district in which the beer drinker lived. He included the legislators' relevant views and votes, if available, plus suggestions for writing, calling, or sending a mailgram. If the representative sided with the Beer Drinkers of America, the member was asked to send a reinforcing missive saying, "Thanks for your support, and please ask your colleagues to follow your lead." If not, then the suggested communication would give reasons that the representative should reconsider.

Nelson and his associates—one of whom, Bill Schreiber, is now president of BDA—reasoned that beer drinkers had a more pragmatic approach to life than the "do-gooders more often associated with a Chablis and brie crowd." Their surmise was correct. From that initial experiment in New Mexico in extending the grassroots coalition building process to include an industry's primary consumers, Beer Drinkers of America now numbers over 750,000 people in all 50 states.

Notes Schreiber:

> We touched a couple of raw nerves. The industry had spokespeople, but no one was speaking for the beer drinker. The preponderance of them are of modest means—less than $40,000 per annum—and view their consumption not as some luxury, but as one of the few pleasures they can afford. Further, while they enjoy their beer and are loyal to the product they also, by and large, buy into the notion that they should be responsible drinkers, and frown on drunk driving and underage drinking.

Aside from their political activism, the group has become one of the primary national forces for moderation in drinking. Members are sent information about and encouraged to become active in a program called "Party Smart." Through the organization, efforts have been underway at major sporting events like the Super Bowl and the Kentucky Derby to have designated drivers. Additionally, programs have been set up in cities known to be oases for college students at Spring Break. Part of the kit is a breathalizer that tells someone they've had one too many.

In many ways, Beer Drinkers of America resembles the National Rifle Association. They have received support from the brewers as well as major wholesale and retail beer distributors. Their members tend to be politically aware, registered voters who speak their mind and vote accordingly.

Mobilizing Strangers

The group we call "strangers" are those who neither care or even know about the issue at the time it surfaces. On any single issue, with a few notable exceptions, most people are strangers: They have no clear emotional or economic stakes, they have no position.

What is key to building bridges in each instance is, we believe, a complete and creative analysis of all the potential dimensions of any issue. That skill often comes from a background in another field, in journalism or political campaign management for example. In both those fields, practitioners are trained to be skeptical, to question assumptions.

Good grassroots organizers apply the same inquisitive logic, the predisposition to acknowledge that any issue thought to be of interest to only a few may have appeal to others, to some "strange bedfellows." One case worth citing is the effort by Hershey Foods Corporation to deal with an issue it felt equally affected "strangers" to the issue.

The NO-ALCC Story

The Hershey case was launched in 1986 when Congress passed the smokeless tobacco bill banning advertising of smokeless tobacco products from the airwaves. What was little noticed at the time the bill went through was one line that changed the way liquor could be used as a food additive. That story in and of itself is worth noting.

Since the time of Prohibition, liquor could not be used in foods sold in interstate commerce in quantities that exceeded 0.5 percent alcohol. That smidgen of alcohol amounted to a barely noticeable flavoring. Greater quantities were permissible in intrastate commerce. A noteworthy example are bourbon balls, a delicacy made and sold for years only in Kentucky.

At about the time the Smokeless Tobacco Council was negotiating the best deal it could get on the smokeless tobacco bill, the retired president of the candy manufacturer Mars, Inc., Forrest Mars, Sr., became interested in the manufacturing and sale of liquor-filled candy. He had started a new company called "Ethel M." His problem: He could make the candy in Arizona where his new company was head-quartered and sell it there, but he could not sell it anywhere else.

Enter Tommy Boggs, a named partner in the law firm Patton, Boggs, and Blow. One of the most powerful lobbyists in Washington, Tommy Boggs is unique among his brethren. It is harder to pass something than to stop something, since the legislative process is designed with many hurdles to overcome. Most lobbyists therefore identify them-selves by what they are against and have succeeded in defeating. Boggs is one who is willing to be judged on what he can get passed.

At that time, Boggs represented both Mars, Inc., and the smokeless tobacco bill. Sensing that the smokeless tobacco bill would be enacted without much scrutiny and probably on an overwhelming vote, Boggs got the committee to add one line to the bill that effectively repealed the prohibition on the use of liquor in the manufacturing of food products. The single line said that where states permitted the sale of food products with 5 percent (a tenfold increase from 0.5 percent) alcohol content, the interstate shipment of such products to that state would now be legal.

As a preponderance of legislators were, like everyone else, focused on the primary issue of the legislation, the minor amendment was nei-ther noted nor debated. The bill passed as amended.

Overnight bills began popping up in state legislatures allowing for the sale of liquor-filled candy. As bills moved through Springfield, Illinois, and Sacramento, California, Hershey Foods Corporation was alerted to the new day.

The fact that they were unaware of its dawning was not surprising. Government relations people for candy manufacturers would normal-ly not be monitoring a prohibition on chewing tobacco advertisements, especially one in which a single line had been added without any pub-lic fanfare.

From the outset, Hershey was never opposed to the sale of such products. What they feared were two major problems that could result from the sale of liquor-filled candies at the exact same counter as the traditional candy eaten by children: the possibility that children would eat the candy, get sick, or worse, become addicted; and the possible subsequence that Hershey's products would be viewed less as whole-some snacks in the food category and more like sin products. Hershey management simply believed that such products should not be sold where children could obtain them and certainly not at the same price as they might pay for a Hershey bar.

In the first instance, Hershey could imagine reliving the kid-vid controversy. That was an issue that arose following the banning of tobacco products from the airwaves. Some children's rights activists argued that all candy and games should be banned from advertising on television programs aimed at children. The fact that tobacco advertising had been banned by the Congress established a powerful precedent for other causes to cite.

In the second scenario, Hershey, already fighting a snack tax in many states, could imagine candy being elevated to a new level and taxed at the same rate as liquor. Management decided to gear up to fight Mars and other candy companies who were promoting passage of the enabling legislation in the states.

Caren Wilcox, then director of government relations for Hershey, presented to her management a plan for developing a grassroots organization. She knew that if Hershey representatives approached state legislatures by themselves, they would be accused either of trying to restrain trade, a charge subsequently made by lobbyists for at least one of the manufacturers of liquor-filled candies, or of jealousy. Several proponents of the new product argued that Hershey was opposed because it did not have a product with which to compete.

The organization Wilcox proposed was to consist of people concerned with child welfare, people associated with the problem of dealing with alcohol and drug dependency, people involved in the more fundamental religions, and people involved with law enforcement. The final group was added when it was found out that the liquor-filled products were already being sold in states *before* enabling legislation had passed. In one situation, pro-Hershey forces were able to point out to the committee considering legislation that liquor-filled product was already for sale in the state capitol building itself. The proposal was defeated.

The organization was called NO-ALCC, which stood for National Organization Against Liquor in Candy for Children. Its goal was to present to the legislatures in each state where bills were pending the view that, while the product should be sold, it should be sold in specialty stores, in quantities that no child could afford, and with warning labels.

The location of places for sale and the price were important as the earliest presence of the liquor-filled candies was frightening. One of the manufacturers was producing candies shaped like liquor bottles, hollowed out to contain about one-fifth of a shot of booze. These liquor-bottle look-a-likes were being sold for 25 cents each, the same price as a Hershey bar.

A letterhead advisory committee was recruited and included prominent people from all four groups. The initial chair was the president of

John Jay College of Criminal Justice, Dr. Gerry Lynch; its subsequent chair was Mimi Hewlett, head of the Boston Children's Society.

From the beginning, as NO-ALCC board members were recruited, literature written, and the press contacted about the first press conference, it was made clear to everyone that the principal funding was coming from Hershey Foods Corporation and other like-minded candy companies. Hershey's role was never concealed.

Thus, when some representatives from the other side called all members of the NO-ALCC board to find out if each of them knew of Hershey's involvement, or when the pro-liquor-in-candy proponents noted in their testimony that Hershey had set up the organization, or when they talked to the press about Hershey's involvement, the tactic bombed. It was not news to anyone.

Board members, especially those asked to testify in their state capital, told the, often anonymous, callers and the legislators alike that not only did they know about Hershey's involvement but that they were also willing to praise Hershey Foods and its coalition of like-minded companies for doing something important to protect children.

Noted Lynch at the first press conference: "We applaud Hershey's willingness to spend money to show it cares about the welfare of its customers, the children who buy candy." Letters received by Hershey underscored this appreciation of the company's effort.

The press not only countered that they knew of Hershey's involvement but also began to raise questions about who was funding the other side and why. They also carried stories about two giants—Mars, Inc., and Hershey—in the industry squaring off.

The net results included: an outpouring of support for Hershey from consumers, especially from religious leaders and fundamentalist congregations; legislation enacted in 21 of the 24 states in which the issue was fought in accordance with the proposals put forward by NO-ALCC; and a rousing round of applause for Hershey's management for their civic leadership at the annual stockholder's meeting.

Waste Management and Tort Reform

Two other examples are worth noting—Waste Management Corporation and the American Tort Reform Association (ATRA). In York County, Pennsylvania, Waste Management Corporation minimized opposition to one of its proposed facilities by reaching out to new allies. Nationally, ATRA is bringing together individuals and groups that had, heretofore, not been energized as a single coalition for tort reform.

Waste Management had plans to build a medical waste treatment facility. It did not take a genius to figure out that there would be a vocal and active not-in-my-back-yard group opposed to the plan. The company took coalition building steps in advance of any public announcement.

It was agreed that those who stood to gain the most should be mobilized. That included the physicians in the community, the veterinarians, the dental community, and others who either dealt with waste or would acknowledge the need to have a local facility for dealing with the problem.

That expanded group included hospital administrators and those who served on the boards of directors of the local hospitals. The result was a welcome turnout when the announcement was made. The press knew of the opposition, but they and the community reacted favorably to the reasoned position of the health professionals.

Waste Management has followed a similar outreach process in other communities.

> In Naperville, Ill., where it eventually won an extension of up to 20 years on the life of a 234-acre dump, the company hand-delivered about 3,000 promotional packages—explaining how carefully it handles and buries garbage—to residents within a two mile radius. When opposition remained strong, it went to a county-wide lobbying effort using hundreds of employees who live in DuPage County. They stressed the fast-growing area's need for dump space and the lack of alternatives. That helped split a county commission vote, with officials representing the dump's immediate neighbors opposed but a larger group favoring the extension.[6]

Tort reform is another example. Spurred on by the American Tort Reform Association, organizations suffering from the iniquities of excessive punitive damages and the uncertainties of not always knowing when one might be liable had long labored in vain in several states to make tort reform a reality.

Many had slightly different agendas, the tort reform umbrella embracing at least three separate aspects of the problem. Many had given up hope given the lack of success over the years. People talked about tort reform much as they talked about the weather with an equal impact on both situations.

What was needed was a way to broaden the coalition, to reach out to many who either had not realized the extent of tort action on their lives or who had been unable to see how they, as individuals, could become part of a unified approach. The key to their success, credited by most observers, is the involvement of a savvy political campaign manager, Neal Cohen, executive vice president of APCO Associates, Inc.

Cohen realized that what the tort reform movement needed was a political campaign, and that to accomplish that goal required a broadening of the coalition normally associated with such efforts. To broaden the coalition, he recommended a strategic message that was easier to understand than the arcane arguments associated with indemnification and the like. It was agreed to, and a new effort was launched in 1993 in several states.

The messages were simple and straightforward. First, the system cost too much. The opportunity to create jobs in industry was being stifled as corporations set aside funds to defend themselves against potential judgments. Those funds might be used to expand the work force. Similarly, communities were unable to spend money on essential services as they, too, had to set aside funds to protect themselves from lawsuits.

Second was the question of fairness: Did a tort judgment benefit the plaintiff fairly or the plaintiff's lawyer's estate grandly? These were messages many people could understand.

Cohen also recommended a change in the way the campaign was to be waged. Instead of being an inside-the-capital coalition of associations, it would become truly statewide and grassroots. Each state coalition was to recruit a well-known and respected chair and employed the trappings of a campaign with adequate staff, TV, direct mail, phone banks, billboards, print, personal meetings, editorial board sessions, patch-through to legislators, 800 numbers for volunteer recruitment, and signed cards for the use of volunteer's names in advertisements. One key to success has been customizing the campaign strategy and tactics to fit the state in which it was implemented.

It worked. Joining the coalitions were physicians, local city council members, small-business owners, retailers, athletic directors, and influential citizens, all gravitating toward the broader theme.

Over 10,000 people eventually joined the Texas Civil Justice League, which had been working for reform since 1986, while 1200 private citizens, community leaders, and others became part of Mississippians for a Fair Legal System. Another 7000 people joined the effort in Louisiana to prevent the trial lawyers from reversing a tort reform law that had been enacted in 1992.

In Alabama, the coalition attracted some 2000 volunteers. The breadth and quantity of the support is solid evidence that with creative thinking about the issue, a clear message, and a broad outreach effort, strangers can come together to build a winning coalition.

In all three examples—liquor in candy, a waste treatment facility, and tort reform—those who sought to change public policy or public perception had to mobilize a group who initially either had not focused on the impact of the issue on their lives—who sometimes appeared not to care, seeing other issues as more significant—or who knew little about how to get involved in doing something about the issue.

Yes, care and concern for the issue was aroused. But, initially, many who got involved had no emotional or direct economic tie to the problem. What sets the strangers apart is that as a group they are people who should *intellectually* support the coalition.

Typically, the group we call "strangers" represent anywhere from 80 to 98 percent of the public. The family and friends usually have 1 to 10 percent, same for the foes. Strangers can be organized into categories or subgroups in order to refine and target the message.

Business could be a category, or small business a subcategory, or small business owned by women as an even more finely tuned group. Unless the issue is going to be decided by initiative or referendum, that is, in a mass election, there is rarely the impetus to reach out to all the strangers.

Increasingly, though, in legislative battles, there is a need to find common ground with one select group of people among those who know nothing about your issue. These are the influentials, those people in our society, sometimes self-selected, to whom others turn for advice and for whom others feel great respect. The Roper Organization has tracked this group for many years.

Rebecca Piirto has written about these people with clarity and insight in *American Demographics:*

> About one American in ten enjoys [a special] standing. They are Influential Americans, according to studies conducted over the last 47 years by The Roper Organization in New York City.
>
> Influentials have strengthened their position as America's product leaders, social activists, advisers, and information seekers. These four qualities make them the prime consumer targets of the 1990s.

Piirto quotes Tom Miller, Roper's senior vice president, on the influentials: "'They are willingly and frequently involved in their communities, both socially and politically.'"

She continues:

> Roper defines an Influential American as someone who has done three or more of the following in the past year: attended a public meeting, written a legislator, been an officer or committee member of a local organization, attended a political speech or rally, made a speech, written a letter to the editor, worked for a political party, worked for an activist group, written an article, or held or ran for political office.
>
> Roper [says about this group] that they are growing more frustrated with government but not with their communities.
>
> One of the things Influentials take seriously is politics. Influentials are likely to put themselves either to the left or right of

the political center. Democrats outnumber Republicans in the general population, but among Influentials the two parties are almost tied at 38 percent for Democrats and 37 percent for Republicans.

Influentials still believe in the power of government to solve problems. They are more likely than other Americans to say the government is doing too little to improve education, help the homeless, solve health problems, find a cure for AIDS, and protect the environment. Yet they have less confidence in U.S. political and business leaders than they did in 1984.

Influentials are more likely than other adults to believe that what's good for business is good for the average American.

What really sets Influentials apart is their status as role models. People trust them; people ask them for advice [emphasis added].

According to Roper, influentials were much more likely than other people to be asked for advice on 16 of 20 specific topics. Leading the list were government and politics:

The Influentials' influence is most important for products and services that depend on word-of-mouth recommendations [emphasis added].

Influentials are also "greener" than other Americans. A significantly higher share of Influentials recycle their garbage, use products made from biodegradable and recycled materials, and avoid aerosols. 28 percent of Influentials say they avoid buying products from environmentally irresponsible companies.

As consumers and citizens, they show a rock-solid commitment to intellectual substance, high quality, good value and fairness. Businesses [read also any organization, profit or not-for-profit] that meet these standards will emerge stronger from the 1990s.[7]

Mobilizing the strangers has become increasingly more important, especially as a counter to the charge that those who support a particular position are self-serving. The involvement of the strangers, more particularly that leadership group among them known as "The Influentials," lends credibility to an organization's arguments that the position they advocate has support within the community.

In the next chapter we will examine the application of technology to the process of mobilization. For the use of modern technology makes mobilization both easier and more potent.

Notes

1. Sometimes "family" includes stockholders. But the fact that a stockholder's allegiance to a company is often no more than the size of the next dividend check makes their automatic inclusion somewhat suspect. However, the issue may prompt their involvement.

2. Peters and Waterman, *In Search of Excellence,* New York, HarperCollins, 1982, p. 57. (Copyright © 1982 by Thomas J. Peters and Robert H. Waterman, Jr. Reprinted by permission of HarperCollins Publishers, Inc.)

3. Ibid.

4. Ibid., p. 74.

5. Toni Martinez-Burgoyne's success at ARCO led to being selected in 1994 as Vice President. Charitable Contributions, by First Interstate Bank of California. The data bank she built for ARCO remains formidable

6. Jeff Bailey, "Tough Target. Waste Disposal Giant Often Under Attack, Seems to Gain From It," *The Wall Street Journal,* May 1, 1991, p. A11. (Reprinted by permission of *The Wall Street Journal,* © 1991 Dow Jones & Company, Inc. All Rights Reserved Worldwide.)

7. Rebecca Piirto, "The Influentials," *American Demographics,* October 1992, pp. 30 ff.

7
Using the Technology

*The database is the second most important
component of a good grassroots coalition. The
first being the volunteers themselves.*
                              BARBARA L. TRACY
               Corporate Grassroots Programs
                                 Glaxo, Inc.

Ponce de León, some medical researchers, and many in communications have one thing in common. They have all believed they could find the impossible: With Ponce it was the Fountain of Youth. With a few medical researchers it is the "magic bullet" that will end all diseases. With many in communications it is the great database in the sky that will magically deliver the right message to the right person at the right time, and, on every occasion, in the right way.

While the good Ponce may have died frustrated in his attempt, his followers in haute couture, cosmetics, and plastic surgery manage to keep alive the belief among some that eternal youth is but one product or procedure away.

Similarly, the reemergence of viral and bacterial diseases long thought conquered suggests that, despite our best efforts, viruses and bacteria have a desire to survive that matches our own. That said, some immunologists think that the potion to end all potions is still just waiting to be discovered.

Many in communications and particularly in public affairs suffer from their own illusions, especially when it comes to technology. They see technology as an elixir that will enable them to avoid developing the relationships in the community on which true problem-solving power can be built.

Many would prefer to believe that just around the corner there is the hardware, software, or database system that will solve all their challenges. If only that were true, this chapter could be finished right now. All we would have to do is to include the price and mailing address for you to purchase that panacea.

Since that is not the case, what we hope to accomplish is to frame the discussion of technology in terms of what it can and cannot do. Technology is simply a tool, a tool that is being forever improved upon but one that can never replace the one-on-one part of making connections between people that will lead to success in public affairs.

Seen in that context, it is possible to use technology to identify quickly those with whom it is either necessary to build a relationship or with whom it is more likely that a relationship can be built. Technology can be used to assist in monitoring and servicing that relationship building process. But before seeing how it can be used, let us explore some of the problems people have in dealing with technology, problems that need to be overcome in order to control the technology rather than be mesmerized and, possibly, controlled by it.

One major problem is the current analogue to the old boss-secretary relationship in which the boss took no responsibility for his (and in those days it was always a "his") files. If anything crossed his desk that needed to be filed, he would simply say "file this," and it would disappear into the bowels of those gray metal cabinets controlled by, always then, her.

Recovery of the document or the information it contained was dependent upon the secretary's being available at the moment it was needed plus her uncanny ability to retrieve some scrap of paper, no matter whether or not he remembered the date it came in, the subject matter, the person who sent it, the affiliation of the sender, or the tenor of the note. He stood there helpless, as the stereotype would have it in the comedy routines, with no idea where to look. She, the ever-faithful secretary, momentarily irritated, would refile all correspondence according to the first names of the wives of each of her boss's clients.

As computers replaced typewriters, a number of interesting things happened. Initially computers were viewed, and used, as nothing more than electronic filing cabinets. Those who view computers as nothing more than electronic file cabinets continue to see them as part of a file clerk's job. There are class and perhaps even sexist elements to this.

We know of offices in which the placement of a computer on one's desk is tantamount to being considered part of the clerical versus the managerial group, a fact not lost on female managers who, in turn, refuse to have a computer for fear that its use by them may be demeaning. Those who hold to this notion see having a computer on one's desk as a sign of weakness instead of power.

A corollary view has been that computers are little more than word processors. Surveys of public relations people, for example, have tracked the fact that some 90 percent of all professionals in that field use their computer for word processing alone. It is no surprise that many people see them as resources for clerks.

A third image of the computer is that it is part of the "back room," as if the back room were not important. That notion may have been justified when computers were doing only number crunching, the task for which the term "to compute" was assigned. Order processing, numerical data entry, repetitive tasks probably do belong in a back room assigned to entry-level employees who have little need to ana- lyze the information they are entering.

But today's technology, especially for the communications industry, is more than numbers processing. It is text processing whereby essen- tial information is compiled and analyzed. The decisions about what information to gather and how it is to be organized and analyzed is most clearly a management function. Those managers who remain detached from the process risk having a system that outputs large amounts of useless information. And they may also risk leaving them- selves personally unprepared for the future.

Certainly the day is coming when senior managers cannot be divorced from technology. A middle manager who is in his or her mid- thirties in the mid-1990s will retire around 2025. With some technology already part of most workplaces, and increasingly more sophisticated technology part of the learning and training environment of most new hires, it makes sense to suggest that promotions may soon be as much based on the creative use of technology as on creativity itself.

There are signs that that day is rapidly approaching. Organizations in the 1990s have pared their staffs to the fewest number of people and replaced with technology those who cannot increase their productivity. As Arnold Brown, a partner in Weiner, Edrich, Brown, Inc., and one of those rare futurists who tells it like it is rather than like the client wants to hear, says: "Organizations did not spend $3 trillion on computers over the past two decades in order to maintain the same work force. People can be and are being replaced in functions that computers can handle."

While most communicators are beginning to understand and use some technology, there remains, in our judgment, some confusion about databases, in particular, how they are developed, by whom, and under whose control. One reason, we suspect, may be in the lack of clarification as to the role the public affairs group is to play in the communication's process versus that which is to be undertaken by the public relations group. Another reason may be that, while there are similarities between the databases used by the two, the very role assigned to public affairs suggests the need for a different approach to the construction and maintenance of the databases supporting that activity.

A third reason may be a lack of understanding as to what we mean when we use the term *database*. For many, the term *database* in public relations or public affairs means simply lists of names. That may remain true for those engaged in public relations, as we shall discuss. But the continuing need for current and relative intelligence on each community of importance to an organization makes the role of the database supporting a public affairs person engaged in lobbying or external affairs far more complex than simple list manipulation.

Different Databases for Different Tasks

Let us begin by examining first a distinction in roles. Not everyone will agree with our distinction as many engaged in public relations now say they are also engaged in public affairs. But by making the distinction, we are at least able to focus both on two separate tasks— whatever they are called—as well as on the difference in the use of technology, especially in terms of the care required in the development of databases for the public affairs professional.

For both communications professionals, a name and an address is what a number is to a financial analyst—pure gold if valid, fool's gold if not—but one communicator may not be as concerned with the carat quality of the names as another. The reason: The assigned task.

To Create Awareness

The task most often assigned to public relations or advertising is to increase awareness, create a climate, establish a mood or propensity for a sale if one is dealing with a product, or a vote if one is working in the political process. The allure of the advertisement, the favorable mention in the media, the attention drawn to the product or the candidate—all establish a framework for increasing sales or winning elections. Mass mailings are a part of the advertising–public relations arsenal and can accomplish as much as any form of mass media. The goal in every instance is impressions made which affect behavior.

When mass mailings are to be part of the media mix, lists may be bought from any number of vendors. But, as the goal is mass impressions, the degree of accuracy may be irrelevant. In fact, with few exceptions, no vendor will guarantee that the list for sale is 100 percent accurate. Yet full-blown accuracy matters little if the number of impressions is high and the number of leads or responses is within an acceptable range.

For example, if someone in advertising or public relations involved in direct marketing sends out 1000 pieces and gets back 4 or 5, that may be a phenomenally high response rate given the product. The same can be true for a fund-raiser or for a campaign manager simply trying to create awareness.

If the number of direct impressions is high—to repeat, the response within a range that experience has taught to be decent—the program can be viewed as successful. That's because such direct marketing is based on *impulse buying,* the emotion of the moment when, standing idly at the checkout counter awaiting a turn or opening the envelope for lack of anything better to do, one says to oneself, "I need that," despite having never felt that way before.

Advertising and public relations provide a powerful backdrop to marketing of products, services, and ideas. In political campaigns, advertising and public relations alone can move a candidate to within a point or two of winning, as many people generally prone to a particular point of view buy into the message being delivered. Survey and focus group research should, in fact, suggest what message will deliver the largest numbers in terms of proclivity or predisposition to a candidate, cause, or proposal.

To Target a Message

But, in a close election, a different skill is sought. As Matt Reese and other grassroots organizers have known and preached for years, the winner is usually the candidate who has an aggressive get-out-the-vote effort, a one-on-one sales job that delivers the margin of victory, sometimes accounting for as much as 5 percent of the vote, a significant number in a close election.

In fact, political campaign managers often use words like *retail* and *wholesale* to discuss different kinds of communications. *Wholesale* refers to mass-marketing techniques, *retail* to direct one-on-one techniques. Both are designed to deliver a message, but the latter is geared toward making the "sale," to determine who, in fact, is willing to vote your way, that is, who you need to get to the polls on election day. For a get-out-the-vote effort, a 4 or 5 percent response would constitute failure. That effort must be virtually 100 percent.

One reason we have suggested that an excellent preparation for the field of public affairs is a stint as a campaign manager is the need to appreciate this distinction between wholesale and retail. Both are important. It is rare that one approach *sans* the other can win. So, it would seem that the skills of a good campaign manager—whether honed in the community or on a campus—bridge the roles or tasks of public relations and public affairs.

Thus, the task of the public affairs professional, to our way of thinking, is different in the sense that it is often measured on a one-on-one basis, somewhat like sales. In fact, we would suggest that there is a greater kinship between the public affairs professional and those engaged in sales. For like the salesperson, the lobbyist or the external affairs professional for an organization is building relationships, one by one.

These may be relationships with legislators, community activists, fellow employees with whom they are building a grassroots network, or voters, be they the influentials or just the next-door neighbors whose acquiescence in the goals of the organization are deemed important. The salesperson is trying to sell a product.

The public affairs or external affairs person is selling an idea. And while both public relations and public affairs professionals are trying to sell an idea, the distinction we make is between selling the idea *wholesale,* in our view a function of public relations, and selling the idea *retail,* the task of public affairs. The outreach is to those in the community among whom person-to-person relationships must be built over an extended period of time in order to develop a reservoir of goodwill, regardless of where that community is located throughout the world.

Thus, the technology required and the databases needed to support public affairs professionals are different in some ways from those that support the public relations person. Unlike those concerned with a wholesale, mass appeal, one cannot begin building sustained relationships simply by purchasing a list, any more than they can be satisfied by simply having at their fingertips a name and an address.

The goal may not be to get out the vote, but it should be viewed as the list the organization can call upon in a crisis to rally behind the organization. Viewed in that light, hitting the mark 4 or 5 percent of the time is unacceptable. A large list that "works" to produce results in so few cases does not work at all. The amount of intelligence needed to make strategic plans and to execute them in good times and crisis is far more comprehensive.

To Maintain a Relationship

If the goal of public affairs is to enhance, at best, or to protect, at the very least, the public acceptance of the organization within the community, then the system needed to support that effort is one that will assure the organization of accuracy that is as close to 100 percent as possible even as the audience to be reached numbers into the mega-thousands, as it will and as it should.

That is because to achieve success in public affairs, particularly in the corporate and trade association community, one can rarely afford to rely on *impulse buying*. It should be a long-term enterprise. The public affairs group should be seeking to build sustained goodwill, the kind that supports intellectually, rather than simply emotionally, the belief that the organization is good, its objectives supportable.

Exceptions exist, obviously. When the public affairs challenge is a short-term one, a crisis situation such as an election or a legislative action, it is possible to stir up emotions and carry the day. What is being substituted in the heat of the moment for sustainable relationship building and community outreach is the huge expenditure of funds for the creation of instant organizations designed to accomplish a single task, usually to vote for a candidate or cause in an election or to press for the solution espoused by the sponsoring group to a legislative issue in a lobbying situation.

These instant organizations, even if successful in the short run, can rarely sustain their clout on major issues over the long haul. That is primarily because their appeal is emotional, seeking an impulsive reaction rather than a truly thoughtful response. Organizations able to sustain such emotionalism usually require astronomical budgets such as those deployed by the National Rifle Association or televangelists in support of their causes. We explore other examples of instant organizations more in the following chapter.

Suffice it to say at this point that the willingness to spend the money to create an instant organization is partly due to the technophobic avoidance behavior we discussed earlier. Unable to see the computer as a management tool, many groups are unwilling to develop a truly useful system to support public affairs strategic planning and management initiatives on an ongoing basis, favoring, it seems, the crisis-driven crash program when all hell breaks loose.

Seeing the computer as nothing more than an electronic filing cabinet, such organizations refuse to spend the thousands of dollars on an annual basis that are required to develop and to maintain an inhouse intelligence system, preferring instead to spend the millions of dollars it takes to identify and communicate with the correct constituent groups when the crisis occurs. To paraphrase Ben Franklin, "a thousand wise, a million foolish."

Every organization thus has to face a threshold judgment: Should we use the technology to develop a coherent, ongoing, and targeted external affairs program; or is it worth the gamble to simply wait for the explosion of an issue?

Because we have seen over and over again the difficulty and the huge expense of responding to a crisis from scratch, our view is clear. Rather than spend millions of dollars on a 30-day campaign, we believe it is almost always a better idea to spend a tenth of that each year for a decade or more, using technology to support a real network of allies that will have positive management and marketing consequences as well as political impact again and again.

Any company, trade association, or nonprofit can do it. Let's take a look at what is required, technologically, and then examine how one company made the decision in the early eighties to build for the long term, a decision that continues to bear fruit in crises situations. The general principles we suggest, as exemplified by the specific case study, can be applied by any organization that understands the need both to build a grassroots external affairs program and to harness existing technology to support an aggressive public affairs outreach effort.

Building a Public Affairs Database

There is a short-term and a long-term view of what is needed in the development of a database to support one-on-one relationship building. Most organizations build simply for the short term, maintaining only the most basic information. One reason may be that they have not thought through what *value-added* information they need in order to have the intelligence at their fingertips for public affairs strategic planning. Another reason may be that they have felt the pressure of either time constraints or staff reductions, or a combination of the two.

We will explore what is needed in terms of *value-added* information to make the technology support a viable external affairs program over the long term. For those who agree who are also caught in the time-staff crunch, an alternative may be to contract with an outside vendor to develop and maintain the database. We will discuss at the chapter's end the various options available. Before doing so, let us explore the short- and long-term considerations and those ingredients of a database we have learned are necessary to support an activist organization's public affairs outreach.

To meet short-term objectives, there is little disagreement that one begins with a name, title, organizational affiliation, address, city, state, zip code, and direct and fax phone numbers, plus a link to political jurisdictions that are important. The various jurisdictions to which a name is linked may include congressional districts, state representative districts, county and city council districts, and even school board districts if the organization is engaged in issues that are controlled by a school board. Even for short-term efforts, both work and home information should be included.

A long-term retrieval system takes more thought. The system must be designed by or at least with considerable input from the end user, the person who is responsible for developing and implementing a broad-based strategy. Deciding what information to gather will depend on what information is going to be needed to build and activate a coalition. Starting at the megalevel, a public affairs database should eventually be asked to help answer the following questions:

- Who is with us?

- Who is against us?

- Who is neutral, but leaning our way?

- How do we reach those who are with us or leaning our way?

- What arguments will prevail?

These are the questions that one poses in any issue situation, be it in the more narrow political arena—as when dealing with an elective situation, as in a referendum, or a legislative or regulatory situation—or be it in the broader political arena, such when one is building-closing facilities, adding-shrinking staff, seeking-rejecting alliances, or introducing-recalling products. In order to answer those questions, the database must be first able to deal with another set of questions:

- Who is impacted economically?

- Who is impacted politically?

- Who knows whom among those affected either way?

- Who is willing to get involved?

- How, or to what extent, are they willing to get involved?

As those engaged in public affairs require the answers to these five questions, we have the basis for at least *nine* major profiles that should be developed and maintained online for any organization interested in developing and maintaining relationships for dealing with issues. At a minimum they should include the people we call "family" and "friends." But the system should also allow for the addition of the influentials in those communities the organization views as being strategically important. The nine we cite include:

- A profile of issues—legislative and regulatory proposals
- A profile of the economic impact of your organization on the community
- A profile of each community of importance
- A profile of organizations of importance
- A profile of the influentials in each community
- A profile of politicians who control decisions
- A profile of volunteers
- A profile of media
- A profile of contributions

We treat them as nine stand-alone components of an active organization's public affairs database for purposes of illustration. But at least three obvious caveats must be kept in mind during a discussion of such multiple databases.

The first caveat is that while we enumerate several, they could, arguably, be collapsed into a smaller number. After all, many represent several ways of looking at one individual or organization. We separate them for functional reasons, both in terms of how to look at them as well as how the responsibility for each is often staffed.

The second is that while many such databases now exist within organizations, they tend to be segregated from one another. This phenomenon is often due to staffing patterns that result in turf battles to protect what each staff member considers to be his or her own data. We would argue that such segregation limits the most senior decision maker in public affairs from having available a coherent picture at a glance, a supposition that, if shared by the senior most people, might lead to sharing of information for analytical purposes.

The third is that providing for such interconnectedness among the various profiles requires a decision to take advantage of relational software. Functionally, we see a need to approach the process from a multidisciplined approach, in order to arrive at a point at which all the information comes together for planning and action. We will explore this further when we use an example of cross-referencing for targeted communications.

For the relational approach to database management enables the senior most public affairs professional to analyze the variables to form a targeted plan of action. It is an approach that has begun in a number of organizations, especially those whose issues continue to mount as staff continues to shrink.

Nine Database Profiles

1. Issue Profiles

An issue profile tracks national, state, local, and, if necessary, international issues, giving both a historical perspective as well as regular updates as to their status. Each issue should be stated from the perspective of the organization so that it is possible to cross-relate people and groups that have taken positions that either agree or disagree with the organization.

In its completed form, an issue profile can serve as a white paper, that is, an introduction to the issue for people only now becoming aware of an issue's existence who need to understand the impact in its entirety. In an abbreviated form, the issue profile should serve as the basis of ongoing updates to senior management on the status of each issue.

Issue profiles can include a definition of the issue, historical background, positions taken by key individuals and organizations, an analysis of the impact of the issue, an analysis of what may occur in its evolution in the near and far term, and bibliographic references that may be applicable for further study or citation in testimony. In short, a white paper.

The better-developed issue profiles include significant events listed chronologically. These may include newspaper editorials, academic musings, the introduction of legislation—or proposed regulatory action—in one or more jurisdictions, letters received on the subject from various influentials in the community, and any inquiries worth chronicling.

Where we part company with virtually every issues management database we have been permitted to see is in the way we recommend tracking legislative and regulatory proposals. We recommend they be seen as subsets of an issue. These proposals may stand alone for purposes of analysis. But in nearly every instance we have noted, the organization begins by describing its issues primarily in terms of legislative or regulatory proposals and either develops an online system or subscribes to one that buys into that thought process.

What we have argued is that if an organization is ever going to shift its public affairs operational mode from being purely *reactive* to agendas always articulated by others, to a point at which the organization becomes actively engaged in helping to shape events by an *adaptive* approach, one thing is essential. From the conceptual phase of its database development, the organization must see legislative and regulatory proposals as flowing from or reflecting the demand for the settlement of the issue, and not vice versa. The issue is not settled simply because an organization beats back or amends a legislative or regulatory proposal.

If the database is constructed in a relational manner, it is possible to cross-relate information that applies to more than one issue or to subissues, as well as cross-relate legislative or regulatory activities from one jurisdiction to another. This approach keeps the issue in focus as being the same everywhere; it is merely being played out in different ways in different forums.

For example, a utility may consider an issue from the standpoint of whether a specific facility may be allowed to open or remain open. Subsets of that primary issue may be the actual need for additional generating capacity, the safety of that type of plant, the treatment of effluents, or the basic security against sabotage. Proposals to regulate one or more aspects may vary from community to community. But the utility should be able to track each variation as well as responses that work in one community that may be applied with equal success elsewhere.

The advantage of maintaining such information online is that it provides both easy access and easy updates as issues evolve on a regular basis. Multiple access permits many people within the organization to be adding value-added data that others need to know in order to help frame a decision. This can be particularly useful in times of crisis when having all that is known at one's fingertips can improve the response time of an organization. Moreover, multiple access also provides volunteers within the organization to assist in the *monitoring* process mentioned in the previous chapter.

2. Economic Profiles

An economic profile tracks the impact of an issue on the individual person, the organization itself, and the community. A proposed solution to a public issue may affect jobs in the traditional sense. That is, there may be a direct correlation between the decision reached and jobs lost or gained.

But the proposed solution may also affect jobs in an indirect fashion, in the sense that costs borne by the proposed solution will affect potential expansion and growth. For example, an argument for tort reform is that money being made available for job creation is now being set aside to pay off legal costs and court judgments in the event of a tort lawsuit.

Or the loss of real or potential jobs may be weighed against a corresponding cost in terms of quality of life. In this latter instance, environmental groups may argue, for example, that, while logging jobs may be lost in the Pacific Northwest, both the spotted owl and the forest the owl inhabits should be saved from further logging in order to protect the environment for the greater good of all humankind. An outgrowth of this approach is the argument that jobs can be created in other industries, such as those that create substitute materials in housing or industries that clean up the environment.

In any approach, be it direct job loss or gain, indirect job loss or gain, or a combination of the greater good coupled with the potential for job gains in alternative industries, an online economic profile can provide organizations with facts to substantiate their position regardless of whether it is the we-lose–we-gain or we-can-do-both argument. Facts are essential, especially economic facts. As we have seen, they tend to carry the day in any political argument, even if carrying the day means only holding off the other side from a wipe out.

Trade associations need to maintain economic data on their members that can be printed out at any time to bolster their position when presenting a case for legislative redress. Individual organizations need to maintain up-to-date economic profiles that provide such relevant data as number of jobs in a community or political jurisdiction, taxes paid, dollars spent with vendors in the community, purchases of commodities, actual dollar contributions to the community, contributions of time and talent, spin-off sums spent in the purchase of goods and services by the various employee groups, and any other facts that help flesh out the economic profile of the company in the community.

Such additional facts will vary with the organization, but among those we see as having potential relevance are the following:

- The number of minority employees (divided by subsets such as Latino-Hispanic, Asian, African-American, and Native American), the number of female employees, the number of physically impaired employees, and the levels of jobs held by each of these groups
- The gross payroll and the average salary of those who would be most affected by layoffs
- The relative elasticity of the products sold, or how much additional cost can be borne by the consumer before rebellion sets in if the resolution of some issue is going to add measurable costs to the unit sales.

For an association, knowing such facts on a member-by-member basis will provide a profile of both the industry generally and the average member in particular. And, as these facts form the basis for measuring the economic impact of any issue, maintaining the currency of the information is essential.

A good model worth following is that developed by the Philip Morris Companies, Inc. Entitled *Our Commitment to Jobs and Economic Growth*, the brochure lists state by state not only the number of employees of Philip Morris, the salaries paid by the company, the total purchases made by it, the federal and state taxes paid, and the community and cultural contribution made, but it also breaks out the company's impact on agricultural activity.

A graphic illustration shows, by each product purchased, the quantity and the value of the product, the employment sustained by that purchase, and the compensation to those employed who produced the products purchased. All in all, a powerful statement of one corporation's impact on the economy of each state.

3. Community Profiles

A community is more than a set of demographic facts surrounded by a border. It has a modus vivendi, that is, a way of approaching change and dealing with issues that is unique. It is sometimes what we call a city or state, but it is just as often only a neighborhood, or some combination of blocks in which residents think, feel, and deal with change and issue resolution in their own, special, fascinating ways.

Having a profile on each community—however it is defined on a given issue—in which an organization hopes to do business or to bring about change is very important. It is certainly important in a country like ours in which local communities can have major impact on an issue. It is equally important if an organization is confronting issues in a foreign country, a case we will deal more with in Chap. 9.

The community profile includes information on the resolution of similar issues in the past, including editorials from the full range of local media outlets, from metropolitan dailies to neighborhood newsletters. The organization doing the tracking of the community is like a candidate for office. It is necessary to know both the territory and the people as one seeks supporters on any given issue. Thus, the total community profile provides an online snapshot of the territory.

A community profile should stand alone as an analytical tool that portrays the demographic and psychographic information one needs to understand a community. It should provide an analysis of the civic and social structure, the various current issues being dealt with, a reference to the various political jurisdictions that embrace the community, and the results of any surveys done that may impact your own organization.

But it must also be cross-related to profiles of other organizations within each community as well as individuals, be they political leaders or community activists or one's own volunteers. For it is possible to analyze a community separately, but not distinctly, from the individuals and organizations within that community.

4. Organizational Profiles

Many organizations within a community may impact an issue. A division of organizations may begin as being either for-profit or not-for-profit. They may be active in issues of interest to your organization or not, potentially involved or not. They may have maximum or minimal impact. But to make a sound judgment, one should have various bits of information in a database that can be used for evaluative purposes.

This would include the officers and directors and issues of concern to that organization whether for-profit or not-for-profit. In the not-for-profit area, the profile of each community group should include:

- Name, address, phone(s) (home, office, fax, e-mail)
- Organization structure (chapter of a national group, independent, membership or staff run, number of members)
- Funding sources and annual budget
- Positions taken on issue of importance
- Meeting types (welcomes outside speakers, day of meetings, time, usual turnout, audiovisual equipment available)
- Newsletters and other publications (submission requirements, deadlines, recipients of publications)

Beyond this basic information, each community organization's profile should be cross-referenced to include who among its members are also affiliated with your group, either as an employee or as a volunteer. Thus, when planning a campaign for public outreach, it should be possible to analyze organizations within the community by at least the following types of criteria:

- By type of organization (business, women, social, Hispanic, and the like)
- By whether the organization takes public positions on issues
- By whether the organization accepts outside speakers
- By whether the organization being tracked includes among its members individuals who are employed by your organization or who are volunteers within your organization

- By related organizations based elsewhere with which your group has had positive or negative experiences
- By whether volunteers from your organization have contributed time or talent to the organization you are tracking
- By whether the organization has among its members individuals who impact your issues

5. Individual Profiles

An online profile of individuals begins with the influentials in each community. Profiles we have seen tracked include not only those who are elected and appointed as officials but also the chairs and boards of directors of those organizations that tend to get involved and have impact on the outcome of an issue. All information is from publicly available resources, with documentable facts, and is stored in a sensible and sensitive manner.

These profiles include, at the very least, the following information:

- Name, address(es), phone number(s), title with organization
- Biographical sketch
- Employment, if different from organization
- Past leadership positions
- Positions taken on issues important to your group

Positions taken by individuals on issues of concern to your organization may be obtained from news articles, letters to the editor, and thoughts rendered in public gatherings. If the goal is a zoning variance, for example, it is important to know who in the community has made progrowth statements and who has opposed any development, just as knowing where a member works can be helpful in terms of how best to approach that person, if at all.

Each individual's profile should be cross-referenced to every other key individual within your organization and to all the other for-profit and not-for-profit groups to which that person belongs. The profile should indicate who one's fellow board members are so that you know who each person knows. That will become particularly important if the individual is willing to take a position, as a third party, advocating your organization's view. You will know who they can help you reach.

Figure 7-1 illustrates how this is accomplished. Mary Doe serves on the board of three local groups. In total, there are 32 people with whom she shares board membership in one or more of the groups. Mary has agreed to join and to endorse the third-party group you are forming, which is wisely called W.I.S.E. A good move.

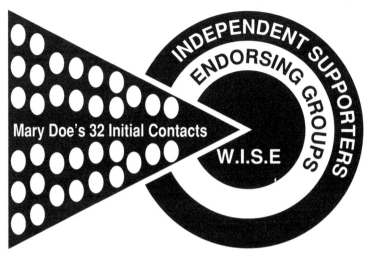

Figure 7-1. Constituency building.

She asks how she can help. You indicate you would appreciate having more prominent people in the community join W.I.S.E. She says she'll sign a letter explaining why she supports your cause and inviting those she knows to join with her as third party and independent supporters. Instead of asking her to come up with a list of who she knows (often a painstaking process for a volunteer), you are able, from publicly available documents, to secure the names and addresses of her fellow board members.

You have been able to support her as a volunteer, and you have a volunteer who, at a minimum, can reach 32 people. It's called the *multiplier effect* in constituency building and works in any grassroots development effort, whether that is to assist in an issue or to help your CEO raise funds for a worthy cause.

6. Political Profiles

Many organizations do maintain political profiles, keeping online information that includes a biographical sketch of those elected officials who have an impact on the organization's issues. This information should include major recent financial contributors and public statements on the relevant issues.

Keeping a log of pro or con statements or general observations is particularly useful if the system allows a search on all elected officials who have made a statement in favor of a situation and/or who are in opposition to the organization's view. But too few databases of those that we have seen go much beyond those elected to Congress. If an organization is dealing with transnational issues or issues that affect local communities, these profiles should reach from city council to foreign parliaments.

Here's an example of where such information in one town made the difference. In a community in North Carolina, a zoning board turned down a proposal for the construction of a new plant. The vote was three to two.

A review of the biographies of the three who voted against the new plant revealed that all three were associated with a major company in a different industry that had been in the community for several decades. One member of the zoning board worked at the other company, the other two were vendors. The other company paid its workers $10 an hour after 20 years on the job; the newcomer was planning to start workers at $12 an hour. Thus the opposition from the existing company and those aligned with it.

When the public affairs people for the incoming plant made known the real reasons behind the negative vote, they were able to stimulate a massive outpouring of support, in which some 3000 local people demonstrated outside the county courthouse. The vote was reversed. The plant was built.

Good political profiles add such links as organizations in which the elected official has a membership or a particular interest. If, for example, an organization makes contributions to the arts, it would be useful to maintain information online identifying those elected officials who share that interest and the particular local arts organizations in which they are involved. This information would be useful when drawing up lists of who to invite and who to ask to be part of any presentation of a contribution.

Political profiles that various organizations maintain include some or more of at least the following:

- Position, if elected or appointed
- Biographical sketch
- If elected, results of last election
- Past votes on issues of relevancy to the organization
- Key staff
- Addresses (capital, district, home)
- Phone numbers, including fax
- E-mail address
- Other employment, if elected position is not full time

- Source of wealth
- Major and consistent campaign contributors
- Contributions made by your organization's political action committee[1]
- Committee assignments
- Personal data such as hobbies, family, birthdate
- *Most importantly,* as we have said, positions taken on issues of relevancy to your organization
- Who within your organization knows the person

Many programs also enable an organization to connect their employees or members to legislative and congressional districts. One notable program is offered by Legislative Demographic Services, a Washington, D.C., based division of System Dynamics Incorporated. Their software provides organizations with an online system to reformulate lists of one's close associates by their federal and state legislative districts as well as to show on what committees that elected representative is a member.

But even this information is becoming too rudimentary. A really effective political profile will connect the organization's people to the politicians not only geographically but by personal relationships. Who knows whom, and how well? The answer to those questions should be cross-related between the political profiles and an organization's volunteer profiles.

7. Volunteer Profiles

This profile should represent the mother lode, for it should tell you who in your organization is willing to get involved and to what extent. These profiles should include who each volunteer knows politically and how well—as a next-door neighbor, a relative, a campaign volunteer, a contributor, school ties, past employment connections, whatever. These profiles should also include the names of other organizations in which your volunteer is either active (if your volunteers are also employees of your organization) or employed (if yours is a not-for-profit group). Further, if your organization is a trade or professional group, this profile should be cross-referenced to the economic profile of the volunteer.

A quick checklist of the kind of information on volunteer programs we have seen at some companies includes:

- Title with organization

- Work and home address
- Work and home phone numbers
- Fax number
- E-mail address
- Community involvement, including degree of participation
- Political involvement, including degree of participation
- Current involvement in company programs (PAC, company-supported volunteer programs)
- Whether trained as a public speaker
- Issues able to address
- Willingness to become involved in public affairs activities

All of the above information would have been provided by the volunteer as part of a survey that is updated annually. Volunteers should be assured that the information is to be used only by the public affairs group and be kept away from any employment records. Any information collected that is not voluntarily supplied would be considered a gross invasion of privacy. But volunteers should be told also that the survey is designed to elicit information that will enable the organization to pose and get answers to such questions as:

- Who among our organization's employees or members knows a specific legislator who sits on a committee that has original jurisdiction over issues affecting the organization?
- Who among our organization's employees or members has contributed to the campaign of a specific legislator who sits on a committee of concern to the organization?
- Who among our organization's employees or members has met with a specific legislator, attended a hearing, testified on behalf of the organization, when did these events occur, and what transpired as a consequence?

Such information can be invaluable in planning and executing a grassroots effort. We know of one situation in which a relational database produced information about a mayor that indicated a not-for-profit organization to which the mayor belonged and in turn showed who, from among several thousand employees in the for-profit organization, was also active in that group. The contact point had been found.

We know of another in which a 1400-member trade association was able to have an existing law amended because its volunteer and economic profiles provided the necessary grassroots touch. The organization is the National Association for the Specialty Food Trade (NASFT), which represents the small food processors who make gourmet foods. Frankly, they were not focused when the Nutrition Labeling and Education Act passed the Congress. They awakened to realize that companies marginally able to keep afloat would have to spend thousands of dollars they did not have to make labels for products purchased and used, on average in most instances, once a year for one meal.

With a new executive director in the saddle, John Roberts, a hard-driving, retired chief executive officer of a member company, and a responsive chairman, John Beers, they decided to organize a grassroots coalition. Their goal was to pass an amendment to the existing law that would permit small entrepreneurs an opportunity to gradually comply under circumstances that would enable them to stay in business.

Virtually overnight, a database was assembled. A survey gave the association the necessary economic data as well as who knew whom and who was willing to help and to what extent. Key states and districts were selected because of the role members of Congress from those areas played in the outcome of the battle. Eventually, 58 percent of the membership participated in the effort. It succeeded because Roberts had the information at his fingertips that told him who, among his 1400 members in any given jurisdiction was ready, willing, and able to deliver the association's message to the right person at the right time.

Such information can also be useful in helping to identify areas in which volunteer activity is weak and needs to be improved before a crisis erupts. In a moment, we will cover the use of such database information to build a plan for public affairs outreach.

8. Media Profiles

Media profiles in the way we define them are often nonexistent in many organizations. Yes, they have press lists. And, yes, they often know who likes them and who doesn't. But tracking is generally limited to a manual clipping file.

What we have seen in some organizations is an electronic link between lineage or on-air time for an issue over a period of time. This gives, theoretically, a picture of the intensity of the issue and a sense of the kinds of activities that trigger its eruption. Some organizations now claim that they can predict which communities are more inclined to become active on an issue. That may be so. But we have also seen pedestrian uses that appear to have more practical value on a day-to-day basis.

For example, with a database the substance of a news article or editorial can be linked to the issue with cross-references to the media outlet and the media person. This has enabled at least one organization to have at its fingertips a quick synopsis of a journalist's point of view when an inquiry comes. This particular organization has many issues in many jurisdictions, making such a capability more useful than it might necessarily be for an organization with a single issue or for an organization that deals with a very small press corps.

Beyond that, some organizations, in anticipation of an environmental crisis, have begun to develop and maintain online public-speaking opportunities that include, in addition to organizations within each community, various radio and television public affairs opportunities. These organizations maintain a file on a community-by-community basis that tells them whether each station has a forum for discussing issues, whether it takes positions, whether it would welcome a spokesperson, whom to contact if they want to schedule a speaker, how far in advance this needs to be done, and any known biases of the host. Such information comes in handy at any time but particularly when a crisis erupts.

9. Contributions Profiles

The contributions made by a for-profit organization usually follow some guidelines. More often than not these guidelines link contributions to some goal. It may be to improve the quality of a community, an educational program, or to support a product. The rationale varies widely.

Cause-related marketing has gone to new heights with a company called Fifty-50 which has agreed to contribute 50 percent of its profits to those doing research on a cure for diabetes, the fourth largest killer in our society. The company makes snack foods for diabetics.

What we would argue is that philanthropy should have a purpose, that it should be part of some strategic goal for the giving organization. For those who argue it should remain altruistic, we would simply counter that choices must be made, especially at a time when the number of dollars to give away has shrunk at least in proportion to the dollars available to be earned in a difficult economy.

Linking the dollars to a strategy also implies to us the willingness to link the contributions to the organizational, individual, and political profiles used for grassroots purposes. We have noted organizations that track who asks whom and how they responded, a process that enables them to determine who, in turn, owes them a favor when they set out to raise money for a candidate or cause.

We know of many situations in which, without any thought of a quid pro quo, an organization was able to prosper politically for something it did in a charitable situation. The company received a call shortly before Christmas. The person making the call on behalf of the group in need said that, somehow, the local group had been left off lists of organizations that would be eligible for money to provide gifts for the children they assist. Could the company help?

The company knew of the organization, its assistance to many in need in a poor part of town. The company, however, had spent most of its contributions budget for the year. But the company had a grassroots volunteer organization. The appeal went out, and the volunteers responded. Gifts were available for every child when Christmas arrived.

Part of the story is that the call had come from the state legislator who represented the district in which the local group was located. None of the company's volunteers were aware of that connection, so their generosity was motivated simply by a need to help. And at the time, the company had no issue pending before the state legislature.

Two years later, an issue the company knew had the potential for adverse reaction finally brought about a legislative proposal. The governmental affairs group began making calls on members of the committee. When they had finished their presentation to the legislator, they had helped that one Christmas, he told them not to worry. The legislator said he felt comfortable with the company's presentation because he had learned firsthand that the company was responsive to the community.

Whether the data was cross-referenced or not, it is an example of how such information can be useful when building a program. Let us examine that concept more closely.

Cross-Referencing to Target Outreach Efforts

Take, for example, the issue of unisex insurance rates requiring that women be charged the same for automobile insurance as men. It would be important for an auto insurance company to know which women's organizations in a community take positions on issues affecting women. It would also be useful to know which women's organizations have meetings at which outside speakers are welcome.

Knowing that women tend to have better driving records than men and therefore might want to oppose any attempt by states to force the insurers to charge both sexes the same, the company would also want to know who among their employee-volunteers can open the door for them to make their case to an audience of women.

By cross-referencing the issue profile on unisex insurance, the economic profile of its impact, the organizational profiles on women's groups, the contributions profiles, and the volunteer profiles, the database should be able to provide a list of targets for outreach. It would include which women's organizations exist in the communities in which the company does business, which employees are members of those women's organizations, how active the employees have indicated they are willing to become in the company's public affairs program, and whether there are other links between the company and the leaders of those groups, for example, contributions made, a bona fide record on opportunities for women within the company, or public support for women's issues worth ballyhooing.

If the employees have provided information about their own community involvement, cross-referencing the database may reveal an employee who shares a board membership or even just an active role in a community organization with someone who is in a leadership position in one of the targeted women's groups. Knowledge of that link is vital.

As names of key individuals from the community are added to the database for purposes of mailing invitations or other pieces, the internal source of that name should be included. In this way, it will be possible to know quickly who within your organization knows a particular individual to the targeted organization. This information is particularly helpful when the organization is setting up a phone bank for a solicitation of some kind. You are able to get the right person within your group to make the pitch.

Such data answers the questions posed initially: Who knows whom, who is willing to get involved, and how much are they willing to get involved. With such information at one's fingertips, a campaign of any kind can be waged: political, legislative, fund-raising, or simply the beginning of a community outreach effort. A good volunteer database will also tell the organization what it does not know, or does not have, in order to build the resources it needs.

Planning

Planning becomes easier with a relational database system that encompasses all of the profiles we have mentioned. Using the targeting example mentioned above, a plan can be developed and executed which includes at least the following opportunities:

1. Target constituent outreach by location.
2. Target constituent outreach by group, for example:
   - Young people
   - Seniors
   - Members of minorities

- Women
- Men
- Environmentalists

3. Target constituent outreach by issue, for example:
   - Offshore drilling
   - Health care reform
   - Auto insurance
   - Liquor in candy

4. Target constituent outreach by messenger.

Getting volunteers to serve as the organization's messengers leads to a second phase of planning. The three charts in Figs. 7-2 through 7-4 suggest the kind of information the computer can produce about its volunteer group that will enable an organization to plan for strengthening those areas in which it needs help in advance of any crisis.

As an example, let us assume the company depends on city council decisions and is seeking to build outreach among organizations in each councilmanic district. To accomplish this, the company should gather information by jurisdictions.

Figure 7-2 shows the number of employees involved in various types of organizations. Figure 7-3 shows the number of volunteers involved in organizations on a district-by-district basis. Figure 7-4 shows the number of volunteers trained as public speakers on a district-by-district basis.

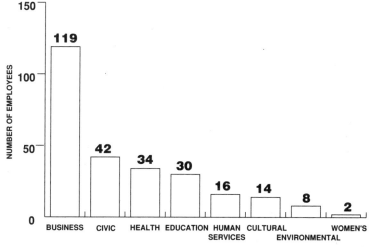

Figure 7-2. Types of organizations in which company volunteers are members.

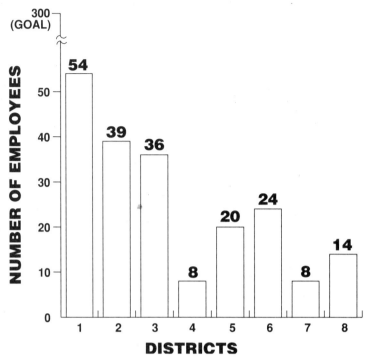

Figure 7-3. Employee volunteers by city council district.

There are a number of ways such information can be used in planning for outreach. For example, if the elected councilman for District 4 is crucial, the organization may wish to recruit more volunteers to get their message out to that district's constituents. If the community groups in District 7 are heavily involved in issues of concern to the organization, the organization may choose also to train more public speakers for that neighborhood.

Another way of looking at the information for planning purposes is to evaluate participation of volunteers in various activities. For example, public affairs people for environmental organizations tell us that in a number of communities, particularly on the West Coast, garden clubs are now raising questions about environmental matters. They are holding seminars, inviting speakers, making known their positions.

Garden clubs are not particularly strident, but they are an important voice within the community, one that can, if courted, help present a balanced view of your organization's environmental record, quite possibly as a counterweight to more radical presentations by other organi-

SPEAKER BUREAU MEMBERS
BY CITY COUNCIL DISTRICT

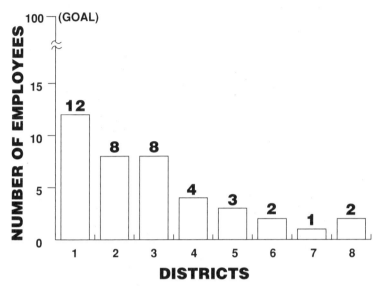

Figure 7-4. Speaker bureau members by city council district.

zations. Companies with many environmental issues should begin to realize that garden clubs are becoming an increasingly important part of their public affairs community.

Printing out charts such as those depicted here, the company can identify how many employees are now active in garden clubs and whether those employees are also active in the company's public affairs volunteer program. The data may reveal that the company needs to encourage employees to become more active in garden clubs and can help by charting garden clubs according to employee home addresses and legislative districts.

At the very least, it can connect employee volunteers who are willing to do public speaking to key garden clubs in their own communities. The potential for planning and building a relationship in advance of a need is obvious.

To this point we have been discussing the use of technology to support a public affairs effort aimed primarily at one's family, friends, and the influentials within those communities that are of primary concern to the organization. The ability to cross-reference and cross-relate information such as we have described is technically possible today because of the development of relational database management systems.

It becomes feasible when a strategic commitment is made to proceed. They are being developed among those organizations that are truly on the cutting edge of corporate activism. One company that has had the foresight and fortitude to persevere in the creation of a major grassroots organization supported by sophisticated computer technology is General Mills Restaurants, Inc.

General Mills Restaurants, Inc.

General Mills Restaurants, Inc. (GMRI), is a $3 billion, wholly owned restaurant-oriented subsidiary of the General Mills Corporation. It began as a single Red Lobster Restaurant on January 18, 1968, and was purchased by General Mills in 1970.

From that humble beginning, GMRI has grown to some 1200 restaurants, 1100 of which are located in the United States. It employs 110,000 people in North America. GMRI is divided into three lines of business: Red Lobster, a seafood business; Olive Garden, an Italian business; and the newest, China Coast, a Chinese food business.

Joe Lee, currently vice chairman of General Mills, is the person most point to as being primarily responsible for the tremendous growth and success of the business. He is also credited with promoting strategic planning for government relations long before any of his chief executive contemporaries did so in the food industry. He was way out in front of his colleagues and competitors both in thinking about grassroots organizing and in using sophisticated computer technology to get there.

In 1981, Lee had commissioned a study by Computer Research Group in New York to analyze how best to build a grassroots network both for his company and for the other multi-billion-dollar restaurant chains that were members of the National Restaurant Association. The recommended plan was put on hold because it arrived at a time of a major economic slump both for the country and the restaurant industry. But in 1984, Lee revived the idea and brought in Rick Walsh to head up government relations and make it happen.

Walsh's primary recommendation to Lee from the outset was that the General Mills Restaurants build a solid grassroots structure in advance of, and even at the sacrifice of, a political action committee. At the time, the notion of grassroots political education and involvement was novel.

PACs were the rage. Some people thought Lee and Walsh were going down the wrong road. History has proven otherwise.

With Lee's whole-hearted support, Walsh set out to build his grass-roots network by developing a massive database to support grassroots activities and by implementing an employee education program that stressed the importance of grassroots activities at all levels—federal, state, and most critically for a restaurant, local. To develop the data-base, Walsh created six different programs, most of which were housed elsewhere within the corporation, but all of which would ultimately be tied together through his seven-person government relations office.

The first thing Walsh realized was that his office could not maintain the files on employees. In his restaurant operation there are as many as 175 personnel changes per week. New people are employed, some leave, others get promoted or reassigned. It's an updater's nightmare. With Lee's support, the personnel office agreed to tie into the govern-ment relations operation so that Walsh would have an up-to-date list of all employees by restaurant location and title. Adjustments were made so that the location would be linked to the correct federal and state legislative districts.

A second program, maintained by the market research department, provides a sophisticated economic model of the community in which each restaurant is located. It tells Walsh important demographic infor-mation about each congressional and state legislative district. This information includes current population, household income, number of businesses, number of employees, average age, average income, and ethnic breakdowns.

Such numbers have been developed by the company for site acquisi-tion or site development. They are also factors that might be impacted by an issue were it to be settled adversely to the restaurant. It is infor-mation that is essential when presenting a position to a state legislator or member of Congress.

A third database was initiated to provide economic particulars on each of the individual restaurants by legislative district. That included the number of employees, the number of units, the amount of sales tax, property tax, payroll tax, use tax, and the number of alcoholic bev-erage licenses. It also shows the number of meals served and the gross sales of the company by legislative district.

The fourth database was the political profile, providing Walsh infor-mation on the people who represent the districts in which the compa-ny has restaurants. That told him the legislative and district address of each representative, the committee assignments, and when they are up for reelection.

The employee database indicates who has contributed to the company's Good Government Fund. The political action committee database also contains information as to whom contributions have been made.

Walsh's staff is currently working on a Rolodex database that adds, by legislative district, who employees know, including social and professional contacts such as employees of other, related companies that may be impacted by an issue affecting the company or simply key community figures whom the company might want to keep informed if an issue is brewing.

All of this information is useful when planning a campaign. But what makes the system tick is a sophisticated direct response program. It allows Walsh and his people to pull together all of the economic data and to create as many as 10 different letters, each with variable paragraphs adding important details about the economic impact of the company's restaurants within a representative's district, each on different color stationary and in multiple typefaces. From the point that the letters have been created until they are ready to be shipped to the key people at each unit takes nine hours, or as Walsh points out, from about the time his people leave the office until they return to work the following morning.

These letters are prepared for the signature of one of the four key management people at each unit in each of the targeted legislative districts. The four key people include the general manager, the assistant manager, the associate manager, and the dining room manager. They are sent the letters overnight together with a variety of suggested postscripts each may add *if they choose* to sign the letter that has been prepared for their signature.

At that point, the program is voluntary. Whether any of the managers sign the letter prepared for their signature and send it along in the envelope provided and with a suggested postscript is up to the individual. Walsh does not even ask for verification. He knows only that letters have, in fact, been sent when he is told by the legislator's office.

Similarly, he knows that the press has picked up the views of local managers when he gets clips from local papers or reports of local television coverage. Each of the company's units has the ability to send a localized press release to the local ABC, NBC, CBS, or Fox television station and to the two principal newspapers that cover each restaurant's area.

Getting the managers to buy into the program is the political education part of Walsh's job. He and his staff have been able to accomplish this by piggybacking on an existing employee education program designed to teach their employees the correct way to handle every aspect of running a restaurant operation, from preparing the food to serving the meal.

Among some of the creative videos Walsh's people have produced is one, taped in a congressional office, that illustrates the importance of letters and how correspondence is handled by a legislator's staff. The video also addresses the significance of personalized letters and what a legislator looks for in a letter from a constituent.

Political education continues in other ways. A quarterly newsletter provides stories about managers who assisted the company in a particular political situation. By citing examples of how the company was helped, it encourages others to participate.

For quick alerts, the public affairs staff members have access to an electronic mail system that ties all the restaurants together. A further integration of the normal business operation with government relations is the addition to the regular business plan of restaurant managers of a section on dealing with government relations issues in the community. They are asked to think through their handling of a local issue.

The result of this training is an enthusiastic response from the restaurant managers and, when appropriate, other employees such as servers and maintenance people. It has also stimulated something equally vital that has given rise to still another database.

Restaurant managers now use E-mail to keep Walsh's government relations staff apprised of issues that are surfacing or moving in their area. This is tracked by one of Walsh's staff members online, both giving them a picture of what issues are bubbling up and helping them to determine legislative priorities. This monitoring aspect of the program has proved to be critical on more than one occasion.

For example, in one recent situation in Fairfax, Virginia, Walsh's staff learned of an effort to add a meal tax by the local county council. Using their electronic-mail alert system, they were able to help mobilize not only their own employees but also other restaurant owners and patrons to help defeat the initiative at the polls.

While Walsh maintains he started out with little or no knowledge about computers, he has become a bit of a visionary in this business as he sees a day in the future when restaurant patrons will be added to those who comprise the company's grassroots resource base. Restaurant owners in California have begun limited experiments with using tent cards at table to enlist customers' involvement in issues, but no systematic approach had ever been attempted. With his company serving over 220 million meals annually, Walsh points out that the capacity to communicate effectively with even 1 percent of his customer base would be a powerful addition to his grassroots network.

Walsh and his staff have already started linking corporate friends to the database. GMRI has 46,000 vendors. They are affected by issues that affect the restaurant business and are keen on becoming involved.

Walsh sees the addition of this resource as a natural next step beyond organizing his employees, the company's family.

Walsh views his use of technology as evolving. As he says:

> When I started this job I was a computer illiterate. But as a manager intent on building a grassroots network that could respond to issues at any level, I knew a couple of things. For one, I knew we had to have the facts to support our case. All of our data is tied together so that legislators know we are giving them an accurate picture of the economic impact on our business and their district.
>
> Second, I knew that we had to build the trust and confidence of our people, not just among those who are participating who see what we do as something important that they can join on a voluntary basis without distracting from their primary mission, which is running a two to four million dollar restaurant, but also from our management. Our top people have begun to see us as a profit center, winning issues that, had we not been so well organized, might have been lost, possibly adding a great expense to our Company.
>
> Third, I knew I needed the best people to help develop the system. Lindsay Parrett, our Manager of Government Relations, and Betty Salves, our political action committee Administrator, were central to the success of our system.

As to the cost and time it has taken to build a system to this level of sophistication, Walsh is even more emphatic:

> We may have spent—given staff time, programming, equipment, and the like—perhaps a million dollars over the past seven years. But, compared to what it would have cost us to gear up each time to deal with an isolated issue versus our ability to deal with multiple issues in multiple jurisdictions all of the time, we have truly taken an approach that is enormously cost effective.
>
> Clearly, it has been far cheaper than it would have been if we had simply waited to do something each time we needed to deal with an issue. That was our vision at the outset and I think we have been successful so far although new opportunities await us. And that should be very, very exciting.

Some Final Considerations

We are talking about the new corporate activism, cataloguing those who, in our judgment, are actively engaged in building relationships in order to be part of the solution to the political issues resolution process. Seeking to be adaptive rather than reactive, the databases developed by such organizations reflect that commitment to active relationship building.

What activist organizations, Rick Walsh, and others have learned about the creation of a public affairs database is that first, the information must be correct. For the system itself is nothing if the information gathered and stored is not being maintained with unerring accuracy.

Second, gathering and maintaining data is an expense. No one knows the costs exactly, but there are some ways of calculating both how much it might cost as well as some ways of balancing the cost versus waiting for disaster to strike. And third, the information must belong to the tracking organization itself.

There is no great database in the sky one can plug into to obtain the necessary information. And while external databases are useful, many find that the information they provide is often too general, too little, and, sometimes, too late to be of any real value.

Nor are there vendor-developed databases that can relate to one's organization the *value-added* information that relates the general information to the specific organization. Issues may affect a group of organizations. How the community views individual organizations within that group may vary widely.

Having one's own database assures greater reliability and timeliness, permitting the identification of targeted audiences critical to the organization and the means for launching a targeted communications program. To that end it is the data, not the hardware or software, that is important. It must be current, accurate, and available for analysis and action.

Gathering and maintaining such information on an organization's database can be done in one of three ways:

- By the organization itself
- By an external vendor
- By a combination of the two

In the combination situation, the vendor, acting as a service bureau does the research, builds the database, and maintains the overall integrity of the system. Being interactive, the customer is able to access the information and make changes at any time.

In either situation the process is labor intensive. Some estimate that whatever the hardware system costs, the software to provide for targeted communications will cost an equal amount. But maintaining the information can cost as little as 4 and as much as 10 times that figure, depending on how inclusive the data are and how regularly they are updated. The heavier end of that equation is usually at the outset, as maintenance, especially if undertaken exclusively by the organization, is a far more modest cost.

Bearing that cost depends on a number of factors, not the least of which is the consequent cost of *not* maintaining such information if the issues are being lost as a result of poor communications with those who make policy and those who have impact on the outcome of issues. If an organization is unprepared, it may lose both the battle and the war.

That said, however, we recognize that another factor is whether, at a time of downsizing, it is possible to have staff on payroll to maintain the information required for a truly targeted external communications program. For some organizations it is cheaper to have outside vendors maintain the information.

Computer Research Group (CRG), the organization that did the preliminary work for Joe Lee in 1981, develops and maintains huge databases for some of America's leading companies. Founded by the late Thomas C. Miller in 1979, CRG developed one of the first mainframe relational database management systems for public affairs, initially for Philip Morris, then adapted for Bankers Trust, the New York Power Authority, American Telephone & Telegraph, and others.

We predict that research service bureau support will grow in the future. All the information needed for external communications will be gathered and maintained for the client. The client will own its proprietary data and have direct access online to their database. The advantage to the client, beyond having a source of information they can depend upon, is the avoidance of increasing fees when staff additions are not possible. If coupled with public affairs counsel, the client will have both the tools necessary to direct a targeted campaign and assistance in the strategic planning process.

Meanwhile, for those disinclined to build their own external affairs program percolator-style, there remains the instant organization, a function of crisis communications, our next chapter.

Note

1. We have chosen not to discuss political action committees as much has been written about them. However, we do believe they are an essential part of an organization's public affairs activity and that they should be integrated into the databases we describe. For an excellent discussion of how to establish and run a political action committee, we recommend *Managing the Business-Employee PAC*, published by the Public Affairs Council. We suggest to anyone interested in this subject that they contact either Peter Kennerdell or Peter Shafer at the Public Affairs Council in Washington, D.C.

PART 4

Hanging in There

**Reining in Situations
That Appear Out of Control**

8
Dealing
with Crises

Crisis. The very word sets the nerves on edge, causes the blood to rush, and activates the senses into a flight-or-fight mode. Within an organization beset by crisis, the mood is like a castle under attack. Should the drawbridge be raised for defense or lowered for an offensive, who is supposed to decide, and when does the decision have to be made?

First, we need a definition of what we are talking about, or what we are not talking about. There are lots of types of public crises that an organization might face. And there has been a lot written about managing public crisis.[1]

We are not concerned here with some of the more celebrated varieties. We can put aside for our purposes business calamities such as the demise of Drexel Burnham Lambert or CBS's troubles with General Westmoreland; consumer confidence issues such as the product-tampering problems faced by Tylenol, Pepsi, and Gerber Food Products or the defective products situations dramatically dealt with in product liability lawsuits; and human tragedies such as the downing of PanAm Flight 103 or the shooting of customers at a McDonald's Restaurant.

These crises may have had political fallout. But dealing with terrorists or product tamperers or stock manipulators is not our fare.

Our focus is on what we think of as *public affairs crises,* as distinguished perhaps from public relations crises. We are looking at those crises that are played out in the governmental system or in the political process.

They may be focused on a formal part of the process such as legislation or regulation, tied into an election such as a referendum, or simply political in a broader sense such as a community protest or an organized boycott driven by issues such as facility siting or racial discrimination. In any of these cases, the view of the common good, as perceived by some important segment of the public or of the influentials in the community, is inimical to the interests of the corporation or organization as understood by their own leadership.

The source of the crisis may be truly accidental such as an act of God or human error, which causes the organization to be seen as a bad citizen needing to be reigned in by some governmental or citizen response. It may have been avoidable, as in the backlash from NIMBYs (not in my backyard) or concerned citizens against some action the organization is taking in the community without having developed a consensus in its behalf in advance.

Or it may have been the product of the agenda of some group, seeking to gain political advantage for itself at the expense of the organization that is the object of the attack from NIMBYs or concerned citizens.[2] The source doesn't matter. The characteristics of the public affairs crisis are the same.

The corporation or organization suddenly finds itself behind the curve, fighting a battle that it needs to win against serious odds. What makes a public affairs problem a crisis is that the other side has a head start, the time is short, the threat is palpable, and the negative impact of not successfully resolving the crisis is measurable.

To some extent, crises occur only because the kind of long-term permanent grassroots public affairs program we have been advocating throughout this book has not been implemented. The purposes of such a program are twofold: first, to lay a foundation of public understanding and to create goodwill for your enterprise among family and friends so that when some attacks increase, they are more easily addressed by the troops on the ground without your ever even having to call them into action. But second, if the attack is powerful enough to require a countereffort, you have a broad-based, knowledgeable, and credible organization ready to be activated in your behalf. So what we are dealing with in this chapter are those public affairs crises that occur for organizations that have not developed a grassroots network.

Some types of public affairs crises have special qualities, derived from the source of the problem, which suggest core elements that must be included in any response strategy. Consider an accident, such as an oil spill or a fire. The goal is to prevent the accident from becoming a successful rallying point for a new law or regulation that would undermine the company's mission. The public understands that accidents do happen. People can relate to that reality from their own experience.

What the public demands in those situations is accountability. Pointing fingers elsewhere is not acceptable behavior when such accidents occur, even if the blame rightfully ought to be shared. Assuming control and responsibility, right from the outset, is essential.

Or consider the problem caused by the organization having not completely thought through all the consequences for a group or groups that might be affected. Suddenly people say "ouch," and a possible public affairs crisis is right around the corner.

What is essential here before any other step is taken is to candidly acknowledge the lack of foresight and express sympathy for the pain experienced by the aggrieved parties. The capacity to sympathize with someone else's grievance is one step on the path it is necessary to take to deal with another category of potential public affairs crisis, the crisis stemming from someone else's agenda.

Avoiding a full-blown crisis of this type, or successfully surviving one, usually requires a willingness to truly see the world from the antagonist's point of view. It is, in a sense, the opposite from looking in the mirror and taking responsibility; it requires having gone 'round to the other side to see how your organization looks when looking through someone else's eyes.

Some common principles apply across the board to the diffusing of any public affairs crisis. These include having a plan, responding quickly, being candid, telling your story, and placing yourself in the shoes of those most directly affected by your provocation, whether it was intended, or accidental, or innocent, or whatever.

Having a Plan: Accidents and Action

More often than not, those who make the right decisions are those who have a plan in place to deal with crises. Those who don't have a plan become the fodder for "how-not-to" business school case studies. The purpose of a plan is to prevent a problem from turning into a full-blown public affairs crisis.

Developing a crisis plan is an internal exercise, one that requires the direction of a senior manager and support from the chief executive. It starts by acknowledging that crises will occur in any organization and that certain kinds of crises are most likely, even inevitable, in your own organization. A good plan has absorbed the lessons from other crises, both within and outside, particularly the public affairs dimension we address.

Here's an example of a plan developed by the BP Corporation for responding to an environmental accident, the type that can be planned for simply because for them, with acts of God and human error, it is not whether an accident will occur, but when. Their plan incorporated most of the basic principles.

In February 1990, a tanker carrying BP crude was punctured by its own anchor as it was docking, tearing a 3-foot hole in a compartment of the vessel and causing 295,000 gallons of oil to spill within 2 miles of Huntington Beach, California. After the Exxon *Valdez* spill in early 1989, BP's management had organized a planning group with the mission of learning what they could from the Exxon experience. Their efforts paid off.

They decided that the keys to containing the problem were to respond quickly, to be a reliable source of up-to-date factual information for the media, and to reassure the public that the company took responsibility for the spill and was already working cooperatively with the communities affected to clean it up and repair the damage. Within two hours after the spill occurred, BP had senior executives airborne en route to the scene and local BP people on the beach seeking to be interviewed by the media.

The company took the initiative from the start to bring together everyone who might be affected by the spill (local, state, and federal public officials, local businesspeople, residents, heads of local organizations), anyone who could offer suggestions. That included people who could assist in a cleanup operation that had the company's commitment and resources and the community's input.

As the [at that time] BP executive in charge of managing public crisis issues, Charles "Chuck" Webster explained:

> Our people were highly committed to doing it the right way. Our basic goal was to respond as though the spill had occurred in our own backyard. We were determined to never allow a situation to arise in which anyone could accuse us of being arrogant.
>
> The basic concept was, if some fact existed, get it out as a fact, and don't try to delay or dress it up. As a consequence both the media and the local people began to respect us as the best source of facts because of the candor, accuracy, and consistency with which we responded.
>
> We felt that we had to understand how others viewed the crisis, to see it from their perspective. For example, the normal policy was to wait to pay claims until all claims are in. We understood that such a procedure might make sense to a corporation, but if a local business were a "cash" business, perhaps it would be better to be flexible and make partial payments. That allowed the tourist trade to stay afloat at a time when they might have gone bankrupt without any tourists and while they waited endlessly for insurance claims to help them get reestablished.

We set up a collaborative planning group that included city, state, and federal officials as well as those most directly affected. Through twice daily meetings, held simultaneously in three communities, we were able to get everyone's ideas on the table. As a consequence things were done immediately that might not have been BP's priority.

For example, the Huntington Beach pier had been oiled by the spill. And while cleaning up the oil was of critical importance to BP, the local people at the meetings suggested that cleaning the pier was of *equal* importance as a symbol to them. So we redeployed people to clean and restore the pier—an issue that would not have surfaced if we were not meeting regularly, and listening.

Our plan followed a simple three-leg response. First, to share the problem; second, to share the solution—determine who could do which job best; and third, to share the decision making. The third portion of our plan was, by far, our biggest challenge, but one we would recommend anyone follow who is trying to deal with a societal or an environmental crisis of this type. For while you recognize that others may not always do it the way you would do it yourself, by allowing others to share in the decision making, the results will probably be better.

The collaborative process paid off for BP. Webster notes that the coordinating sessions, while not without some bickering, greatly reduced the potential conflict. Local residents were sufficiently supportive that they began to supply sandwiches and coffee as a way of saying thanks to the crews working around the clock to clean up.

Press response was not only fair to BP, it often showered praise. *The Donahue Show*, having planned to use the spill as another example of corporate disdain, decided instead, after learning the facts, to focus on the effort by BP as an example of how responsible companies respond to crises.

Three weeks after the cleanup was completed, a dinner was held in the community, and 160 people attended. Lifeguards, police, fire marshals, local businesspeople, and officials at the city, county, state, and federal levels came to receive BP's thanks for their cooperation and, at BP's urging, to offer ideas for improvements so that the company could handle things even better the next time around. BP believes that they made lifelong friends during that cleanup simply because there was a plan for including and responding to all those affected, treating their community as if it was BP's own home.

Putting yourself in the shoes of those who have been hurt is central. What that means may be different in different cases. It may mean, as it did for BP, breaking the insurance payment routines. It may mean having the chief executive on site or pulling stock from a shelf. No two crises are identical.

Meeting the Resistance and Lining Up Allies—In Advance

Whenever an organization is contemplating an intervention in a community or in the lives of a group of people, it is necessary to accept the idea that there will be resistance, even if it is only to the notion of change. Identifying the pockets of resistance and dealing with them in advance is an essential step in preventing that resistance from moving from a containable understandable reaction to a serious problem for the initiative and for the organization itself.

Similarly, turning potential support into actual endorsements before there is a broad public announcement balances whatever local opposition exists in a way the corporation itself could never do convincingly. The process of identifying potential resistance *and* support in a crisis is called *stakeholder analysis* in the issues management business. The process and ideas are transferable.

Edith Weiner and Arnold Brown have written and lectured frequently on the subject of stakeholder analysis as a prerequisite for developing a plan to avoid doing something that may have repercussions. In a thoughtful piece in *Planning Review,* they suggest a way

> to identify the various stakeholder groups [by considering] the following reasons why a group might mobilize around any element of the issue:
>
> The element affects the personal health and safety of that group
>
> The element could result in economic loss or gain for that group.
>
> The element reflects a change in the values or life styles characteristic of that group.
>
> The element can serve as currency for exchanging support among groups—"I'll join your fight on this issue if you'll join mine on that one."
>
> The element is important to constituency protectors (politicians, labor leaders, corporations with stockholders).
>
> The element can serve as a lightning rod for the disaffected (both generally and particularly).
>
> The element is of vital importance to those most directly linked to it— that is, it goes to the root of their reason for being.
>
> The element is attractive to opportunists.[3]

The more attuned organizations are involved in that kind of analysis, preparation, and planning. We know of a major pharmaceutical corporation in New Jersey that was trying to build a new factory to produce some potentially sensitive materials. In advance of their announcement, they hired a firm to conduct surveys and focus groups in the three communities under consideration for the site.

As a result of the research to determine the level of acceptance or resistance to a factory of the type envisioned by the company, one community was eliminated from consideration. Residents of that community talked about wanting only retail businesses and were prepared to make a public show of their opposition to a new facility that did not fit in with their vision. In the community finally selected, meetings were held well in advance of the announcement with key groups identified in the survey as both influential and most likely to be supportive.

The examples we have used so far share one important characteristic in common: The problems were foreseeable, and in that sense planning for them was somewhat in control of the corporation itself. But how do you plan for the crises that arise because of someone else's agenda? How do you anticipate situations in which you are being used by others for their own purposes which may not be connected to you at all except that you are a convenient target? We call these *other-directed crises.*

Dealing with the Other-Directed Crises

A typical other-directed crisis stems from one group's feeling slighted in the workplace, which ultimately leads to a public confrontation. Confrontations lead to demands and action steps, such as calls for product boycotts, which often are effective in bringing the manufacturers of a consumer product to the bargaining table. We are concerned here with the other-directed crises that are focused in a legislative or regulatory forum, although some of the techniques used in developing a program for dealing with such crises can be applied as well in the confrontational situation.

In the legislative or regulatory arena, there are at least two distinct premeditated scenarios: a crisis launched by some other organization seeking to further its own agenda and one precipitated by a political leader seeking to enact new laws or regulations. A crisis generated by another organization often blindsides the target group and is unanticipated and perhaps unanticipatable. A crisis stimulated by a politician's initiative is often telegraphed, either through election oratory or the introduction of some proposal before a legislative or regulatory body.

Other-directed legislative or regulatory crises are distinctive because they tend to be presented as something close to zero sum games, pitting one organization or ideology against another, creating winners and losers. There are often possible compromises or even win-win results, but how the crisis plays out will be influenced by the perceived and actual relative power relationships between the parties early on. That is why, when your organization is seriously threatened by an other-directed crisis, either in terms of actual survival or reasonable economic growth, you need to reach out to opinion makers in the community, even if you have never been in contact with them before.

Typically, the dominant emotion experienced by an organization at the beginning of an other-directed crisis is the sense of reacting, of being on the defensive. Whether the crisis sneaks up stealthlike or is telegraphed, the feeling is roughly similar to the sickening sensation when taking a blow to the solar plexus. Some group, however noble or misguided, is trying to gain a legislative or regulatory, that is, political, advantage over your organization.

Catching up to someone else's initiative is not easy. You are behind before you begin. You have to gain ground just to get back to point zero. Your organization senses that it is not in control, that the other side is setting the agenda and framing the debate, that your people are simply reacting.

There are some advantages to being on the defensive, although it usually doesn't feel that way. First, the other side has probably let loose its best shot. Second, the ball is in your court. It's up to you to decide how to proceed, how to fight to win. Ideas gained from others in crises may help your organization respond.

Alar and Apples

There are acts of God, like Hurricane Andrew or Iniki. There are acts of lunatics, like the people responsible for the sabotage of PanAm Flight 103. There are the acts of fools who cause accidents either through ignorance or apathy or both. And there are those who view their position on an issue as justifying any tactic to achieve their ends whose acts combine the traits of all three. Such was the case with the Alar scare.

Alar is a chemical commonly used in the ripening process for fruits, among them apples. In February 1989, according to an article by Malcolm Gladwell in *The Washington Post,*

> The CBS news show *60 Minutes* broadcast a segment calling the presence of Alar on apples an "intolerable" threat that put one preschooler in every 4,200 at risk for cancer.
>
> The exclusive report, based on data from the National Resources Defense Council (NRDC), said the Environmental Protection Agency had known since 1985 about studies linking UDMH, a breakdown product of Alar, to cancer in rats, but had not yet acted to ban the substance.

The effect of the broadcast, followed by the general release of the NRDC report the following day, was immediate and dramatic. Sales of apples and apple juice plummeted, some school boards banned apples from their cafeteria, and health officials were deluged with calls from parents worried about the health of their children.

But, in the following weeks, government and industry officials told a different story about Alar. The study cited by the NRDC, they pointed out, was considered and rejected by an EPA advisory panel four years [previously] as "seriously flawed," and what results were in from a subsequent study commissioned by the EPA were so far inconclusive.

In the meantime, the EPA, FDA, and the Agriculture Department all said publicly that the amount of UDMH on red apples was negligible, since Alar only produced UDMH when it was heat-processed. And in those products that have been processed—apple juice and apple sauce, for example—average UDMH levels were at a tiny fraction of the safety standards set by the government.

Perhaps most important, Alar—which keeps red apples on the tree longer, increasing yields and making harvesting easier—is only used on between 5 and 10 percent of apple orchards, following a general industry move away from the product over the past three years.

Almost everyone who joined the opposition to the NRDC report, however, has said that they had difficulty getting this message out.[4]

That was an understatement.

While the defenders of Alar pointed out that a person would have to ingest huge quantities of the chemical over a lifetime to duplicate the results seen in the two studies on rats, they were unprepared for the power of public panic. The protestations of the Alar defenders were lost in a barrage of conflicting media stories that went on for weeks.

These conflicting stories were the handiwork of the NRDC. Not content with all the joy that comes from creating a less-than-half-truth, the NRDC "needlessly fanned the flames by launching a series of public service spots featuring Meryl Streep," according to an analysis of the crisis by Peter McCue.[5]

The actress also appeared on the talk-show circuit to spread the gospel. Her basic message, beyond inveighing against the greed of corporate America, was for parents to wash all fruit and vegetables before serving them to their children. Generally speaking, that probably is sound advice. It is a simple and effective way to remove pesticide residues from the fruit.

The trouble is, her helpful hint failed utterly to address the issue that she and the NRDC had raised. Substances such as Alar are used to regulate growth and promote uniformity of color. They work inside of the apples and other crops rather than on the surfaces. No amount of soap and water or hard scrubbing can remove Alar from apples.

So instead of providing consumers with some reasonable way of responding to its warning, the NRDC treated them to the sorry spectacle of Ms. Streep addressing a separate issue. This added to the confusion and convinced many consumers to avoid apple products altogether until the controversy had passed. The resulting erosion of sales, in turn, caused a secondary panic among growers and producers and reinforced the impression that the public threat was more serious than it actually was.[6]

By the time it was over, it is estimated that the apple growers in Washington State alone had lost $125 million, "and one of the leading producers of apple juice admitted publicly that its sales were down 25 percent."[7]

Could the Alar crisis have been avoided or at least its impact lessened? Hindsight is always easy, but in this case the apple growers who used Alar were up against some factors that made their fight extremely difficult.

As we have suggested, the first step in dealing with a serious, threatening blindside crisis is to reach out to close constituencies and to opinion leaders to find support and increase the power of your response. As for opinion leaders, the anti-Alars had Meryl Streep.

Frank Young, the then U.S. Food and Drug Administration commissioner, who might have been able to provide outside expert support for the side of the Alar-using growers, was preoccupied with sorting out the alleged contamination of grapes imported from Chile. In any event, the FDA had been subjected to enough criticism from Washington-based public interest groups so that its support might not have helped much anyway.

What made reaching out even more problematic for the Alar users and the Apple Processing Institute, their trade association, was that the short-run interests of their natural allies cut the other way. Non-Alar-using apple growers saw the crisis as an opportunity to increase their market share.

The same was true of the growers of other fruits. Retailers who stood to lose revenue as a result of customers' fears of Alar had to choose between helping the Alar growers educate consumers and riding the fears by stepping up the marketing of Alar-free products. Guess what they did.

According to the *Post* story, there was a "reluctance of the people most directly in touch with consumers—apple producers and retailers—to confront the Alar issue directly." The article quoted one frightened retailer who had pulled apple juice from the shelves, saying, "'We're dealing with perceptions here. 'We're not dealing with reality.'"[8]

The only way for the Alar users to have had the advantage of their natural coalition in this situation would have been to have created mutual defense arrangements beforehand. Those arrangements could not be made once the crisis began. If the fruit industry had agreed in advance to take the long view, that "we all win together or hang separately," it might have been a different story. That certainly was the case when the poultry industry confronted inaccurate accounts of salmonella poisoning.

The Salmonella Chicken

As with Alar, the crisis erupted with the broadcast of a segment on CBS's *60 Minutes*.[9] Entitled "One Out of Three," the March 1987 story became the cornerstone of a well-orchestrated campaign on the part of the American Federation of Government Employees (AFGE), the union that represents the U.S. Department of Agriculture's inspectors, in an alliance with a number of self-styled consumer groups, to save their jobs by positioning "the inspector as the lonely figure in assuring that giant corporations don't get away with short-changing the consumer."[10]

They might have succeeded in their effort had not the National Broiler Council, the industry's trade group, brought in Fleishman-Hillard's Jane Redicker, who mounted a successful counterattack. Her effort is a textbook example of how an industry group, working together, can combat an unfair but potentially devastating public charge.

The industry's critics had gone for the jugular. "They charged that the USDA's inspection system had become 'increasingly lax,' allowing poultry companies to 'routinely violate health standards' and 'ship products tainted with harmful bacteria.' They further pointed to chicken as the culprit in a 'dramatic increase' in reported cases of food-borne illness."[11] As Redicker acknowledges, asserting that a conspiracy coupling corporate greed with product safety produced "a story that the media couldn't resist."[12]

> In 1986, Congress gave the USDA the authority to vary the type of inspection in meat processing plants, depending on the product, the compliance history of the plant, and the commitment of plant management to control its operations. With this legislation, the USDA would have been able to make the kinds of changes modern science supported—changes that could threaten jobs of meat and poultry inspectors.[13]

The act was never implemented, but "buffeted through the 1980's by budgetary anxieties and threats of temporary shutdowns, job security had become an increasing concern within the ranks of the USDA inspectors." To offset "the successful implementation of a streamlined inspection system," the union shifted attention away from trying to protect their jobs to food safety. Taking down the poultry industry seemed like a good strategy.[14]

The poultry industry persevered, however, thanks to Redicker and her agency's program. In a two-pronged effort, the National Broiler Council was able to convince the public that (a) all fresh animal products—beef, fish, pork, and other meat included—have salmonella on their surfaces and (b) that bacteria can be removed and the food made safe for consumption by following basic food handling and preparation techniques, such as cooking the food completely and avoiding the use of the same utensils on the uncooked meats and the raw vegetables used in salads.

> Perhaps the best indicator of success is industry sales. By the end of 1988, chicken consumption was up to 58.7 pounds per person (from 55.4 pounds in 1986)—[just prior to the launch of the union's scare technique]—and wholesale sales had risen to $13 billion (up $1 billion from 1986). In 1992, for the first time ever, chicken topped beef as America's most popular meat.[15]

As *The Washington Post* piece on the Alar story noted, the apple industry chose to view the crisis as one of marketing, with some succeeding at others' expense. In contrast, the poultry producers saw their crisis as one of science and education, raising the consciousness of all consumers toward the proper preparation of all foods. They realized that by not defeating an attack on one element of one segment of a big industry, they were asking for government regulation or laws that would hurt them all. The poultry people hung together and succeeded.

Instant Coalition Creation

It has been said of the press that they voted for Bill Clinton, then grew to dislike him after his inauguration as President. For many consultants engaged in the business of creating instant coalitions for dealing with political issues, the opposite may have become true. While many may not have favored Clinton's election, their business has boomed since he came to power with his lengthy agenda for change. He promised renewed prosperity for the entire nation, and he has certainly delivered, at least for the grassroots consulting industry.

Any proposal that affects legislative or regulatory activity will provide lobbyists with work. But with those proposals that are grand and sweeping in their approach, that challenge the status quo and affect lots of people and industries, the opportunity for growth and profit arrives for people who specialize in quickly creating coalitions to fight for the status quo.

A proposed change in the way the nation is taxed, an overhaul of the health care system, legislation to provide student loans without the private banking sector involved, a shift in the way the government views questions as diverse as gays in the military, abortion rights, the availability of guns, or the application of environmental rules in a new setting, all mean big bucks for the firms who specialize in identifying and enlisting armies of opponents (or proponents, for that matter) of the proposed change.

This is especially true in an age in which technology enables us to find those with shared views, recruit them, and provide them with an easy way to express their sentiment. It is also true in an age in which leadership more often appears to be a function of weighing mail, faxes, phone calls, and telegrams—the modern equivalent of hoisting a wet finger in the air to determine which way the wind is blowing—than truly seeking a consensus for solving problems. Coalitions created to "Just Say No" seem to have more success with preventing change than inhibiting the use of narcotics.

On the other hand, while the force for the status quo always has the upper hand, all the tools available for preventing change may also be used to bring about new policy. The process is the same in either situation.

When a political leader makes a proposal that is inimical to the organization, the proposed change is a threat—in our definition, it is the prelude to a public affairs crisis. When a political leader welcomes a proposal that favors an organization, the proposed change is an opportunity.

But unless that opportunity is approached in the same way, not only might the opportunity be reduced or even lost but also a further crisis may ensue. In short, dealing with the process of identifying and mobilizing strangers is as applicable in dealing with a threat as with an opportunity.

If an organization has the resources, it is not only possible, it is also prudent to reach beyond the family, friends, and influentials to individuals and other groups who might be interested for one reason or another in rallying behind the position of the organization either opposing or advocating change. The question is whether an organization should await a crisis to reach out to others or do it as part of a strategic public affairs plan.

We advocate the strategic public affairs approach. For we believe that this is the essence of relationship building. When a long-term relationship is maintained, in our judgment there is not only a better guarantee of dealing with a crisis successfully but there is also a better chance that the results achieved will be sustained.

But, First: Some of the Cons

We know instant organizations work. We will mention some of the better-known firms in the business currently. But we would issue a word of caution at the outset. While many of these organizations are successful in specific, well-defined situations, we continue to be amazed at the contrast between what telemarketers report about the effectiveness of instant organizations and what we have been told by legislators and others.

Some public officials who admit to having been mauled in the process tell us that there is often a bitter aftertaste. They say that the setback is temporary and that they maintain a long memory of having been pilloried, a memory that may well come back to haunt the client of the telemarketer. And at least one, Steven Englebright, questions whether the effort mounted in his venue was as effective as some have been led to believe.

It started in Suffolk County, New York, 1987. The county legislature was wrestling with two problems. The first was a state landfill closure law that required the closing of landfills in the county by 1990. The second was the indignity of watching each evening, with the rest of the nation, the odyssey of a barge, filled with Suffolk County bulk, disposal overflow, floating around the world looking for a place to dump its load.

For a over a year public hearings were held. Based on those hearings and the necessity to deal with its landfill problems, the county passed the first legislation in 1988 virtually banning the use of all plastics. It was a far-reaching document, according to *The New York Times:*

> The law forbids food establishments to use products made of two major types of plastic, polyvinyl chloride and polystyrene, unless they could be shown to be as biodegradable as the old fashioned brown paper grocery bag. Violators faced $500 fines.
> Banned were plastic grocery bags, foam take-out containers, most straws and even some plastic knives, forks, spoons, but only when used in restaurants, cafeterias and the like. Plastic bags were still permitted in department stores, and foam cups could still be purchased in bulk for use at home.

It was, as *The New York Times* noted in the same article, "the first of dozens of laws across the nation banning some of the non-degradable plastic products filling up landfills, and it was hailed as the answer to the wasteful excesses of a 'throwaway society.'"[16]

Stung by the severity of the law, the Society for the Plastics Industry initiated two actions. The first was a lawsuit challenging the Suffolk County law. The second was the hiring of a firm—Jack Bonner & Associates—to organize a grassroots group to oppose the law.

As a consequence of these activities—the lawsuit and the grassroots effort—it would appear that the legislature reversed itself. Having voted initially 12 to 6 in favor of the law, they subsequently voted 12 to 6 to suspend implementation of the law. However, the author of the legislation claims that the grassroots effort had little, if any, impact on the subsequent vote.

Steven Englebright sponsored the Suffolk County law. Today, he is a member of the New York State Assembly. He recalls what happened from his perspective:

> When the lawsuit was filed, the argument was made that we should hold off enforcing it until the courts had ruled as to whether or not we had jurisdiction. The industry approached the Legislature and asked if we would agree to pass a one-year moratorium. While a number of us opposed the moratorium, it seemed a prudent request to many who had voted for the bill.
>
> Two others who voted for the moratorium did so because I had failed to vote with them in caucus on a tax matter. I know that for a fact, because they told me why they were voting for the moratorium. So, the vote for the moratorium was strictly "inside baseball" stuff. The law had already been enacted. There was no reversal, and grassroots played no part in changing what the courts have ruled is perfectly okay for the County Legislature to do.[17]

Englebright is one lawmaker who questions the effectiveness of orchestrated grassroots efforts. Whether his reservations about such activities affect how he deals with legislative efforts in the future remains to be seen.

That said, a properly developed grassroots effort can be enormously effective. Let's discuss how.

Some of the Pros

Jack Bonner is probably the best-known person in the country in the crisis coalition building business. He and his firm have been the subject of many articles. These include pieces in *National Journal* in 1987, *Fortune* in 1990, *Newsweek* in 1991, and both *The New York Times* and *The Los Angeles Times* in 1993. They recount his exploits on behalf of many clients.

As *The New York Times* noted:

> [His] company is among a new breed of Washington firms that has turned grass-roots organizing techniques to the advantage of its high-paying clients, generally trade associations and corporations. [They specialize] in seizing on unformed public sentiment, mar-

shaling local interest groups and raining faxes, phone calls and letters on Congress or the White House on a few days' notice.[18]

The Los Angeles Times recounted how "millions of cards and letters generated by the Bonner firm helped keep Northrop Corp.'s B-2 Stealth bomber alive, helped auto makers fight off tougher fuel economy standards, and helped banks defeat a forced reduction in credit-card interest rates:

> The Stealth campaign in 1991 and 1992 involved getting 5,000 groups—including farm, senior citizen, minority, even religious groups—in more than 100 congressional districts to write their representatives, supporting the radar-evading bomber.
> It was a tough sell—the Cold War was ending and the $800-million per copy bomber was under heavy fire as wasteful. But, Bonner's phone bank operators won over the groups' leaders by arguing that the plane would save lives; they noted that the stealthy F-117 fighter built by Lockheed Corp. in Burbank [CA] had flown 3,200 missions in the Persian Gulf War without a loss.
> In turn, the groups' letters to Congress sounded precisely that theme, helping keep Los Angeles production lines going on a projected 20 planes.[19]

Bonner is not alone as a builder of grassroots coalitions. Other firms include The Clinton Group, The RTC Group, Direct Impact, PM Consulting, Inc., The Wexler Group, Burson-Marsteller, and Fleishman Hillard, Inc., according to the Public Affairs Council's newsletter *Impact*. Where Bonner may stand alone is in the fees his firm is able to command.

According to *The New York Times,* "A campaign aimed at a handful of lawmakers on a subcommittee could cost in the tens of thousands of dollars, but one trade association in an uphill fight on the Senate floor paid $3 million for a single month's work."[20]

What each firm tries to accomplish is to find those people for whom the issue can be framed in personal terms, to make the issue come alive with a human face rather than a corporate face. A reduction in the percentage of the cost of a meal corporations may claim as a business expense becomes the reduction of tips and income to an individual waiter or waitress. Forty-mile-per-gallon standards for autos manufactured and sold in this country becomes a burden for a sheriff requiring the fastest car possible for responding to an emergency.

In the crisis situation, telemarketing can target a community of prospects. Once found, such people may then be asked to sound off their support of the organization's position by being instantly patched through on the telephone to a legislator or regulator. Or through two services offered by Western Union (OpinionGram or Action Hot Line), the just-signed-up volunteers may be asked either to send their own mailgrams or to allow their names to be added to the text of one or more prepared messages.

The recruiter on the telephone may ask for the names of those who share board memberships, for example, in order to multiply the number of prospects and to provide a working list for the volunteer to mine. In some situations, the volunteers may be asked to attend a hearing or invited to actually testify.

Finding those individuals can be fairly simple, though time-consuming. It can be done more quickly, but with a commensurate increase in cost. It may be as straightforward as going through the Yellow Pages and calling companies or individuals whose business or profession matches a profile of one that could be affected directly or tangentially. Or, on the high end, computers can be used to cross-index many variables to develop a profile—some call the development of such profiles "modeling"—of potential allies, or to cross-reference who knows whom by developing tabulations of friends of those who have already volunteered. Modeling, or building a profile, begins by identifying lifestyle clusters.

Lifestyle Clusters

Ralph Murphine, incoming president of the American Association of Political Consultants and a leading political consultant both in the United States and abroad, is a proponent of reaching out to strangers in a crisis situation through the selective process of targeting lifestyles clusters. He credits his introduction to the process to two veterans in the political consulting business, Matt Reese and Jonathan Robbin.

Reese had the political savvy and Robbin had the technological capability. Together they developed techniques for finding potential supporters through lifestyle clustering. They launched their collaborative efforts in the early 1980s. Murphine has since used their ideas in this country and has been introducing them in South America and in Eastern Europe.

"We moved from the very simple concept that some demographics were more persuadable than others—especially the univariable demographics such as black-white, rich-poor, or male-female. Robbin and Reese created geodemographics in which multivariables such as election results, polling results, and demographics were combined. They then added the psychographic concept of 'clustering' lifestyles to give a more accurate picture," said Murphine.

Like the concept of market segmentation, the concept of clustering came to the political process, and to crisis communications in the issues arena, from marketing. Three primary companies provide their own trademark approach to the process. Robbin's former company, Claritas, calls its program PRIZM. The others include ClusterPlus from Donnelly Marketing Information, and Acorn from C.A.C.I.

Does it work? According to Murphine,

> It's great in those situations in which you need smart bombs. If you only need one bomb to win, like the A-bomb on Japan, it doesn't matter. But if you need to be selective in whom you hit, this approach increases response rate and decreases costs normally associated with direct mail or broadcast. It can save the client money and increase response rate.
>
> Accuracy does vary. A lot depends on the neighborhood. You can come up with a message or set of messages that should work, but there is always the exception—the Puerto Rican living in the middle of a Lithuanian neighborhood. But those are the exceptions you can live with.
>
> Targeting gives a good direction. It allows you to reach the people you want to reach, to persuade only people who are persuadable who are going to turn out to vote, or make that call, or sign that mailgram needed to win an election or convince a legislator.

In the preceding chapter, we discussed building bridges to one's family, friends, and the influentials, those in the community who tend to get involved and have the most impact. When the issue is severe, the community more involved, and the crisis is upon you, it may be necessary to build bridges to a greater number of strangers. When that occurs, using the techniques of targeting through clustering may not only be cost efficient, it may prove to be more economical in the long run.

Affinity Grouping

Lifestyle clustering is important as a first step. It helps you identify who should be with you. But, as an indicator, lifestyle clustering does not go far enough. What is needed is the additional process of identifying who within the cluster shares an affinity. For it is the affinity group that will act, a step beyond simply identifying who might be willing to act.

Affinity marketing is the cutting edge of targeted communications today. It is made possible by the computer's ability to cross-index many characteristics that the marketer believes share some affinity. It is done by cross-indexing categories of people from multiple computer lists or tapes. The process is referred to by some as *database layering*.

For example, by cross-indexing car ownership listings on computer tapes that indicate a level of purchase with tapes that indicate income, age, and work type habits and other parameters, the computer can produce lists of individuals who fit a profile of people who might share an affinity for a new product. These lists can be used for either direct mail or for telemarketing purposes.

In the magazine field, the degree of sophistication has reached a point at which advertisements can be run only in issues going to one select group of subscribers. Publishers are also able to schedule special inserts for readers who have been identified as having special interests.

As an example, a magazine can tell the manufacturer of baby products that their advertisement will be run only in those copies received by mothers of newborns. Information regarding products for newborns can either be placed in those issues or be the subject of a special mailing from the magazine sent to the subscriber. The affinity is not only to the status of the subscriber but also to the fact that there is a relationship of trust between the reader and the publication, a level of trust on which the manufacturer is trading.

The concept of finding people of like-mindedness, aside from party affiliation, in the issues or political arenas dates back the 1960s when pollsters began to realize that there were voters in some areas who were more persuadable, more prone to switch from a steadfast view, if presented with plausible reasons for doing so. Prior to that time, it was assumed that everyone in a given area would vote a certain way regardless of the issue, that there was no way to get people to split their vote between the two parties, or switch their assumed allegiance. The primary focus was *demographic.*

The addition of computers has made the job easier to find and target groups of people more inclined to support an organization's position on an issue, be it in the legislative, regulatory, or campaign environment. Computers have been able to add *psychographic* data, a more subjective analysis of lifestyles. Facts regarding a person's age, income, marital status, sex, race, and other objective criteria can be matched against responses on a survey.

The difference, say, between one $50,000-per-year male, college graduate, age 40, and a second person with the same demographics may be that the former lives in a suburb, drives a Lexus, and enjoys attending rock music concerts, while the latter lives in midtown, drives a VW Bug, and goes to the opera. If a survey shows that the suburbanite is more inclined to support the economic or cost-to-comply side of an environmental issue while the city dweller leans toward the "green" side, a coalition builder has a good indicator of where to target which message. Such targeting is especially useful in building a coalition among strangers since the mass appeal, whether by electronic media or mail, will reach many people who are unconvincable and may even intensify the commitment of those who are opposed.

To elaborate, we know of a situation in New York State that took place in the early 1980s when two issues collided. One issue involved efforts to shut down existing nuclear power plants. At the same time, the nation was reeling from escalating oil prices. Survey research showed a number of interesting things.

For one, two groups with different demographics and possibly psychographics, upscale Jewish communities and upwardly mobile black communities would support keeping the nuclear facilities open—the same message—if the arguments were made pertinent. To the former, it was control of foreign policy, not letting the oil-producing Arab nations dictate policy with respect to Israel; to the latter, making cheap power available to those who understood how the price for electricity could add to existing hardships.

However, the research also indicated that people with similar incomes—a demographic—but different lifestyles—one or more cars versus no car—would also support keeping the nuclear facilities but for different reasons. Those with multiple cars may not have felt the economic pinch, but they disliked long lines and alternative days for refueling. Those with no car bought into the argument that the cost of a subway ride would rise, a problem for their employees, if not for them.

Coors Brewing Company

There are times when the issue is so pervasive that one must begin at the beginning, a time when even the most sophisticated techniques may pale in comparison to good old-fashioned shoe leather and an earnest approach. One classic example involved the Coors Brewing Company.

We discussed the Coors case in Chap. 4 as an example of how best to deal with the press. For in that one episode, Coors's candor with respect to the press was worth citing. But the handling of the entire crisis is worthy of a further review here as a study in good crisis management.

In the late 1970s, a dispute erupted between the Coors management and some of the workers at the company's headquarters in Golden, Colorado. From that dispute a boycott followed in which the AFL-CIO sought to convince people in the 10 southwestern states in which Coors marketed its brew to cease buying the product until the labor dispute was settled.

While the union boycott had little effect, what had caused the fracas to escalate was the lack of a program in place to continue the negotiations. About a year after the problem started, in 1977, talks broke off. No more meetings occurred until 1985.

In the interim, the company appeared vulnerable and was hit with additional boycotts from groups promoting their own agendas by claiming that Coors was unfair. African Americans were outraged at a comment attributed to Coors's chairman that was misquoted in the paper. Hispanics were mobilized by a whispering campaign claiming that the company was anti-Hispanic. Then gays were energized by the assertion, which later proved false, that the company had contributed to Anita Bryant's effort in Florida to prohibit gays from teaching in the Miami schools.

As these and other unsubstantiated charges continued, Coors's share of market dropped precipitously. It is estimated that the boycott drove Coors's market share among Hispanics from around 50 percent to around 15 percent. As the company sought to add new markets in different areas of the country, it faced organized protests. The National Education Association (NEA) announced a boycott in 1985.

By that time the company had in place a response team and program, headed by John Meadows. Meadows contacted the Colorado Education Association, which put him in touch with key people at the NEA. In their initial meeting, the company expressed an interest in bringing to a close all of the boycotts, in particular the one that had started it all in 1977. Through the good offices of the NEA, meetings were arranged between the company and the AFL-CIO, and eventually the dispute was settled.

In analyzing the situation and how it got out of hand, Meadows has been most candid:

> We suffered from a policy of silence. From its founding in 1873 until 1975, the company had a policy of saying "no comment" to the press no matter what the story might be. The story could be about a wonderful grant we had made for a worthy cause, a story praising us, and when the press called for a statement from the company, the stated policy was, "no comment."

Coors did some research and learned some lessons. They discovered that the community rarely, if ever, knew of good things done by the company, such as grants made to local schools, funds provided for youth activities, and other contributions the community valued. Plus their surveys showed that when people were informed about the company's good works, a significant chunk of heavy beer drinkers would consider switching to Coors.

The process by which this research was completed included the cluster and layering techniques we have discussed. The survey isolated census blocks by lifestyle in order to determine on issues of interest to the company and attitudes toward the company who might switch and under what circumstances. That survey data were then linked to information gained from a leadership survey among 100 community leaders.

Beyond the use of such sophisticated research, however, Meadows would be the first to say there is a very simple way, and a far less expensive way, to avoid all the problems of confrontation, be it in a labor dispute or in a legislative venue: "You gotta talk, and keep talking, until the issue is resolved. No matter what the cause of the dispute may be, if you understand that it is real from the other person's perspective, then you keep talking until a solution is found.

> Too often, there is a tendency to say either that the situation is hopeless, which it is not; or, for management to take the attack personally. If you can get everyone to agree that the other side is attacking your organization because they have—at least in the mind—a legitimate complaint, then you can take control of the problem and resolve it instead of letting the problem control you.

Meadows and others who deal with consumer complaints offer the notion that the response effort must include research that is real. Simply taking as gospel the fact that everything is falling apart in the community just because a local salesperson says so is not prudent. It's important to get on the scene, learn all the facts, determine whether the complaints are legitimate, the group raising the question for real, and the damage as extensive as initially perceived before taking action. That is as true in the natural disaster as in the legislative arena.

We believe issues start because at least one person in one community says, "Ouch!" They reach crisis proportion when they are ignored.

If an organization can anticipate a problem because it is in the nature of things for accidents to occur, then a plan should be in place so that the organization is prepared to deal with that crisis when it occurs. Just as there should be in place a modus vivendi that says, let's find out what the complaint is about and deal with it before it escalates into a war.

We have spoken often about the fear of engagement many executives suffer from in both the for-profit and not-for-profit world. Often that fear manifests itself in an unwillingness to reach out to affinity groups and develop a meaningful relationship, to prefer instead for a "quick fix" from those who would create what we have called an "instant organization." These groups may win, at a very high cost, but they often remain superficial.

We believe that if those responsible for the public affairs of organizations under attack begin to put themselves into the shoes of those who feel aggrieved, they will find that they, in fact, share an affinity with many in the community. Developing a relationship with one's affinity group may not mean never having to say, "I'm sorry," but it does mean there will be a group in the community that believes the organization shares the goals of the group, a good way of avoiding crisis.

Notes

1. One of the best books on this subject is Jack A. Gottschalk's *Crisis Response: Inside Stories on Managing Under Seige,* Visible Ink Press, Detroit, 1993. Gottschalk has compiled a superb chronicle of some of the most celebrated corporate crisis management cases in recent years.

2. In this last category we would include the confrontation tactics associated with Saul Alinsky, *Rules for Radicals,* Random House, New York, 1972. These tactics have been discussed in a number of books including, notably, Otto Lerbinger's *Managing Corporate Crisis,* Barrington Press, 1986.

3. Edith Weiner and Arnold Brown, "Stakeholder Analysis for Effective Issues Management," *Planning Review,* May 1986, pp. 27 and 28.

4. Malcolm Gladwell, "Some Fear Bad Precedent in Alar Alarm, Scientists Criticize Pulling of Apples Without Proof of Danger," *The Washington Post,* April 19, 1989, pp. A-1 and A-12.

5. McCue's analysis, entitled "Repealing Gibson's Law," appears in Gottschalk, op cit., pp. 229 ff.

6. Ibid., p. 236.

7. Ibid., p. 235.

8. Malcolm Gladwell, *The Washington Post,* p. A-12.

9. For a complete account of the effort, see Jane E. Redicker's playfully entitled chapter "A Red Herring in the Chicken Coop," as told in Gottschalk, op cit., pp. 159 ff.

10. Ibid., p. 169.

11. Ibid., p. 159.

12. Ibid., p. 161. To which we add: Public safety is a far more compelling argument than mere money. That reality was one of the lessons government unions learned from the failure of the air traffic controllers. The controllers misfocused their argument. The perception was that they were already far better paid than the average worker and simply wanted more money. They might have won if they had sold the traveling public on the safety issue.

It is a point that has not been lost on others, most notably those in the weather forecasting government union who see the new Doppler technology as a threat to their job security. These forecasters claim that the long-range forecasts provided by the fewer Doppler stations are unsafe, suggesting that the public will be ill-served with fewer human forecasters on the job.

13. Ibid., p. 168.

14. Ibid., pp. 168–169.

15. Ibid., pp. 172 and 173.

16. Josh Barbanel, "Suffolk County's Ban on Plastics Loses Allies," *The New York Times,* December 31, 1991, pp. A-1 and B-6. (Copyright 1991 by The New York Times Company. Reprinted by permission.)

17. While Bonner concedes that the lawsuit did have an impact on the legislature, he maintains that "people did show up to protest the law, and several legislators indicated that they would vote for the moratorium based on the new information generated by the grassroots campaign." And in fairness to Bonner, the grassroots effort he helped launch was eventually successful. In March 1994, the Suffolk County Legislature amended the law passed in 1988, eliminating the ban on plastics and calling for more recycling instead. The industry seems to have prevailed.

18. Stephen Engelberg, "A New Breed of Hired Hands Cultivates Grass-Roots Anger," *The New York Times,* March 17, 1993, p. A-1. (Copyright 1993 by The New York Times Company. Reprinted by permission.)

19. Paul Houston, "Phone Frenzy in the Capitol," *The Los Angeles Times,* March 16, 1993, p. A-12. (Copyright 1993, *Los Angeles Times.* Reprinted by permission.)

20. Stephen Engelberg, op. cit., p. A-17.

9

Public Affairs in a Global Economy

Tip O'Neill's observation that "all politics is local" is as true on the international stage as here at home. That said, we have identified some seven broad cultural-political differences between the United States and most other democratic nations that have significant strategic implications for influencing the course of public policy deliberations there.

(We are here dealing only with those countries with democratic values. The rest of the world is different. There are some nations that still operate by a golden rule they interpret to mean "he who has the gold, rules." In such nations, government and other organizations tend to be dictatorial or oligopolistic, and influencing public affairs means working closely with those in power according to their rules.

(A "royalty" payment is aptly termed, coming as it does from the notion that one pays the ruler—not his people—for the privilege of doing business there. Such an approach, while repulsive to many, may be the only practical way of doing business in such countries. Perhaps world pressure and the development of a strong middle class in such situations will bring about reform. Meanwhile, getting along business-wise means going along, being willing to be part of the network that sustains the government in power.)

Three Cultural Differences between the United States and Everyone Else

The first important distinction is that this country was born out of a distrust of government, and that deep skepticism plays a bigger role in public affairs in the United States than anywhere else in the world.

The American ethic is to distrust bigness in general, be it big labor or big corporation or big media or big church, but to distrust big government above all else. The Constitution institutionalized that distrust by dividing power among three independent branches of government, building in a series of checks and balances among them, maintaining a federal system in which the individual states retain significant power and reinforcing the notion that governmental power derives from the people.

In most democratic countries, the government confers rights upon the citizens. That difference can be seen quite starkly in a look at the U.S. Bill of Rights versus, say, the French Constitution. Whereas the French, following their revolution, adopted a constitution in which it is stated that the government guarantees its citizens the right of free speech, the U.S. Bill of Rights says that the government shall pass no law that in any way inhibits freedom of speech.

In the United States, campaigns for national office, the presidency, and Congress have often been run on an antigovernment theme, the notion that it is the government itself that is the problem, that getting government off people's backs and out of their lives is the issue. The Perot phenomenon is based in part on the assumption that the people of the country are okay, but the system of government is rotten. Conservative talk show hosts have successfully exploited this same theme.

Time has taught us that government has a role in our society, most especially as a force for leveling the playing field. But the issue of whether the government should enter a new arena and be empowered to serve as referee and rules enforcer is still often the place at which activists on either side of an issue begin their campaign.

Whether Americans want government involved in whatever the question on the table happens to be—whether it is the doctor-patient relationship or the need for a seat belt or environmentally based constraints on an individual's use of his or her own land—is still often the central issue in public policy debates. In many other democratic countries, the majority view is that government plays a predominant role in making life better and that the legislative process is one of defining a problem, seeking, through consultation, a consensus for solving that problem, then moving on to enact a proposal that reflects the general will of the populace.

S. Prakash Sethi, associate director of the Center for Management at The City University of New York's Baruch College, commented:

> There is not the degree of animosity between public and private interests elsewhere that exists here. Corporations, for example, rather than being adversarial toward social programs, have bought into the welfare state. In that sense, a Volvo is different than a General Motors, Volvo having accepted the cradle-to-grave benefits it is expected to provide for its employees, while GM, like its American counterparts in the auto industry and elsewhere, remains opposed.

Flowing out of that distinction is the second: that in the United States the public interest is best served by the pulling and hauling among special interests, a brokered government with concurrent majorities on individual issues sorted out through advocacy and confrontation. In most other democratic nations, public decision making is done in a more collaborative mode.

Unless a crisis is clear, the U.S. representative system is designed to give weight to special interests and to make it difficult to effect change. This creates a presumption in favor of the status quo, an invitation to gridlock, to do nothing or next to nothing unless absolutely forced to do so.

The U.S. government tends to lurch forward in fits and starts, with great reluctance, and struggling toward half-a-loaf solutions rather than trying a higher-risk great leap forward. In other democratic societies, as we shall discuss, the process tends to be consultative, evolutionary, and the solutions more complete the first time a problem is addressed.

Outside this country, the process is based on the notion that a solution to a publicly defined issue will be found. The group seeking change assumes that they will have to make some accommodations, possibly a delay, but rarely outright defeat. Collaboration is welcome. Confrontation is usually hopeless.

The American sense of fierce independence may find such an approach uncomfortable, but the reality is that much of the free world—especially in the European Community—operates that way. Doing business in such nations, many of which constitute huge consumer markets, requires a different way of thinking.

It requires being part of the process and being willing to accommodate those in opposition to achieve mutually shared goals, not as some public relations gimmick but as a way of achieving mutually agreed upon objectives. One theme heard repeatedly in interviews with public affairs executives with international responsibility is the problem faced by "ugly Americans" who display an unwillingness to compromise, saying their company will become involved only as long as things are done the American way.

A third distinction is derived from the first two, or may even be a precursor to them. The culture of the United States values the individual over the collective good; in most of the rest of the world, it's the other way around. From its earliest days, our nation bought into the notion of pure capitalism in which people, unfettered by government interference, could make contracts with one another and just do their own thing.

For a hundred years even children were thought to be able to negotiate their own employment contracts without government guidelines. Antitrust and consumer protection laws and the right of workers to organize were late-coming responses to the obvious shortcomings of a reluctance to restrain individual freedom in the marketplace.

Four Political Differences That Flow from the Cultural Distinctions

The first difference that flows from these cultural distinctions is that, in order to maintain the cherished separation of powers and system of checks and balances, the U.S. Constitution established the legislative branch as an independent branch of government. What distinguished us then and now is that other democratic governments tend to have parliamentary legislative systems.

In parliamentary systems, political parties develop platforms on which they go to the voters, and the voters know that it is very likely that the measures proposed by the party will be enacted if that party takes power. Thus, influencing public affairs in a parliamentary environment requires a distinctive strategy.

Individuals do not write to their elected representative with a view that he or she will vote differently from the platform that representative espoused as a candidate of his or her party. Individuals in other democratic nations are less likely to write their elected representative on a matter of policy.

Rights are conferred by government, including the right to vote. Once the voters have spoken, those elected to govern assume they have the power to act. Holding all power within the ranks of the majority within the parliament, the leadership demands and obtains fealty to those positions put forward to the voters at the time of the election or to those positions deemed by the leadership to be in the best interests of the nation and embraced once they are in power.

If a group seeks changes in the proposed solution to an issue, change must come about either during the time of the framing of the platform or prior to the time the party in power caucuses between elections. There are two public affairs tasks in such nations.

The first is to develop a plan based on reliable intelligence about what is happening. The second is to build alliances with like-minded groups in order to be part of the decision-making process.

For while lobbying in a parliamentary nation is different, it not only occurs, but in most instances is welcomed, so long as it is aboveboard; and, while building a grassroots constituency as we know it is not part of the tradition, there are existing and emerging opportunities to form coalitions at the grassroots level to assist in the lobbying effort that are not only worth considering but also, as we shall see, on the cutting edge of the new corporate activism abroad.

Second, in societies that are less prone to confrontation and explicit advocacy, it is understandable that whatever old-boy network exists continues to have influence and that grassroots perspectives are relatively less important. Knowing a country's history of operating through an old-boy network of those who have attended the same schools or belong to the same clubs as those in power, groups seeking change are more likely to accomplish their goals by having one of the right old boys on retainer.

As Baruch College's Professor Sethi says, "In other developed nations of the world, there is an oligopoly in the sense of power being shared among an elite that attended, for example, the Sorbonne or Oxford. But, there is also a sharing of common values in which all the players see government playing a constructive role. All are willing to work together for what they view as the common good."

Third, the U.S. press, reflecting the cultural values we have discussed above, cherishes its independence, which is manifest by an arm's-length, if not hostile, attitude toward government and those in positions of public and private power. Even in the 1990s, the press in most democratic nations identifies with the governing class and sees itself as communicating public issues from the government to the people rather than holding the government accountable to them.

Finally, the distrust of government, the primacy of the individual, and a belief in market systems all contribute to a presumption in the United States that in public policy debates the economic arguments will trump the philosophical and other arguments nearly every time. The view of economic determinists that the U.S. Revolution was inspired solely by economic interests has been hotly debated. Yet, to this day, the most powerful arguments against government proposals such as environmental cleanup or access to adequate medical care tend to rise or fall on the question of who is willing to pay and how much, a point not only made repeatedly by us but also proven daily by messages to that effect from commentators and critics alike of public policy proposals.

Americans often buy into an idea on an abstract level, then impale its adoption on the question of having to pay for it. For example, a significant majority of Americans agree with the notion that a woman, not the government, has the right to make a decision affecting whether or not to have an abortion but not on whether the taxpayers should pay for it or even ensure that the baby has adequate care if the woman decides to go to term.

Transnational Coalition Building

For all the reasons we have presented above, the process of coalition building in developed nations other than the United States is new and possible only in selected situations. Nevertheless, there is a growing body of evidence that supports our contention that it is a tool to consider in any public affairs strategy. Its use as an effective tool, however, depends on a greater commitment on the part of an organization. It cannot be ad hoc, and it must flow from a plan in which the organization has both stated long-term goals and interests as well as a sensitivity to needs of the potential partners in the coalition.

We have spoken at length on the need for public affairs strategic planning throughout this book. That is sound advice in any jurisdiction. In many parliamentary situations, however, such strategic public affairs planning may require a much earlier warning mechanism or monitoring process in order to get in early with one's facts and figures. In every nation, the United States included, we recommend becoming part of the deliberative process early on. That becomes paramount in parliamentary situations.

When a bill is introduced in a U.S. legislature, it may be either ignored or subsequently defeated when put to a vote before the full body. Proposals put forward by the governing party in a parliament or by the bureaucrat responsible for oversight in an area in the European Commission are serious and ignored only at the peril of the organization affected. Becoming part of the dialogue late usually means being frozen out of the decision reached.

As Margaret Klaus, an executive with Monsanto, notes:

> Successful public affairs abroad depends on building consensus. That means developing a network of contacts and keeping up with

literature advancing ideas among the community leadership in order to learn as early as possible what is being proposed. Then, if it is important to your company, being willing to get in early to deal with the situation before it becomes an issue.

Part of dealing with the situation may mean having to educate people who are operating with too few facts. Then, it is helpful to be able to work through what we in this country often refer to as the "grasstops"—local, respected leaders in a particular field, such as academicians or physicians, to achieve the consensus. The goal is less to oppose then to recognize that, while the idea has merit, it may be better achieved in a way in which everyone wins—the community, the company, and its products included.

As in the United States, the coalition process begins when a company or an industry or not-for-profit group has developed a plan in which it sees that the issues with which it is dealing are, in fact, transnational. Such a plan should factor into it the possibility of alliances based on economics or philosophy.

To date, the most successful rallying point for transnational grassroots activity among democratic nations outside the United States has been on the philosophical level. Three come to mind as being among the most successful grassroots coalitions over the past two decades: first, human rights activists, in particular those who led the fight to boycott South Africa until that nation rid itself of apartheid; second, those concerned with food safety and food labeling issues, especially those who organized to protest the marketing practices of the manufacturers of infant food formula and to lobby the World Health Organization for action who now seek the promulgation of standards for processed foods worldwide; and, third, the "greens."

The "green" lobby, that is, the environmental activists, has succeeded in raising the consciousness of people concerning the environment and achieved many legislative successes worldwide, not the least of which are the 1987 Montreal Protocols, at which some 300 delegates from the industrialized nations agreed to halve the chlorofluorocarbon emissions thought to cause the global greenhouse warming by the end of the century. In some nations, the greens have achieved other, direct successes as a separate political party.

From our studies of these efforts, two observations emerge that are relevant to the strategic considerations for successful public affairs work outside the United States in the years ahead.

The first is that these groups have formed international networks, some loose, some formal, that provide for horizontal channeling of ideas and legislative aspirations across jurisdictional lines. That network includes not only the grassroots groups themselves but also governmental functionaries.

As a result, counterparts in environmental or food and drug agencies in many nations, as well as activists, are in contact with each other. This has led to the emergence of transnational trade associations and the strengthening of trade associations in many free nations of the world and to the posting of individuals to foreign capitals who understand the coalition building process.

It was just such philosophically based social activism at the grassroots level in the United States in the 1960s, inspired and often designed by Saul Alinsky, that gave birth to grassroots activities on the part of the corporate community. Many of those 1960s activists became consultants to or employees of major corporations. And while some of the issue activists abroad may never work for a profit-making organization, the techniques they are using at the grassroots level there are beginning to be copied, just as those used here were co-opted.

The second observation is that nascent networks based on economics are emerging to counter those networks whose basic agenda is philosophical. Here are a few examples.

The manufacturers and users of nonreturnable bottles have faced the threat and fact of compulsory deposits on their products in several states and several nations of the world from those who view mandatory deposit laws as a way of keeping the environment free of litter. A key argument in the opposition to the deposit requirement is the potential loss of jobs.

Either fewer people would be needed to make new bottles and cans, or fewer people would be required to clean and fill the bottles that had to be returned. In any event, those jobs created for the task of cleaning and filling would be earning far less. In short, the number of high-paying jobs required to make new bottles would diminish.

Such facts brought union and management together in a number of states to avoid deposits and promote recycling. The same approach was applied in Canada and Australia.

In the late 1970s, in the province of Ontario, the Progressive Conservative (PC) Party had a plurality but were dependent on the New Democratic Party (NDP) for a majority. The NDP is a democratic socialist party and is treated as the political wing of organized labor.

The NDP's socialist agenda separates it from the more pragmatic Liberal Party. Its nonpragmatic approach includes a peculiar procedure. The bylaws of the NDP require that its elected representatives vote for any proposal that has been approved as part of the NDP's platform in convention. One plank in the platform approved by the NDP convention called for mandatory deposits on all bottles and cans and an end to the use of nonreturnable bottles.

In order to hold together its plurality, the PCs had agreed to accept some of the proposals put forward by the NDP. One the NDP pushed for was the prohibition on nonreturnable bottles. It appeared as though the proposal would be adopted by the Ontario legislature without much dissent.

When the manufacturers presented their case to their union employees, the job-conscious unions rose up against the NDP platform, and the NDP reversed itself. At the time, the reversal was said to be unprecedented, but considering the source of the party's strength, the reversal was viewed as politically wise. Recycling was initiated instead, a move favored by both management and unions in the bottle and can manufacturing industry.

Management and union coalitions have not been restricted to Canada. One example in Australia involved the automotive parts industry. When the Parliament in Canberra decided to revise a tariff structure that would have crippled the automotive parts industry, the industry coalition hired Jon Gaul, head of Canberra Liaison and the past president of the International Association of Political Consultants.

Gaul set about organizing each company's employees and the employees of the industry's allies by parliamentary district, not unlike the process an organizer would use in the United States. It was one of the first times an approach of this type had been tried in Australia on a national scale.

Earlier, Gaul had been involved with bringing together the owners and workers in timber-related companies when one of the Australian states had attempted to pass environmental legislation that would have constricted that industry. He succeeded, but a national issue was considered far more difficult.

Part of what helped Gaul succeed was that he had structured his firm on a multipartisan basis, like most U.S. public affairs companies but unlike many non-U.S. firms. Because of the intense party loyalties, consulting firms in most parliamentary settings tend to be from one political party.

Gaul himself is a liberal, which, despite its name, is more like the Republican Party in the United States. His partner, Peter Sekules, is a Labor Party supporter. Between the two they worked out a strategy to bring management and the unions together and to win over the endorsement of their position by the Australian Council of Trade Unions.

With the blessing and support of both the management and the shop stewards, 180 in-plant meetings were held. A petition and letter-writing campaign followed in which every member of Parliament was contacted. The campaign checklist looked much like one that would be used to organize an effort on a congressional district-by-district effort in the United States. For every federal electorate, the industry's check-list indicated:

1. The state_____ (Australia has six states and two terri-tories.)
2. The federal electorate
3. The member of Parliament's name and address
4. The percent swing vote required to unseat the member
5. The major suburbs
6. The local councils and shires
7. The Federation of Auto Parts chairman (the key contact)
8. The Federation of Auto Parts manufacturing plants
9. The number of Federation of Auto Parts employees
10. The results of meeting(s) with the federal member of Parliament

The effort was a success. The tariff was lifted and the industry perse-vered. Based on Gaul's success with the timber industry and the auto-motive parts industry, Ken Youdale, the then president of the soft drink division of Amatil and head of the Australian Soft Drink Association, retained Gaul's firm, Canberra Liaison, to establish a sim-ilar and equally successful grassroots advocacy program.

Advocacy Abroad

What appears to be a key element here is the adaptation of ideas for developing grassroots *advocacy*. Many may argue about the origins, but we do know that organizations such as the International Association of Political Consultants, which recently celebrated its twenty-fifth anniversary, have had an impact on political campaigning around the world.

Organized by Joe Napolitan, for years a leading campaign strategist for the Democrats, and Michel Bongrand, an equally well respected political strategist in France, the group grew out of a felt need to explore and share ideas on the campaign—read "grassroots"—process. As tested U.S. ideas in polling, media, voter identification and even fund-raising have been exported to democratic nations with some suc-cess, it is not surprising that the adapting campaign techniques for issue advocacy would not be far behind. Jon Gaul certainly thinks so, as do many in Canada who have done similar work.

The Canadian Federation of Independent Business (CFIB) is one of the more effective grassroots advocacy programs in Canada. CFIB President John Bulloch is highly regarded by ministers and backbenchers alike. He may also, quite possibly, be a better-known and more dominant figure in his nation's capital than is the National Federation of Independent Business chief in the United States.

CFIB considers itself a political action organization. It gets directly involved in the policy planning process. Over the years it has been a player in a number of major battles, many over taxes. Where it has gained its respect is in its ability to generate grassroots support in order to bring public pressure to bear on politicians already committed to a position.

CFIB's grassroots activism sets it apart among business groups. Some say that the Business Council on National Issues (BCNI), open only to CEO-level membership, is more influential. And certainly BCNI's effort in support of Canada's acceptance of the free trade agreement with the United States was awesome.

But BCNI, we are told, tends to restrict itself to the megaissues like the need for more research and development support, free trade, deficit reduction, and other broad issues associated with fiscal and monetary policy. It may be similar to the Business Roundtable in the United States, but some say not as assertive at a grassroots level.

There is certainly good reason to avoid grassroots, as we know it, in Canada. As we have said, party discipline in the parliamentary systems of the world makes it difficult to get changes once a party has caucused and agreed to stand by a specific position. It is one of the reasons why an organization must make its views known early.

In Canada, that means getting into the act *before the caucus.* It has been said of Bulloch's organization that it is one of the few that have been able to get members of Parliament to carry into the caucus the thoughts and feelings of constituents of their *riding*—the term for a Canadian district—in order to suggest changes in the proposals of the leadership.

Bulloch's organization represents some 83,000 individual small firms and partnerships, the largest such business organization—on a per capita basis—in the world. Seasoned observers consider Bulloch's group among the more successful lobbying organizations in Canada. One reason may be that the CFIB is constantly engaged in the process of educating its members and the public through extensive research on the impact of issues.

With a sophisticated computerized system, the CFIB can generate the names, addresses, phone numbers, and fax numbers of all its members in a riding who have an interest in a specific issue. CFIB then contacts those who are concerned about the issue, gives them the facts, and encourages them to bring pressure upon the member of Parliament.

Such tactics have tended to be successful primarily because the positions developed by the CFIB have credibility. With his organization's ability to flood the Parliament with cards, letters, and phone calls, Bulloch has given ministers reason to pause before rushing to enact rules that would stifle the development of the small-business community.

In the mid-1970s, Bulloch's group was credited by many with the creation of the Ministry of State for Small Business. In direct response to one major effort by the CFIB, the Canadian Cabinet ruled that all regulations affecting business must include an accurate calculation of the amount of paperwork the proposed regulation will require of each business. If the paperwork required for compliance is considered an overload and therefore unduly expensive, the rule is to be revised. Most of CFIB's victories, however, have been linked to improving the tax burden on smaller firms.

Bulloch has also been credited with transporting the idea of organizing small independent businesses around the world. In 1975, he was one of the pioneers that brought together representatives from 12 nations to form the International Small Business Congress.

Today, 60 nations send representatives to the group's annual meeting. And while many of the nations sending representatives are in their early stages of development, the group's work has been beneficial in the cross-pollinization of ideas to foster market-driven economies and in the development of policies that will foster job creation, community development, and the distribution of income through economic activity.

While geopolitical arguments remain paramount, coalitions can be influenced by economics, especially as the positive aspects of capitalism are being exported and realism sets in as the cost of achieving some of the issue-oriented agendas are added together. For example, it is not surprising that even as the Maastrict Treaty moved the European Community closer to unity, the question of a common currency loomed as a possible deal breaker. Countries with a strong currency may resist giving up their economic advantage to create parity.

Similarly, the success of the transnational environmentalists, culminating in the 1987 Montreal Protocols, may be eroding as the economic realities set in. A 1990 article by James K. Sebenius for *The Christian Science Monitor* entitled "Of Red Ink and the Greenhouse" raises this question. Sebenius teaches at the Harvard Business School and cochairs the joint Harvard Business School–Kennedy School Negotiation Roundtable, which is focused on international environmental negotiations. He wrote:

Ironically, greenhouse politics may turn out to resemble, of all things, budget deficit politics: Nearly everyone rates the [federal U.S.] deficit on a scale from displeasing to demonic, yet it persists.

[A recent] Economic Report of the President estimates the United States' costs of compliance with the Montreal accord at $2.7 billion. That's one measure of the costs motivating skeptical policymakers and corporate opponents of the treaty.

Greenhouse activists should take note: Unlike those who have blocked real deficit cuts, the powerful coalitions that will arise to resist major greenhouse action are now mostly asleep. Keep an eye on Canada, a country in the rhetorical vanguard of greenhouse concern. If serious actions are proposed, however, will the Canada that pumps oil, cuts forests, and builds cars, really just go along? And are those Brazilians who profit from burning rain forests really going to buy arguments about future world benefits? If only a few countries bear the preventive burden, others will get a free ride. Since no country wants to pay first and end up the sucker, the list of real climate volunteers will be short. Much more complex and time-consuming "trades" will be required (e.g., technology and resource transfers, debt-for-nature swaps).

So, when it comes to making common cause in a collective greenhouse war, think of the persistent deficit that nobody wants. Both problems are cumulative, quiet, contested, in and out of mind. Both compete with other priorities, and attract phony solutions. Costly action seems to promise future benefits for all, but faces blocking coalitions today.[1]

Those who seem best able to mount coalitions abroad are those who are equally attuned to the political process here at home. This does not mean that the processes themselves are identical, just that all politics is very human at its core.

For example, it is not worth a short-term victory if the price is the humiliation and embarrassment, and thus the long-term wrath, of those on the other side. It does not make any difference whether they are elected officials, bureaucrats, or group leaders. Retribution will come, eventually.

That is as true in Frankfort, Kentucky, as in Brussels, Belgium. And that is why many of those people who have had success in the halls of government in Albany or Sacramento are now plying their trade abroad.

Paul Buiar is a New York City–based public affairs consultant as much at ease in Albany, New York, as he is in Moscow. It helps that he speaks fluent Russian, but, of equal importance, he has spent more than 40 years in the political process, as a reporter for the Associated Press, a political campaign manager, and as a consultant to corporations and causes.

Buiar says his experience has taught him one thing: "I advise clients to adhere to the principles suggested in the old Russian proverb—'The truest friend is one you build a house with.' It means, quite simply, that you have got to build a relationship. First, on trust. But, also, on being able to work together, to help those from whom you seek help so that everyone wins."

Exporting Grassroots Lobbying Is Already Big Business

One who has written extensively on the subject is James N. Gardner, a former staff reporter for *The Wall Street Journal*. He is also a lobbyist in Oregon, a named partner in the firm Gardner, Cosgrove & Gardner.

In an article for *World Link*, "Transnational Lobbying: End to National Borders," Gardner notes that "the soaring growth in transnational lobbying by giant global corporations is one of the least discussed but potentially most significant consequences of the increasing globalization of commerce."

He defines *transnational lobbying* as "legislative or regulatory advocacy by companies, trade associations and public interest groups in national jurisdictions, other than their home bases" and maintains that it "is a roaring growth industry throughout the so-called Triad of Japan, the United States and Europe."

Gardner contends that the rapid growth of transnational lobbying has been due to one simple cause: "Although the marketplace for most products and services sold by large corporations is global, the regulatory standards with which they must comply are typically promulgated at national or even local levels."

He credits the advent of transnational lobbying to a prophet, the Japanese management guru Kenichi Ohmae. Gardner reports that in *The Borderless World,* Ohmae

> foretells a 21st century in which the very concept of corporate nationality will gradually erode. Global companies, he predicts, will increasingly disregard national borders in a relentless search for competitive advantage and access to those lucrative consumer markets.
>
> If Ohmae is correct, then in the world of the 21st century corporate competition, three great poles of political power—Tokyo, Brussels and Washington—will hold virtually equal sway over the fortunes of transnational firms.

Gardner sees three potential benefits from the expansion of cross-border lobbying:

First, transnational lobbying can be a strong new force for free trade [as it tends] to advance the interests of European consumers and taxpayers more consistently than will lobbying by domestic special-interest groups bent on limiting competition from foreign-based firms or foreign agricultural products.

Second, cross-border advocacy can help disseminate the results of regulatory experiments conducted in laboratories of democracies across the globe. Third, the practice may help bring into focus an emerging debate about whether the individual nation-state is equipped to cope with the regulatory demands of the global economy.

Jim Gardner's checklist of guidelines for effective transnational lobbying:

The watchword is low key. Swagger is out. Humility is in.

Keep communications short and substantive.

Get in early.

Use the bottoms up approach. Focus on the lowest staff level first.

Catch the wave. Don't fight it.

Remain vigilant. Never assume you've won an issue, once and for all.

Speak the language and know the culture.[2]

For those contemplating the start of a lobbying operation to deal with the Common Market, Gardner's book *Effective Lobbying in the European Community* is must reading. He rightly sees lobbying as a useful communications tool that is welcomed, if forthright, by those who must make decisions in any democratic structure. He echoes our assumption that grassroots lobbying is a tool with great future potential abroad. It is the first of the "unused tools" he mentions when discussing new trends and strategies.

"Grass-roots lobbying," Gardner says,

in its classic form, might well prove initially disconcerting to MEPs [members of the European Parliament] and Council ministers. On the other hand, the Rules of Procedure of the European Parliament explicitly contemplate at least one form of grass-roots lobbying. These rules provide for a Committee on Petitions, which is responsible for reviewing and reporting on petitions sent to the Parliament from EC citizens. Rule 128 declares expressly that "[e]very citizen of the European Community shall have the right, individually or jointly with others, to address written requests or complaints (petitions) to the European Parliament."

This petition procedure furnishes a framework for a grass-roots lobbying campaign aimed at the Parliament and indirectly at the Commission and the Council. The fact that this possibility is real and not fanciful was confirmed in a speech by a recently retired British Conservative MEP who spoke with undisguised dread of

the danger that the British Labor Party might try to embarrass
Margaret Thatcher and her political allies by "flooding the
European Parliament with petitions on human rights issues from
Britain" which "could influence the next round of European elec-
tions."

One possible use of petitions as a grass-roots lobbying technique
would be to give a stronger voice to European consumers concerned about the impact of protectionist laws on the price or availability of products or services. Another potential use would be to
underscore the adverse impact on European taxpayers of restrictions on the eligibility of foreign firms to compete for public procurement projects.[3]

Already there have been instances of grassroots networks achieving
legislative goals in the European Community. The most obvious example are the greens who have forged a network among the member
countries and have forced working relationships with some elements
of the business community. For example, the manufacturers of catalyt-
ic converters worked with the greens to achieve their goals on emis-
sion controls.

One technique that may be adopted is the identification of individuals within a parliamentary district who have an interest in an issue.
Only the British currently elect their MEPs from specific districts; other
nations choose them at large. But the French, for example, allow their
politicians to hold more than one elective office simultaneously as long
as they are not a minister in the French government.

Thus, an MEP from France may also be mayor of a city or a member
of the French National Assembly. In that case, there is a constituent
base with whom communications can take place. Should Italy allow
their MEPs to be directly elected, as some current discussions suggest
they are now planning to do, their MEPs will also be open to grassroots influence.

Absent direct election, *grassroots* lobbying may take the form of
grasstops lobbying, in which the professional leaders of important
groups—as opposed to the actual members—are enlisted into a coalition to carry the message to the MEPs. In this era, the process of building coalitions at the grassroots begins with trade associations, recognized and accepted as part of the deliberative process.

Impediments to successful grassroots lobbying as a technique outside the United States are noted by Bernie Robinson, one of the
transnational public affairs strategists who has plied his craft in virtually every state capital in the United States and numerous capitals in
Europe and the Middle East. Robinson has been an activist for more
than 20 years, and 6 of those years he was headquartered in Lausanne,
Switzerland. He maintains that for many multinational corporations,

senior management doesn't yet support a transnational public affairs function organized in alignment with existing governmental activities.

"For example," says Robinson, "within the European community of nations, a corporation should have one public affairs executive responsible for the entire corporation's public affairs activities in the European community. And, the strategic plan implemented for the corporation within the E.C. should be integrated within the corporation's global public affairs plan."

Cecilia Anderson, the author of *Influencing the European Community*, argues for creating what she calls a "strategy of interaction":

> Business involvement in the [European] Community decisions," Anderson writes, "requires that companies determine what they want to achieve, know the openings provided by the Community policy-making structure, and use various channels to express their views....[4]
>
> [Then], if action is required, a campaign is planned. Lobbyists [should] know how to work with the media and build credibility by, for example, [obtaining] support from neutral, respected, and knowledgeable people (third party endorsement) in a well-orchestrated public-affairs campaign.[5]

Not bad advice for public affairs professionals working at home, or abroad. Not a bad place to inquire as to how many associations and corporations here at home have begun the process of coalition building through outreach to their natural constituents. For that we turn now to the results of a survey taken among 2000 public affairs people.

Notes

1. James K. Sebenius, "Of Red Ink and the Greenhouse," *The Christian Science Monitor,* September 12, 1990, p. 19.

2. James N. Gardner, "Transnational Lobbying: End of National Borders," *World Link,* vol. 5, no. 4, pp. 40–42.

3. James N. Gardner, *Effective Lobbying in the European Community,* Kluwer Law and Taxation, Cambridge, Mass., 1991, pp. 109–110.

4. Cecilia Anderson, *Influencing the European Community,* Kogan Page, London, 1992, p. 87.

5. Ibid., p. 100.

10

A Survey of Public Affairs Professionals

Question: Is there an organization you would point to as having done a poor job in grassroots coalition building, one you would point to as how not to do it?

A respondent to our survey: Yes. My organization. ANONYMOUS

In an effort to develop some data on current best—and not so best—practices of public affairs specialists and to see just how widespread grassroots organizing had become for large corporations and trade associations, we sent a questionnaire to 2150 individuals selected because their titles designated them as public relations or public affairs professionals. They represented some 880 different organizations.

Our survey was designed to build upon research undertaken in the summer of 1992 by the Foundation for Public Affairs, the educational arm of the Public Affairs Council. The foundation surveyed 517 senior corporate public affairs executives. Designed to establish a benchmark on "The State of Corporate Public Affairs," the project was spearheaded by the foundation's executive director, Leslie Swift-Rosensweig.

Swift-Rosensweig and Ray Hoewing, the Public Affairs Council president, are among just a handful of professionals in public affairs who have an overview of what is happening in the field—what works, what doesn't work, as well as what trends are emerging. Their survey helped to augment their extensive anecdotal knowledge.

It was the first comprehensive survey of the profession undertaken by the foundation, and it covered a broad range of topics, from functional responsibilities to staffing patterns. Following two mailings—an initial request to respond and a follow-up reminder extending the deadline—163 U.S. companies of Public Affairs Council members responded, some 31.5 percent.

Their responses provide an excellent snapshot of the role of the public affairs person within the corporate community today. The foundation's hope is to update the information every three years. Eventually they would like to add responses from Canadian and Australian firms.

Three sections of the foundation's survey report were particularly relevant to the focus of our work on grassroots organizing: (1) the checklist of existing functions for which public affairs executives are responsible, (2) the checklist of recent assignments, and (3) the analysis of political involvement programs.

The checklist of existing functions provided a sense of the relative importance of grassroots in the corporate community today. Recent assignments suggested the extent to which grassroots has become more central in the last few years. And the analysis of political involvement programs provided some insight about whether grassroots organizing had become integrated with the more traditional efforts. It also tells us how far many have to go if they are to realize the full potential of grassroots efforts. Here's what the foundation's survey found.

The Foundation Survey

Grassroots was a functional responsibility of 73 percent of the senior public affairs executives within the companies responding to the survey. But that made it only the seventh most prevalent, tied at that level with issues management at 73 percent. The top six are: federal government relations (86.8 percent), state government relations (84.9 percent), local government relations (79.9 percent), community relations (79.2 percent), political action committee (77.4 percent), and contributions (74.8 percent).[1]

Nevertheless, grassroots was the second fastest growing newly acquired responsibility. Of the respondents 15.7 percent had added grassroots within the last three years, topped only by the 16.9 percent who had added environmental affairs.[2]

In the area of outreach, the use of grassroots for political involvement, the survey reported:

> Communication on public policy is more prevalent than action requests across the board. Companies attempt to influence employees more than any other group. 85.9% of them communicate with their employees on issues, and 68.1% of them request them to take some action.[3]

The foundation's survey results suggest that grassroots organizing have begun to gain a foothold. The vast majority of corporate public affairs professionals include grassroots in their portfolio. But other data from the survey suggest that on the whole the grassroots programs are pretty primitive stuff.

The foundation's survey was of the élite among American corporations. The majority of those surveyed were members of the Public Affairs Council. The rest were taken primarily from the top 200 to 300 corporations in America. The relative size of the respondents was, on the average, $3.5 billion in sales, $6.226 billion in assets, $1.2 billion in operating revenues, and 10,700 employees.

Measured that way, what is surprising is not the large number of respondents who acknowledged that grassroots is part of their job but how few of the companies in the survey seek direct involvement from their employees or from other key constituent groups such as retirees, shareholders, customers, suppliers, and "third parties" (see Table 10-1).

With those resources, their assumed sensitivity to public policy issues, and their membership in the Public Affairs Council, the organization that most embodies corporate activism in public policy affairs, it is surprising that the numbers on grassroots were not higher, closer to 100 percent. The reality seems to be that when it comes to activism at the grassroots level in the corporate community, there is more talk than action.

Our Survey

Our survey sought to examine the views on grassroots organizing of individuals in the field. We were looking for observations both about their own organizations as well as others.

Between our July mailing and our August deadline, we received 119 completed questionnaires, all from different organizations, a 6 percent response. About 30 of those who declined to complete the questionnaire wrote us to say why. Some of those responses were humorous in their own way, revealing more than they intended.

Table 10-1. Companies Responding to Survey Who Seek Direct Involvement from Their Employees or from Other Key Constituent Groups

	COMMUNICATES		ACTION	
	Count	Count%	Count	Count%
Employees	140	89.5	111	31.3
Retirees	73	44.8	45	27.6
Shareholders	61	37.4	30	18.4
Customers	71	43.6	46	28.2
Suppliers	44	27.0	32	19.6
"Third Parties"	70	42.9	48	29.4

For example, a letter from one of the largest oil companies in the world said they do not have the resources to respond. If they don't, who does? Another letter from that same company said that for grassroots efforts, "Jack Bonner is the best." Bonner's expertise is in creating instant, short-lived organizations.

A letter from a big soap company said that information about the possible use of employee-based volunteer grassroots coalitions is to be confidential. That says a lot because if they ever got around to using such a coalition, they better hope it is not a secret. To our way of thinking, the terms *confidential* and *grassroots coalition* are mutually exclusive, for an effective grassroots lobbying effort necessarily has some—if not a lot of—visibility.

And we enjoyed the letter that said our survey "simply doesn't describe any of the activities of our essentially apolitical company." We believe there are probably a lot of companies that remain apolitical, consider grassroots organizing as subversive, and have as little in the way of resources to respond to surveys as they appear to have to respond to environmental disasters.

We even ran into some ideological reactions. Derrel DePasse, vice president government relations, Varian Associates, headquartered in San Francisco stated categorically:

> These grassroots campaigns are another reason the cost of government is being driven up. I'm not in favor of generating loads of mail that Congress needs to answer by hiring lots more staff.

To get another view, Ms. DePasse might want to talk with Mike Hickey, director of national affairs for NYNEX. Hickey wrote us that:

> Business cannot survive in this highly competitive environment without a solid congressional outreach program to generate support for critical public policy/business policy issues.

Most of the comments received endorsed the basic principles and noted the benefits. Here's Bill Gibson, vice president of government and public affairs, The Continental Corporation, headquartered in New York City:

> Grassroots have a positive impact on employee morale because it provides employees with an opportunity to do something about an issue that is as important to them as it is to us.

We were intrigued that there was an almost universal reluctance among respondents to cite instances in which some other organization either did a poor job of grassroots organizing or did not use the approach at all when it seemed to be appropriate and potentially effective in generating a positive outcome. We had guaranteed anonymity, agreeing to cite without attribution or quotation unless given permission to do so.

Twenty-four respondents were willing to mention specific situations in which an unsuccessful public affairs effort might have benefited from a grassroots coalition, might even have changed the outcome. Among those cited was the handling of Proposition 103 in California by the auto insurance industry in 1988, the cable industry's 1992 attempt to stop the Congress from regulating their industry, health reform in New York State, the Empire Blue Cross bailout, no-fault insurance in Georgia, any effort to date to permit the use of pesticides, Martin Luther King, Jr.'s, holiday in Arizona, and the clean water enforcement act in New Jersey.

Let's turn to the results.

The Specific Results

The principal areas of interest of the respondent organizations were:

Area of Interest	Percent of Respondent Organizations
Manufacturing	17
Utilities	14
Finance	13
Medical	8
Service	7
High Tech	7
Agribusiness	4
Petrochemicals	4
Food	3
Retail	1
Other*	22

*Other includes education, aerospace, recycling, pharma-
ceutical, energy, and telecommunications.

In addition, the respondents to the survey varied extensively in terms of their numbers of employees.

Number of Employees	Percent of Respondents
Less than 100	2
101–499	3
500–999	3
1,000–4,999	23
5,000–9,999	14
10,000–24,999	25
25,000–49,999	12
50,000–99,999	11
+100,000	7

Twenty percent of the respondents do no grassroots coalition work, relying exclusively on paid, full-time lobbyists. However, of that 20 percent, almost half have considered using a grassroots coalition at one time or other.

Thirteen percent of those responding have a key contact program in which the leadership of the organization is charged with developing close personal relationships with key political leaders. But less than half of them have called upon their key contact employees to help the organization when facing an issue of concern.

One of those lauding the key contact approach was Robert E. Wood, vice president of public affairs and environmental policy, MDU Resources Group, Inc. He recounted a time when the company used the key contact program to thwart an effort by the local railroad to discontinue service, a proposal that would have been devastating for this utility company serving Montana and the Dakotas:

> In 1979, the Milwaukee Railroad, facing bankruptcy, attempted to drop all rail service west of Minneapolis-St. Paul. This could have proven disastrous for many, including our company, reliant on rails to deliver product. In our region it would have hurt our ability to deliver coal to our power plants and the farmers needing to ship grain products. Our Key Contact program saved the day.

One important area of inquiry was to see the distribution between ad hoc coalition strategies and institutionalized coalition strategies.

Thirty-one percent of the respondents put together grassroots coalitions *only* on an ad hoc or as-needed basis. Most of those organizations, 54 percent, had formed coalitions that went beyond employees of the organization or members of the association.

Thirty-six percent indicated that they had a continuing grassroots coalition with ongoing activities in which their employees or members were involved in specific public affairs efforts. Nearly two-thirds of those with these institutionalized programs said that they had used the potential of their coalition on at least one occasion.

Of the organizations with continuing coalitions, 48 percent limited participation to employees of their organization or members of their association; 35 percent reached out to others, including retirees, shareholders, customers, and suppliers.

One area of difference among coalitions was whether there were any restrictions on employee participation. Almost three-quarters, 74 percent, of those with coalitions said that there were no restrictions. Among the restrictions cited by others were one or more of the following: salary level, tenure with the organization, and position within the

organizatiʘn. Other noted restrictions included only exempt personnel, only those with proven ability to communicate, and only those
who know legislators.

One finding that was particularly surprising to us was that nearly 60
percent of those with some form of grassroots organization reported
that the effort involved the participation of fewer than 10 percent of
their employees. In fact, 32 percent reported grassroots activities
which involved fewer than 100 participants.

This suggests either that too few employees are being asked, a
symptom of the fear of fighting, or that employees are not interested
or that the program to motivate them to get involved is lacking in
some way. People will respond if approached in the right way. One
respondent told us in a follow-up interview: "Among our 24,000
employees, we have 49 people involved in our grassroots coalition.
Those are our plant managers."

Two-thirds of those who have either a key contact program, an occasional ad hoc coalition, or an ongoing grassroots program said that the
grassroots effort had accomplished the goals set out for it. Only 21 percent felt it had not lived up to its goals. The rest had no opinion,
which, in our judgment, is almost as negative as a failure. If the organization is not impressing people with its ability to become part of the
public policy debate process, perhaps the effort needs a jump start.

Ranking the Programs

Of those who ranked their programs, only 12 percent felt that their
grassroots efforts were excellent. Forty-three percent ranked their programs as good. The balance, 45 percent, ranked their programs as fair
or poor or they had no opinion. There is a sense that the effort is not
working up to its potential.

The corporations named most often as being among the best in the
view of survey respondents were, in terms of number of mentions,
ARCO, Philip Morris, and Nationwide Insurance. Among others cited
were Duquesne Light, Warner-Lambert, Schering Plough, AT&T,
Lockheed, Continental Insurance Corporation, Amoco, Hallmark,
Southern Bell Telephone, J.C. Penny, Ford Motor Company, United
Parcel Service, John Hancock, and Sun Oil Company.

The association named most frequently as one worth emulating was
the National Rifle Association. Whatever one thinks of guns or gun
owners, the NRA is the consensus choice as having the best grassroots
coalition. That's why it wins.

Among other associations cited as doing a good job: the Coalition for
Health Insurance Choices (CHIC), National Cattlemen's Association,

American Association of Retired Persons (AARP), Independent State Teachers Association, American Insurance Association, Independent Insurance Agents, Mothers Against Drunk Driving (MADD), the National Federation of Independent Business (NFIB), and the Beer Drinkers of America.

Some Tips for Doing It Right

In response to the questions concerning what makes a good grassroots lobbying coalition, the answers were fairly consistent. A good program, some 51 percent said, depended on clear, continuous, effective education and communications with simple objectives. However, only 21 percent indicated a need for top management *and* employee/volunteer involvement as key.

Twenty-five percent pointed to employee or volunteer involvement as key. Fifteen percent added the need for a clear purpose and simple objectives. Others added an emphasis on the word *voluntary* and top management involvement and support.

Their additional advice to others would be the warning: It takes a lot of time and effort. They also indicated that, for those trying to sell senior management on embracing the concept, it is necessary to make the point that "business cannot survive without it."

Other specific suggestions included:

- Make certain all participants have a stake.
- Encourage all employees to get involved.
- Make sure that all the activities are voluntary, not part of employees' jobs.
- Make sure that all activities are issue oriented and nonpartisan.
- Be completely candid and honest with the volunteers and the community.
- Be aware of consequences, that is, know that you might lose.
- Use your organization only for very important issues.
- Make sure that there are quantifiable outcomes.
- Keep in mind that what works for another company may not work for you.
- Be sincere, use nonboilerplate letters for correspondence with community leaders, and follow up with "thank-yous."
- Reward participation.
- Commit the resources necessary to succeed, and monitor their use.

- Maintain good staffing to keep the program going.

- Maintain a good database and database management system.

- Build on the community's trust of the company.

As John Heino, senior legislative director for Minnesota Power concluded:

> It's clear that three ingredients contribute to the success of a grassroots coalition: direct lobbying, political action committees, and grassroots. Without a doubt, all three are important. But, given the changes in politics and government over the past twenty years, if I could develop one capability, it would be grassroots.

Ray Hoewing summarized:

> The most important characteristic is the credibility of the activists/members of the coalition. Are their activities and their alleged interest the result of an organization formed by an outsider? Ideally, they will be acting on their own. Even if they are being prodded and organized from the outside, they can be credible if their interest is genuine and their activity goes beyond postcards, petitions, and form letters, etc.
>
> Those interested in developing a volunteer employee-based public affairs organization need to do three things first:
>
> 1. Make sure the "management" (whatever form it takes) is firmly behind the program.
> 2. Have a long-range plan or strategy (why you're involved, what you will be trying to do, how you will do it).
> 3. Establish a feedback or two-way communications process.

Beyond the practical rewards of winning a share of one's political battles, Roxanne Danner of State Farm Insurance points to another benefit of their four-year-old employee grassroots organization: "They have begun to use this organization to get involved in community projects."

State Farm's experience is not isolated. We are finding that when an employee grassroots group is set up right—with volunteers, trained in outreach techniques, and encouraged at every step—it becomes a prime vehicle for building solid relationships with the community.

Trade Associations

Only a few trade associations responded. Those responding named as, in their opinion, the best at coalition building: Dow Corning, Nationwide Insurance, Philip Morris, ARCO, and the Beer Drinkers of America. They also offered the opinion that among those who might have fared better had they had a grassroots coalition: Proposition 103 faced by the insurance industry in California in 1988 and educational reform generally.

That said, the responses from association public affairs people were generally pithy and well guarded. A reason may be found in a very candid response from one association executive, Carol Caruso. She is the executive vice president of the Ohio Cable Association.

What puts her in a somewhat unique position to comment on grassroots coalition building from the trade association perspective is her earlier experience. Prior to joining Ohio Cable, she had served as the manager of Nationwide Insurance Company's Civic Action Program. Nationwide's CAP has been cited often as one of the preeminent programs.

She joined Ohio Cable in 1988 with a plan to fashion a grassroots organization for that group. She comments on the frustration of forming grassroots coalitions in an association:

> I was surprised to learn, however, that managing grassroots activities for an association is very different and much more difficult than it is in a corporate structure. What worked at Nationwide didn't work here and, to my disappointment, no one had charted these waters ahead of me.
>
> There are difficulties in managing *association* grassroots program and *coalition* grassroots programs, but they are very, very different.
>
> With association programs, it's like pushing a string up a hill. While we may have the support and encouragement of management, we have no authority. Getting employees to take action without being told to do so by their direct supervisor is just too difficult. We tried to add a second layer to the grassroots network, one which would place special responsibilities on management and supervisory levels, but those efforts were not successful. We have always been successful in getting employees to participate in an ad hoc project, i.e., writing letters on a specific (usually crisis) issue. But keeping an ongoing program alive and meaningful was not worth the enormous effort required of my small staff.
>
> We have moved to a key contact program, which works very well and is much easier to manage and measure. The general manager of each member company is automatically the key contact for the state and federal elected officials for their area. The results have been outstanding.
>
> Coalition grassroots is another story. When it works, the results can be amazing, but coalitions are usually so fragile that managing these projects is next to impossible—depending on the issue to be lobbied.
>
> The cable industry has worked within coalitions during the past two years—with some success. But that work has been limited to coalitions of associations and interest groups. We have not extended it to a true grassroots level. Our allies have been varied; . . . the issues we have lobbied have been of the most general nature; we each have our own agendas once you get beyond the surface.

Our opponent, on the other hand, could not pull an effective coalition together (the local exchange telephone companies). That was a disadvantage to them, but they did a superb job of generating grassroots support from their employees and customers. The phone companies have more money than God and can afford to do just about anything they want. We can't.

It's an ongoing challenge and becoming more difficult. As grassroots management becomes more sophisticated, the skills and techniques required to do a good job change.

Caruso's conclusion is one we share. It is a central theme of this book.

Notes

1. Foundation for Public Affairs Survey on "The State of Corporate Public Affairs," December 1992, p. 14.

2. Ibid., p. 15.

3. Ibid., p. 6.

11
Toward a New Organizational Culture

Public affairs professionals have not been seen as having a key stake in the bottom line of the company nor the function as being crucial to its survivability. RAY HOEWING
PRESIDENT
Public Affairs Council

This book and the ideas in it flow from our experience. They are in context. They are connected to the times in which we live. In that sense, they are both constrained by the current realities and speak to broader current themes in the body politic. That is why, we believe, as we look for principles of coalition building to apply to the twenty-first century, it is worth exploring an analogy from history that may have applicability as we grapple with the economic problems that beset us as a nation currently.

A Reveille for Public
Affairs: Adaptation

Military history is a fascinating topic. Most history courses tend to deal primarily with the problems that led up to the declaration of war, then move immediately to the negotiations leading to the treaty. Courses in military history begin with the first salvo fired and then focus on the day-to-day movement of armed forces in their pursuit of victory.

What has intrigued us about military history, as students of the political process, is a theory posited by some historians that may serve as a useful analogy. The theory we have been told is that democracy, at least in the Western world, followed the development of weaponry.

While armies used horses and swords, only the nobles could afford to fight. In return for their protection, the serfs gave allegiance. Even the crossbow, a step forward—if the introduction of any new weapon can be called "a step forward"—required a higher level of learning in order to master its use. The theory continues that with the advent of the long bow, and eventually the rifle, weapons any peon could handle, armies of mass numbers could be employed.

But mass armies cost lots of money. So, the theory holds, as mass armies became the order of the day, the nobles had to grant to those who could contribute to the financing of the armies, as well as to those whose lives would be at stake, some degree of political power, some say in the decisions affecting their purse as well as their life.

Whether one accepts this theory or not, we can at least accept the notion that participation by the people in the governing process has evolved and grown as people demanded a say in how their money was spent and whether or not they would be called upon to lay down their life. We believe there is an analogy here worth exploring.

Grefe has written extensively on public affairs since the dawn of the 1980s, the beginning of a decade that witnessed unparalleled prosperity, a time many believe we may never see again. His trumpet call has been for employee involvement in the protection of the corporation. A central thesis of his writings has been that the basic strategic goal of public affairs is to assure the future existence of market availability for a corporation's products or services by organizing the most potent force of a corporation—its employees and those dependent upon its continued success—into a coalition to confront government policies inimical to the growth and expansion of the company.

Today, we believe, an organization's assets continue to include those who depend most on its survival. But survival today is more critical, and the chances of doing so are slimmer without some structural change that embraces the concept of employee participation in the survival process.

What that means to us is not simply the organizing of family and friends for the purpose of opposing change but, more critically, organizing them for becoming involved in the process of proposing ways in which jobs can be saved, community problems dealt with, and opportunities for growth stimulated. It is a notion that flies in the face of those who argue that the corporate community has but one task, to provide wealth. For where else, we ask, do we turn to deal with the problems that beset us as we enter the twenty-first century?

As a people, we continue to question the governing process and find it lacking when we do turn to it because of institutional gridlock. We continue to believe that rugged individualism enables us to do better for ourselves than any mandated effort. We continue to believe that those who can turn a profit also have the skills to manage problems beyond producing and marketing a product.

And we continue to believe that the profit-making organizations have far more in common with the not-for-profit organizations, that the corporate community faced with awesome environmental struggles shares more with the Patti Clappers—and her Smuggler Mountain neighbors—than with uncompromising regulators. The people want their environmental problems solved. They can accept a reasonable solution. What is necessary is a coalition of interests to make the government a partner rather than a co-equal adversary.

Our shared belief is that people power can be mobilized beyond merely confronting government proposals to participating with management in solving mutually shared problems, that the grassroots coalitions formed during the 1980s to deal with things we don't like can become instruments for outreach to the community to build a better life for all. That means that management, like the nobles of old, grants employees some degree of participation and adapts corporate policies to work with the community to secure a better future. Toward that end we suggest two models for consideration: an employee and a community participatory corporation.

The Participatory Corporation

In the late 1980s, when the pilot's union first proposed a buyout of United, a group of insurgents organized the Coalition Acting for the Rights of Employees. What was unique about this ad hoc coalition is that it was able to raise sufficient funds from among its volunteers to hire Grefe's firm and mount a campaign that stymied the buyout.

What also set this employee-volunteer group apart was the insistence on the part of the coalition's leadership, notably Captain William H. Palmer, on the at that time unheard of principle of "one employee–one vote" for any kind of ESOP. With guidance from Grefe's firm, Palmer's group was able to get legislation introduced to that effect and make a big enough impact to not only thwart the pilot union's offer at that time but also leave with the organized employees the impression that they should be consulted on future decisions affecting who would own the airline.[1]

What is different about an imposed ESOP and one agreed to by all the employees—the notion of being able to vote on the shared ownership—may be a new form of corporation, one we would term "the participatory corporation," in which the employees have a vested interest in making the company successful both in the short and long runs. To our way of thinking, while the future may belong to "the virtual corporation," it may also belong to "the participatory corporation."

We define such companies as those that, faced with a profoundly changing industry environment, show a willingness to change, to try to adapt to the new exigencies, and to characterize their adaptation by a willingness to share participation in the key decisions affecting the organization. More often, participative programs have been concentrated in manufacturing, linked almost exclusively to productivity. But, as reports about some industries suggest, that degree of participation is now being thought of occasionally in a broader economic way, a share in the risks and the rewards.

Many examples of varying types of participatory programs now exist. These include programs at Xerox, AT&T, General Electric, Scott Paper Company, National Steel, and Toyota Motor Manufacturing, U.S.A. Their success, and that of others, prompted the Clinton administration to form the Commission for the Future of Worker-Management Relations.

The commission's goal was to study successful instances of employee participation in the management of the workplace to discern patterns that may be implemented elsewhere as one way of tackling our current economic morass. It was a joint operation headed by commerce secretary Ron Brown and labor secretary Robert Reich, and it was chaired by former labor secretary and Harvard University professor, John Dunlop. It is now known as the "Dunlop Commission."

The commission was charged with, among other tasks, determining "what (if any) changes should be made in the present legal framework and practices of collective bargaining to enhance cooperative behavior, improve productivity, and reduce conflict and delay." It included individuals from business, labor, and academia. Its report was issued on January 9, 1995.[2]

We applaud such efforts for a number of reasons. We recall referenda in a number of states affecting various industries in which labor's role in helping to either pass or defeat a proposal affecting a client was crucial. We also recall, on more than one occasion, having to show management-level employees involved in the campaign where the union hall was located so they could participate in the victory celebration. And we were dismayed to realize that after the comraderie of the campaign, it was back to confrontation as usual the following day.

To our way of thinking, the public affairs community should be out in front of this effort to seek ways of achieving greater harmony within the organizations. For we believe that the ability to work together in a political situation should be a signal that management and worker goals can be shared in other areas of corporate life, especially when that goal is the very survival of the company. Conversely, if it is possible to work together to rebuild a company when economic issues reach a crisis point—à la the Chrysler Corporation—it seems that the same cooperation can be put to work when political issues arise.

As Ken Dickerson, senior vice president of ARCO notes:

> Change is constant, the order of the day. We must anticipate what the public expects its officeholders to do, and if that expectation is that they pass laws that will penalize business if business does not respond to public demands, business must strive to eliminate the need for the laws by adapting to changes in public perception.
>
> We need to know where the public is going, to anticipate trends, and then, instead of fighting them, accept those that offer community, consumer, and environmental benefits. By aggressively reacting to realistic and legitimate demands for change, we will create a more favorable corporate reputation, attract higher quality employees and be a leader in product development.

We do not know if Dickerson would subscribe to our notion of "the participatory corporation," but his definition suits our purpose. For it is a definition that begins, we believe, with a management as sensitive as he describes and a commitment to employee involvement in the defense of the corporation that is the essence of not only civic action programs but also programs to protect the viability of the organization in every arena of corporate life.

To our way of thinking, those who ask employees to become involved politically in defending the organization are on the right track, especially if that defense is broader than merely passing or defeating legislative proposals. If it is, as we have argued, a program of outreach in which the family and friends of the organization seek to build lasting relationships and alliances with the community in which the organization operates, then that process can serve as the beginning for "the participatory corporation."

The Community
Participatory Corporation

A step beyond, or even parallel with, our notion of "the participatory corporation" might be "the community participatory corporation," one in which the community and the employees share ownership with traditional owners. For tying the interests of the community and the company together may foster relationships that encourage joint problem solving and discourage scapegoating.

Empty buildings from plant closing and defense shutdowns provide communities an opportunity to offer incentives of not only jobs for tax breaks but a share in dealing with community issues such as environmental concerns. David Lawrence, a mayor of Pittsburgh in the late 1950s and early 1960s, and Richard Mellon, the then head of the Mellon banking dynasty, agreed to work together: Lawrence pushed through tough cleanup laws, and Mellon committed to keeping the industries he controlled in town.

When a city council can say to an entrepreneur, "Come, set up shop, earn a respectable profit, but let our people work and be part of the problem solving, and stay and keep people working," there is strong relationship building going on. Everyone involved wants jobs, but they also breathe the same air, drink the same water, and choose to enjoy the same environment. Everyone has a stake in working jointly to solve the problems and build the community.

It is not enough to continue saying—nor will the body politic for long accept—that jobs are someone else's problem. For that "someone" seems never clearly defined. Or if it is suggested that that "someone" be the government as provider of jobs as the employer of last resort, anyone who makes such a proposal is then lambasted for taxing those who work to provide for the unemployed.

Nor is it any longer acceptable to blame those who do not work for their condition. Many of the unemployed were good employees by any measurement. The jobs simply ceased to exist. The problems we face may force us to think globally, but we must act locally, a powerful incentive for the concept of either the community corporation or the participatory corporation.

For example, say we were managing an oil company in Southern California, and we had developed a process for making cleaner gasoline—a product praised by government regulators and environmentalists alike. And say we were thwarted by regulations for expanding present refinery capacity by environmental laws that cannot give a little to get a lot. We might suggest a new way of solving the impasse.

That would be to spin off part of the company to the local community. Guaranteed jobs in order to get permission to expand. Better to have a piece of a pie that exists and could possibly expand than to have no piece at all, a principle that the local government should understand if the goal is to avoid the flight of capital to countries that will make a deal.

One answer to today's economic malaise goes back to Tip O'Neill's dictum: Deal with the problem where it exists, at the local level. Develop systemic relationships in which private organizations are working with both formal local and state governments and with community people to foster a climate of trust and a working engagement that can lead to both the creation of wealth and a protected environment.

Both sides would have to give, but if the benefits are to be guaranteed, then the jobs that would result might be worth the effort. Having a relationship is key. As Arnold Brown says: "There is an increasing demand for business to justify itself on a moral basis."

Short of the "community" or "participatory" corporation, there are signs that some companies are responding in other ways which are consistent with those ideas. A group of more than 50 businesses has established a new trade organization for social responsibility in Washington.

Called Businesses for Social Responsibility (BSR), it states that its challenge is for members to "aim for high performance, innovation and prosperity with practices that are responsive to the well-being of the workforce, consumers, the community and the environment." Like those companies cited earlier that are involved in trying to improve the educational and police practices in Los Angeles, or to work with local environmental groups to solve problems, BSR companies may elect to "participate in a BSR campaign on a timely community or policy issue; or . . . to speak directly to consumers/citizens and build public awareness for an area or program of concern."

In one sense our proposals are not that radical. We have already mentioned a presidential commission that is studying successful participation programs in this country. And we are told that the great German industrial machine—on hold possibly as it absorbs East Germany—succeeded even as it embraced the principle known as *mibestimmung,* roughly "two-hands at the tiller," labor and management jointly plotting the course.

As we were told by Doug Fraser that, while Chrysler Corporation's turnaround was skillfully managed by Lee Iacocca, it could not have been done "without the cooperation and involvement of everyone—the workers, the dealers, the communities in which we operated, and the government. Everyone participated." Fraser is a former president of the United Automobile Workers and a former director of the Chrysler Corporation. He was also a member of the Commission for the Future of Worker-Management Relations.

What we propose may not be easy to implement. As Jerome Rosow, president of the Work in America Institute, has been quoted as saying:

"The biggest factor delaying the spread of participative programs is the mistaken belief by company executives that the human factor in their operation is not as important as capital or technology."[3] Perhaps, then, the "third wave" should be more than information as a resource but the creative participation of our people as well.

To our way of thinking, these are the new keystones in the practice of public affairs: adaptation and participation. The legacy of the sixties is that you can affect power and influence policy-making if you can develop relationships with people whom you want to enlist in your cause. And you can involve people in that way for the long term only if you take them seriously, listen to their concerns, and make the effort to find the shared interests.

The legacy of the nineties, in our judgment, will be that the radical grassroots organizing ideas of the sixties are open to anyone to use, and technology has made it possible to do just that in ways never before imagined. Until the technology became available to target those who share, or should share, in the decision making and to target those who accept or should accept a similar belief structure, discussing an idea as novel as a participatory community corporation would have been difficult, if not impossible.

Today that has changed. If an organization has the will to adapt, the technology exists to identify and to embrace all who participate to assure success. Our reveille call for the practice of public affairs, for influencing public policy-making, and for the professionals in the field who would counsel their organization on how to remain viable in the coming century, is as follows:

- Be bold enough to adapt to change rather than reacting to it and trying to hold it back.

- Be courageous enough to involve all who would prosper from the continued success and viability of the organization.

Any less, in our judgment, may simply lead to taps.

Notes

1. On July 12, 1994, United Airlines became the largest, majority-owned, employee corporation in the world when the pilot's and machinist's unions voted for the ESOP. Included in the vote of the two unions was the automatic involvement of the non-union employees who had no say in the matter. The flight attendants elected not to join the ESOP.

2. The report noted: "The evidence presented to the Commission is overwhelming that employee participation and labor-management partnerships

are good for workers, firms, and the national economy." It urged amending existing laws to remove "the legal uncertainties affecting some forms of employee participation. . . . "

3. "Current Developments: Cooperation Commission Hears of Factors Inhibiting Spread of Employee Participation," *Daily Labor Report,* The Bureau of National Affairs, Inc., Sept. 16, 1993.

Index

About the Authors

EDWARD A. GREFE is chairman of International Civics, Inc., a firm he cofounded in 1979 which provides corporate clients with counseling on coalition building and crisis management. His 40-plus years in communications have covered an extraordinary range of activities including corporate public affairs. A well-known speaker and a former journalist, his previous books include the groundbreaking *Fighting to Win: Business Political Power*, the first book to describe how corporations can use grassroots techniques.

MARTIN LINSKY is currently Counselor to Massachusetts Governor William Weld. He was previously Lecturer on Public Policy at the John F. Kennedy School of Government at Harvard University, a journalist, and a Massachusetts state legislator. His most recent book is *Impact: How the Press Affects Federal Policy Making*.